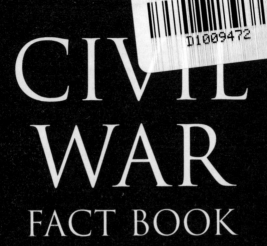

CIVIL WAR
FACT BOOK

Peter Darman

BROWN REFERENCE GROUP

ISBN: 978-1-840-44258-8

The Brown Reference Group plc
First Floor, 9–17 St. Albans Place
London N1 0NX
www.brownreference.com

Editor: Alan Marshall
Designer: Colin Woodman
Production Director: Alastair Gourlay

Printed and bound in Thailand

Picture credits
U.S. National Archives: front cover

Front cover photograph: President Lincoln (center, wearing a top hat)
on the battlefield of Antietam, October 1862.

CONTENTS

ABOUT THIS BOOK

The *Civil War Fact Book* presents a wealth of information about the war between the Union and Confederacy in the form of hundreds of questions and answers, revealing quotations, and fascinating "did-you-know?" boxes. Question topics cover strategy, tactics, battles, uniforms, weapons, espionage, equipment, and the individuals who had a decisive influence on the Civil War, such as Lincoln, Grant, Davis, Lee, and Jackson. This book provides a whole new way to learn about the American Civil War—or to test what you already know about the conflict.

ROAD TO WAR

THE TENSIONS THAT HAD BEEN BUILDING BETWEEN THE SOUTHERN AND NORTHERN STATES IN THE FIRST HALF OF THE NINETEENTH CENTURY WERE BROUGHT TO A HEAD BY THE ELECTION OF ABRAHAM LINCOLN IN NOVEMBER 1860. AS A RESULT, SOUTHERN STATES BEGAN LEAVING THE UNION, LEADING TO THE OUTBREAK OF CIVIL WAR.

Q What was the 1820 Missouri Compromise?

A In 1819 the territory of Missouri applied for statehood. At the time the number of free states and slave states was equal, and so the Senate was evenly balanced between free-state and slave-state senators. Any laws passed had to be supported by politicians from both sides. The addition of Missouri on either side would upset the balance. Jesse B. Thomas, an Illinois senator, proposed that a line be drawn on the map across the country along the latitude of 36° 30' (the latitude of the southern border of Missouri). All states created north of the line would be free, and all states south of the line would be slave. In the future new states would enter the Union in pairs, one free and one slave. In this way peace would be preserved.

DID YOU KNOW

For years before the Civil War the populations of the geographic regions of the country had grown ever more different. Indeed, they had started differently. Colonists in the North settled to do good, while those in the South came to do well. That is, Northern settlers came to create good lives for themselves and a good society for all, often basing this society on religious principles such as those of the Puritans of Massachusetts and the Quakers of Pennsylvania. For the most part, Southern settlers came to make as much money as quickly and as easily as possible, and leave, unconcerned with anybody but themselves. Northern crops were foodstuffs such as wheat and rye, while Southern crops were tobacco and cotton; and though the latter were easier to grow and more profitable to sell, they were nonetheless labor-intensive.

> " NO SIR, YOU DARE NOT MAKE WAR
> ## ON COTTON.
> ## COTTON IS KING
> JAMES HENRY HAMMOND, 1858 "

Q Which territory did the Missouri Compromise originally apply to?

A The territory bought from France in the 1803 Louisiana Purchase (from the present-day state of Louisiana in a northwesterly direction all the way to Oregon). Texas, California, and the rest of the Southwest still belonged to Spain.

Q Which treaty ended the Mexican War of 1846–1848?

A The Treaty of Guadaloupe Hidalgo.

7

Q What territory did the United States gain as a result of the treaty?

A Modern-day California, New Mexico, Arizona, Nevada, Utah, Colorado, and parts of Wyoming.

Q What was the Underground Railroad?

A A secret series of safe houses for Southern slaves to use as they escaped to the North.

Q When did Congress pass the Kansas-Nebraska Act?

A May 1854.

Q Why was the act so divisive?

A The bill created two new territories, Kansas and Nebraska, and provided that settlers who moved to the new territories would be allowed to decide for themselves whether Kansas and Nebraska would permit slavery. As such, it repealed the Missouri Compromise.

Q Why was "Bleeding Kansas" so called?

A The Kansas-Nebraska Act resulted in years of violence in Kansas before the war, as pro- and anti-slavery settlers struggled for control of the state.

> **"** A HOUSE DIVIDED AGAINST ITSELF
> # CANNOT STAND
> ABRAHAM LINCOLN, 1858 **"**

Q Who launched an attack on the government armory at Harpers Ferry in western Virginia on October 16, 1859?

A The abolitionist John Brown and 21 supporters, including five blacks.

Q What was the aim of the attack on Harpers Ferry?

A To inspire a slave uprising that would sweep the South once local slaves had been provided with arms.

DID YOU KNOW

IN THE SEVENTEENTH CENTURY HUMAN SLAVERY WAS INTRODUCED THROUGHOUT WHAT WOULD BECOME THE UNITED STATES. IT WAS IN THE SOUTH THAT IT FOUND THE MOST FERTILE GROUND. THE SYSTEM WOULD DIE BY THE END OF THE NEXT CENTURY IN NEW ENGLAND AND THE MID-ATLANTIC STATES AS FAR SOUTH AS PENNSYLVANIA AND NEW JERSEY BECAUSE IT RAN AGAINST THEIR BASIC ETHICAL BELIEFS, AS WELL AS THE FACT THAT IT MADE LESS ECONOMIC SENSE ON THE SMALL FARMS OF THOSE AREAS. IN THE SOUTH, WHERE FARMERS ASPIRED TO OWN LARGE PLANTATIONS DEDICATED TO ONE OR TWO CASH CROPS, SLAVERY WAS QUICKLY ADOPTED WIDELY. AT FIRST LABORERS WERE BOTH WHITE AND BLACK. WHITES, HOWEVER, SERVED FOR ONLY A SET PERIOD OF YEARS BEFORE BEING RELIEVED OF THEIR DUTIES. THIS SHORT-TERM (OR INDENTURED) SERVITUDE WAS LESS EFFICIENT THAN LIFELONG SLAVERY, BUT SOUTHERN WHITES WERE NOT WILLING TO SUPPORT ANYTHING MORE FOR OTHER WHITES. BLACKS, HOWEVER, FIRST INTRODUCED AS SLAVES IN VIRGINIA IN 1619, WERE QUICKLY SEEN AS HEATHENS LITTLE SUITED FOR, OR CAPABLE OF, OPERATING AS FREE MEN.

9

Q **Who commanded the government Marines at Harpers Ferry?**

A U.S. Army Colonel Robert E. Lee.

Q **Name the principal slave crops in the South.**

A Tobacco, cotton, rice, and sugarcane.

Q Where did Abraham Lincoln live before he became president?

A Springfield, Illinois.

Q What was the Mason-Dixon Line?

A The resolution of a dispute between Pennsylvania (which included present-day Delaware) and Maryland over their common border. A court in London decreed that the border would run north–south between Maryland and Delaware, and then west from Delaware along latitude 39° 43' North. Two Englishmen, a surveyor named Charles Mason and an astronomer, Jeremiah Dixon, were given the job of marking its position.

> " I DO NOT EXPECT THE UNION
> TO BE DISSOLVED.
> ## I DO NOT EXPECT
> ## THE HOUSE TO FALL
> ABRAHAM LINCOLN, 1858 "

Q How was the Mason-Dixon Line originally designated?

A The boundary was marked every mile with blocks of limestone 5 feet (1.5 m) long.

Q Who was president before Lincoln?

A The Democrat James Buchanan.

Q Which city hosted the Democratic National Convention in April 1860?

A Charleston, South Carolina.

Q Name the two factions the Democratic Party divided into after the convention.

A The Southern Democrats and Northern Democrats.

DID YOU KNOW

RACIAL DISCRIMINATION SOON BECAME INSTITUTIONALIZED, BOTH IN PEOPLE'S MINDS AND IN THE LEGAL SYSTEMS OF THE SOUTHERN STATES. BY THE MID-1850S (AT WHICH POINT THE INDENTURE SYSTEM HAD BEEN OBSOLETE FOR A HALF-CENTURY) SOUTHERN THINKING WAS TOTALLY RIGID ON THE QUESTION. GROWING PRESSURE BY MORALISTS AGAINST THE USE OF SLAVERY ONLY FURTHER HARDENED THEIR POSITIONS. IN MAY 1850 SOUTH CAROLINA PRESBYTERIAN MINISTER JAMES THORNWELL PREACHED A SERMON SHOWING THAT HE AND HIS CONGREGATION WERE AWARE THAT THEY STOOD VERY MUCH ALONE IN THE WORLD IN SUPPORTING SLAVERY AND THEY WERE DETERMINED TO DO SO REGARDLESS. "GOD HAS NOT PERMITTED SUCH A REMARKABLE PHENOMENON AS THE UNANIMITY OF THE CIVILIZED WORLD, IN ITS EXECRATION OF SLAVERY, TO TAKE PLACE WITH-OUT DESIGN," HE SAID. "TRUTH MUST TRIUMPH. GOD WILL VINDICATE THE APPOINTMENTS OF HIS PROVIDENCE—AND IF OUR INSTITUTIONS ARE INDEED CONSISTENT WITH RIGHTEOUSNESS AND TRUTH, WE CAN CALMLY AFFORD TO BIDE OUR TIME—WE CAN WATCH THE STORM WHICH IS BEATING FURIOUSLY AGAINST US, WITHOUT TERROR OR DISMAY—WE CAN RECEIVE THE ASSAULT OF THE CIVILIZED WORLD—TRUSTING IN HIM WHO HAS ALL THE ELEMENTS AT HIS COMMAND, AND CAN SAVE AS EASILY BY ONE AS A THOUSAND."

11

Q Who was vice president just prior to the 1860 election?

A John C. Breckinridge of Kentucky.

Q Who was Stephen Douglas?

A The leader of the Northern Democrats in the 1860 presidential election.

> " THAT THE COMPACT WHICH EXISTS
> # BETWEEN NORTH AND SOUTH
> # IS A COVENANT
> # WITH DEATH
> WILLIAM LLOYD GARRISON, 1843 "

Q What was the "soothing syrup" party?

A The nickname given by the press to the Constitutional Union Party, made up of conservative-minded politicians and intended to appeal to moderates looking for a compromise on the slavery issue. It was mostly made up of older statesmen.

DID YOU KNOW

ONLY A MINORITY OF SOUTHERNERS OWNED SLAVES—SOME THREE-QUAR-
TERS HELD NONE AT ALL—AND AN EVEN SMALLER MINORITY HELD MORE
THAN ONE OR TWO WHO ACTED AS FARM HANDS. BUT A COMBINATION OF
THE SOUTHERN CONTEMPT FOR MANUAL LABOR, COUPLED WITH RACIAL
BIGOTRY AGAINST BLACKS, GAVE EVEN NON-SLAVEHOLDERS A SOCIAL CLASS
THEY COULD LORD OVER. THIS REINFORCED THEIR OWN SENSE OF SOCIAL
STATUS AND, FOR THAT REASON, LED TO WHOLESALE SUPPORT OF THE
SLAVEHOLDING MINORITY.

Q Who was its leader and running mate in the 1860 election?

A John Bell of Tennessee for president. His running mate was Edward Everett of Massachusetts, a famed orator.

13

Q How many electoral votes did Lincoln win in the 1860 election?

A 180.

Q Which of the main candidates in the 1860 election died of typhoid fever soon afterwards?

A Stephen Douglas.

Q When did Abraham Lincoln become president?

A November 6, 1860.

Q Who was Lincoln's vice president?

A Hannibal Hamlin.

Q Where was the only major ironworks in the South in 1860?

A The Tredegar Works in Richmond.

> " YOU HAD BETTER, ALL YOU
> PEOPLE OF THE SOUTH,
> ## PREPARE YOURSELF FOR
> ## A SETTLEMENT OF
> ## THIS QUESTION
> JOHN BROWN, 1859 "

Q Who signed the Ordinance of Secession on December 20, 1860?

A South Carolina's state legislators, in Charleston.

Q On Christmas Eve 1860, who issued a proclamation declaring
South Carolina to be separate, independent, and sovereign?

A Governor Wilkinson Pickens.

Q Who was born in a one-room log cabin in Hardin County,
Kentucky, on February 12, 1809?

A Abraham Lincoln.

DID YOU KNOW

SLAVES DAMAGED THE ACTUAL ECONOMIC STATUS OF NON-SLAVE OWNERS
IN THE SOUTH, IN THAT WAGES WERE KEPT ARTIFICIALLY LOW BY OWNERS
BEING ABLE TO EMPLOY SLAVES IN ALL AREAS OF AGRICULTURE AND
INDUSTRY, AS WELL AS INCREASING THE NUMBER OF ACRES OWNED BY
INDIVIDUALS IN PLANTATION ESTATES, WHICH NATURALLY CONCENTRATED
WEALTH IN A FEW HANDS. NO SLAVERY AND NO PLANTATIONS WOULD HAVE
MEANT THAT THE SOUTH WOULD HAVE LARGELY BEEN MADE UP OF SMALL
FARMS WITH MORE EQUALLY DISTRIBUTED WEALTH. BUT FEW IF ANY SMALL
FARMERS IN THE SOUTH PUT THIS ALL TOGETHER. AT THE SAME TIME,
NOTIONS OF RACIAL SUPERIORITY PRODUCED A FEELING OF BEING A
MEMBER OF AN ARISTOCRACY, NOT JUST AN ARISTOCRACY OVER BLACKS,
BUT OVER FOREIGNERS AND ANYBODY WHO DIFFERED FROM ONE'S OWN
CLASS. THIS WOULD NATURALLY INCLUDE THE MANY GERMANS, IRISH,
SCANDINAVIANS, AND OTHERS WHO FLOCKED TO NORTHERN CITIES IN THE
FIRST HALF OF THE NINETEENTH CENTURY. PLANTATION OWNERS SAW
THEMSELVES AS EIGHTEENTH-CENTURY ENGLISH SQUIRES, WHO TOOK CARE
OF THEIR LOCAL VILLAGES AND RAISED REGIMENTS TO FIGHT FOR THEIR
SOVEREIGN IN TIMES OF WAR.

Q **Which leading Southern politician married Sarah Knox Taylor in 1835?**

A Jefferson Davis.

Q **What was unusual about Taylor's honeymoon?**

A On the honeymoon she and Jefferson Davis both came down with malaria, and Sarah died of the disease three months later.

Q **At which battle did Jefferson Davis become a hero?**

A The Battle of Buena Vista, during the Mexican War (1846–1848), where, as colonel of a Mississippi mounted volunteer regiment, he sustained a serious wound in his foot.

Q **Which future Confederate spy was born in Martinsburg, Virginia (now West Virginia), in 1844?**

A Belle Boyd.

DID YOU KNOW

IN THE EARLY YEARS OF THE REPUBLIC, SOUTHERN POLITICIANS DOMINATED THE NATIONAL GOVERNMENT. THEIR STATES WERE THE MOST POPULOUS, ESPECIALLY VIRGINIA, AND ECONOMICALLY ALL THE STATES WERE SIMILAR IN THAT THEY WERE AGRARIAN, RATHER THAN INDUSTRIAL. BY 1820, HOWEVER, SOUTHERN LEADERS BEGAN TO LOSE THEIR POWER. NORTHERN STATES GREW IN TERMS OF POPULATION AND ECONOMIC PROGRESS MUCH MORE QUICKLY THAN SOUTHERN ONES. AT THE SAME TIME, THE NATION BEGAN TO SEE A GROWING MORAL INDIGNATION ABOUT HOLDING HUMAN BEINGS AS SLAVES, A MOVEMENT THAT STARTED IN PENNSYLVANIA AND MASSACHUSETTS. THIS GAVE SOUTHERN LEADERS CAUSE FOR CONCERN THAT THEY NOW HAD TO DEFEND A MAJOR PART OF THEIR CULTURE WITH AN EVER-DECREASING AMOUNT OF ECONOMIC AND POLITICAL POWER. AS A RESULT, THE NOTION OF "STATES' RIGHTS," SOMETHING NOT FOUND IN THE CONSTITUTION, GAINED CREDENCE IN THE POPULAR SOUTHERN MIND.

Q Who was General "Light Horse Harry" Lee?

A One of George Washington's subordinates in the American Revolution and the father of Robert E. Lee.

Q Who married Mary Ann Randolph Custis in June 1830?

A Robert E. Lee, which connected him by marriage to the family of George Washington (Mary was the daughter of Martha Washington's grandson) and cemented his position in the Virginia aristocracy. The marriage produced seven children.

Q What was the profession of Joshua Lawrence Chamberlain before the Civil War?

A He taught natural theology and logic at Bowdoin College, Maine.

Q Which Civil War commander as a child was unofficially adopted by Captain David Porter of the U.S. Navy?

A David Farragut. At age nine he enlisted on Porter's frigate USS *Essex* as a midshipman and saw action during the war of 1812.

Q Who was nicknamed "Little Phil" during his time at West Point?

A Philip Henry Sheridan, who went to the U.S. Military Academy at West Point in 1848 after lying about his age to get in. An average student while at West Point, he was nicknamed "Little Phil" because of his short stature. The name stuck.

18

DID YOU KNOW

BEFORE THE WAR, UNDER CONTENTION WERE THE VAST TRACTS OF LAND TO THE WEST, PARTICULARLY THE NEWLY SETTLED STATES SUCH AS KANSAS. THE SLAVE STATES OF THE SOUTH SAW THEIR SECURITY AND FUTURE IN THE EXTENSION OF SLAVERY TO THESE AREAS, WHILE MANY IN THE NORTH, PARTICULARLY ABOLITIONISTS, SOUGHT TO DENY SLAVERY IN THE WEST AS A WAY OF PUTTING PRESSURE ON THE SOUTH'S SO-CALLED "PECULIAR INSTITUTION" OF HUMAN SLAVERY.

CIVIL WAR TRIVIA BOOK

" **BUT THIS QUESTION IS STILL TO BE SETTLED—THIS NEGRO QUESTION, I MEAN**
JOHN BROWN, 1859 "

Q Who, as a militia volunteer, stood guard at the gallows during the hanging of the antislavery figure John Brown?

A The actor John Wilkes Booth.

Q "Jeb" Stuart served in which regiment before the Civil War?

A The 1st U.S. Cavalry Regiment in Kansas and Texas.

Q Which senior Union commander was born in Cadiz, Spain?

A George Gordon Meade: his father was an American naval agent there.

Q What date marked the beginning of the abolition movement?

A 1831, when a Bostonian named William Lloyd Garrison began publishing the *Liberator*, a newspaper devoted to ending slavery.

Q What was the Free Soil Party?

A An abolitionist party set up in 1848.

> SAVE IN THE DEFENSE OF
> MY NATIVE STATE,
> # I NEVER DESIRE AGAIN TO
> # DRAW MY SWORD
> ROBERT E. LEE BEFORE THE CIVIL WAR

Q What was the 1850 Fugitive Slave Act?

A An act that allowed slave owners to apprehend runaway slaves in free states and territories.

Q What was the "cotton state"?

A Alabama, whose rolling coastal plains were ideal for growing large cotton crops.

DID YOU KNOW

MANY NORTHERNERS SAW JOHN BROWN AS A MARTYR, AND SOUTHERNERS BEGAN TO FEAR THAT THEIR RIGHTS TO HOLD SLAVES WOULD BE TAKEN FROM THEM BY FORCE IF THE OPPOSITION IN THE NORTH GREW TOO STRONG. VIRGINIANS AND OTHER SOUTHERN STATES' CITIZENS BEGAN TO FORM VOLUNTEER MILITIA UNITS IN EARNEST. "AFTER THE JOHN BROWN AFFAIR I WAS SO FIRMLY CONVINCED THAT THERE MIGHT BE TROUBLE THAT I TOOK ACTIVE STEPS TO RAISE A CAVALRY COMPANY IN WASHINGTON COUNTY," REMEMBERED W.W. BLACKFORD, WHO WOULD RISE TO THE RANK OF LIEUTENANT COLONEL IN THE ARMY OF NORTHERN VIRGINIA. "I CANVASSED FOR IT AND THEN CALLED A MEETING IN ABINGDON . . . WE NAMED THE COMPANY THE WASHINGTON MOUNTED RIFLES. I PROCURED A COPY OF *HARDEE'S [LIGHT INFANTRY] TACTICS* AND STUDIED IT INTENTLY, DRILLING THE MEN EVERY COURT DAY. AT FIRST ONLY A DOZEN OR SO TOOK INTEREST IN IT BUT DURING THE WINTER OF 1860–61 MANY MORE JOINED."

21

Q Which former teacher established the American Red Cross?

A Clarissa Harlowe Barton, whose medical service on the Union side during the Civil War earned her the title "Angel of the Battlefield."

Q Who wrote *Uncle Tom's Cabin*?

A Harriet Beecher Stowe, a New England clergyman's daughter. It presented a devastating picture of the cruelty of slavery and became a bestseller.

Q What was the Dred Scott Case?

A A Supreme Court ruling in 1857 that ruled that people of African descent, whether or not they were slaves, could never be citizens of the United States, and that Congress had no authority to prohibit slavery in federal territories.

❝ ALL QUIET ALONG THE POTOMAC TONIGHT, NO SOUND SAVE THE RUSH OF THE RIVER ❞
ETHEL LYNN BEERS, *THE PICKET GUARD*

Q Who founded the *Hartford Evening Press* in 1854?

A Gideon Welles, who also helped to organize the new Republican Party. The *Hartford Evening Press* was one of the first Republican newspapers in the United States.

Q In 1790 there were around 657,000 slaves in the South. How many were there in 1860?

A 3.5 million.

Q What was a cotton gin?

A A machine that automated the separation of cotton seed from the short-staple cotton fibre. The gin was invented by Eli Whitney in 1793. In that year just 94 tons (85 tonnes) of cotton were harvested in the United States. By 1810, after the invention of the gin, the cotton harvest was 45,000 tons (40,800 tonnes).

1861

Despite the North's manpower and industrial resources, the Confederacy mobilized more quickly and inflicted a number of defeats on Federal forces in 1861, chiefly at the Battle of First Bull Run in July. The prospect of a short war disappeared. Both sides organized their resources for a long struggle.

Q Which forts commanded the entrance to Mobile Bay, Alabama?

A Forts Morgan and Gaines, which were captured by Confederate forces on January 5, 1861.

Q What was the first Federal facility in Florida to be taken by the Confederacy?

A The Federal arsenal at Apalachicola, which was seized by Florida state forces on January 6, 1861.

Q What was the second state to join the Confederacy?

" A RECKLESS AND UNPRINCIPLED
TYRANT HAS INVADED
YOUR SOIL
P.G.T. BEAUREGARD, JUNE 1861
"

A Mississippi, on January 9. The Mississippi legislature in the state capital, Jackson, passed the ordinance of secession. The "Republic of Mississippi" was born, and there was rejoicing throughout the state.

Q When did Florida join the Confederacy?

A January 10, when delegates at a special conference in Tallahassee voted by 62 votes to 7 to secede from the Union. Governor Madison Starke Perry and governor-elect John Milton were strong advocates of this move, although ex-governor Richard Call opposed it.

DID YOU KNOW

ORIGINALLY EVERY MALE COLONIST WHO CAME TO AMERICA WAS A POTENTIAL MEMBER OF A LOCAL MILITIA, REQUIRED TO OWN WEAPONS AND EQUIPMENT AND TO BE ABLE TO SERVE AS REQUIRED. SUCH A SYSTEM LED TO WORTHLESS UNITS THAT EXISTED LARGELY ON PAPER. THE U.S. CONGRESS PASSED ITS FEDERAL MILITIA ACT IN 1792 THAT BASICALLY SET UP THE MILITIA SYSTEM MOST STATES USED THEREAFTER. ALL MEN AGED BETWEEN 18 AND 45 WITHIN A STATE WERE LIABLE FOR MILITIA SERVICE, WITH THE EXCEPTION OF FREE BLACKS, INDENTURED WHITES, THE INDIGENT, AND MEN IN EXEMPTED POSITIONS SUCH AS FERRYMEN, MILLERS, OR VARIOUS GOVERNMENT OFFICIALS.

Q What was the Bonnie Blue Flag?

25

A A blue flag with the single white star in the center. It is believed to have been modelled on the flag of South Carolina and the Lone Star flag of Texas. The single star represented secession, the removal of a star from the Stars and Stripes, and independence in that it stood alone on a field of blue. The Bonnie Blue Flag gradually became the unofficial banner of independence and self-government for the Southern states. In January 1861 the women of Jackson presented the Mississippi legislature in the state capital, Jackson, with the "Bonnie Blue Flag," which features a single white star on a blue background and has come to symbolize Southern independence.

Q What was the fourth state to secede from the Union?

A Alabama, after Mississippi and Florida followed South Carolina on January 9 and 10, respectively. Alabama would be followed by Georgia, Louisiana, and finally Texas on February 1.

Q What were the four slave states that remained in the Union?

A Delaware, Kentucky, Maryland, and Missouri. Of these, Missouri, Kentucky, and Maryland had deeply divided loyalties. Troops from these states fought on both sides.

Q Was Minnesota a Union or Confederate state?

A Union. On January 22 a resolution was passed offering men and money to the Union.

26

DID YOU KNOW

WITHIN THE MILITIA BODY THERE WAS A "VOLUNTEER CORPS," MADE UP OF COMPANIES FORMED BY VOLUNTEERS WHO SELECTED THEIR OWN OFFICERS, DESIGNED THEIR OWN UNIFORMS, CREATED THEIR OWN DRILL TIMES AND PLACES, AND TURNED OUT FOR CIVIC FUNCTIONS SUCH AS THE FOURTH OF JULY PARADES. MANY RECEIVED WEAPONS FROM THE STATE ARMORY, WHILE OTHERS PROCURED THEIR OWN. SOME OF THESE, SUCH AS THE RICHMOND LIGHT INFANTRY BLUES, FORMED IN 1793, BECAME AS MUCH SOCIAL CLUBS AS WELL-TRAINED MILITARY UNITS. MEMBERS WERE ELECTED, AND UNIFORMS AND ACCOUTREMENTS COULD COST SMALL FORTUNES.

Q When was Kansas admitted to the Union?

A The U.S. Congress admitted Kansas to the Union as the 34th state on January 29.

" THIS IS ESSENTIALLY A PEOPLE'S CONTEST
**WHOSE LEADING OBJECT
IS TO ELEVATE THE
CONDITION OF MEN**
ABRAHAM LINCOLN, JULY 1861 **"**

Q When did the Confederate Government first meet?

A Delegates from the seven states met in Montgomery, the Alabama state capital, on February 4 and drafted a constitution for the Confederate States of America. Jefferson Davis of Mississippi was chosen as provisional president and was inaugurated on February 18.

Q Where was the capital of the Confederacy?

A The capital was Montgomery, Alabama, until May 1861, when it was moved to the city of Richmond, Virginia.

Q What went on at Camp Curtin?

A Camp Curtin in Harrisburg, Pennsylvania, was opened in April 1861 to deal with Union volunteers in the state. More than 300,000 men passed through the camp.

Q What prompted the Confederates to make a second demand for the surrender on Fort Sumter?

A Confederate batteries resumed heavy shelling of the fort at dawn on April 13. The barracks inside the fort caught fire. At 12:48 hours a Confederate shell dislodged Fort Sumter's flagstaff. When Confederate Colonel Louis T. Wigfall saw the flag go down, he rowed out to the fort to demand its surrender. This time Anderson, the commander, conceded defeat. Fort Sumter remained in Confederate hands for most of the war.

DID YOU KNOW

LINCOLN HIMSELF WAS ON THE RECORD AS BEING AGAINST SLAVERY. FOR EXAMPLE, IN A DEBATE FOR A SENATE SEAT WITH THE EVENTUAL WINNER, STEPHEN A. DOUGLAS, IN 1858, HE SAID: "I SHOULD BE EXCEEDINGLY GLAD TO SEE SLAVERY ABOLISHED IN THE DISTRICT OF COLUMBIA. I BELIEVE THAT CONGRESS POSSESSES THE CONSTITUTIONAL POWER TO ABOLISH IT, YET AS A MEMBER OF CONGRESS I SHOULD NOT BE IN FAVOR, WITH MY PRESENT VIEWS OF INTERFERING, TO ABOLISH SLAVERY IN THE DISTRICT OF COLUMBIA, UNLESS IT SHOULD BE UPON THREE CONDITIONS: FIRST, THAT THE ABOLITION SHOULD BE GRADUAL; IN THE SECOND PLACE, THAT IT SHOULD BE UPON THE VOTE OF A MAJORITY OF THE QUALIFIED VOTERS WITHIN THE DISTRICT; AND, LASTLY, WITH COMPENSATION TO UNWILLING OWNERS." LINCOLN WAS NO ABOLITIONIST IN THE SENSE THAT MANY OF THEM WERE, IN THAT HE PROPOSED NEITHER LIBERATION NOR EQUALITY BETWEEN THE RACES. IN ANOTHER IN THIS SERIES OF DEBATES HE SAID: "I WILL SAY, THEN, THAT I AM NOT NOR EVER HAVE BEEN IN FAVOR OF BRINGING ABOUT IN ANY WAY THE SOCIAL AND POLITICAL EQUALITY OF THE WHITE AND BLACK RACES."

Q What were "90-day men"?

A On April 15 Lincoln had called on the Union states to recruit 75,000 volunteer militia, but they were only to serve for three months. Many regular army officers doubted whether these "90-day men" could be relied on to fight a long campaign.

Q Who was the first brigadier general of the Confederacy?

A Pierre Beauregard. When Louisiana seceded from the Union in January 1861, he resigned from the U.S. Army and was commissioned as the first brigadier general of the Confederacy. He was ordered to South Carolina, where he commanded the attack on the garrison at Fort Sumter in April 1861.

❝ HE WAS A FOE WITHOUT HATE, A FRIEND WITHOUT TREACHERY, A SOLDIER WITHOUT CRUELTY
BENJAMIN H. HILL ABOUT ROBERT E. LEE **❞**

Q Who was Confederate Secretary of the Navy?

A Stephen R. Mallory, who faced a difficult task. When his Department of the Navy came into being in February 1861, Mallory had almost no vessels under his control and only a single naval facility—little more than a coaling station—confiscated from the U.S. Navy at Pensacola, Florida.

Q Who was President of the Ohio and Mississippi Railroad when the Civil War broke out?

A George Brinton McClellan. After he graduated second in his class from the U.S. Military Academy at West Point at the young age of 20, his future looked bright. He was immediately able to make his mark in the Mexican War (1846–1848). Frustrated with his slow progress within the army establishment, however, the intensely ambitious McClellan resigned his commission in 1857 to became chief of engineering for the Illinois Central Railroad.

Q Who was colonel of the 1st Virginia Cavalry at the First Battle of Bull Run?

A "Jeb" Stuart, who led a charge that greatly helped the Confederate victory at the battle.

"

THEN, SIR,
WE WILL GIVE THEM THE BAYONET!
"STONEWALL" JACKSON, FIRST BULL RUN

"

Q What was the aim of Confederate foreign policy?

A The Confederacy's main aim was to achieve diplomatic recognition as a sovereign power.

Q Why did the Confederates think Britain would support them in the war?

A The principal reason for this conviction was the British textile industry's reliance on raw cotton grown in the American South. The Confederacy was confident that Britain would never allow its textile industry to be throttled by a Union blockade.

DID YOU KNOW

Though the militia system was largely moribund by the 1850s, select units in Virginia proved the exception. In 1851 the Virginia legislature authorized its volunteers to unify and form full regiments, and in 1852 they were authorized to form battalions as well. A regiment had a minimum of ten companies, two of which were "flank companies." A battalion consisted of the eight companies left over after the flank companies were removed. A regiment, however, could hold two or more battalions.

Q Where was Robert E. Lee serving before the Civil War?

A Lee served for three years as the superintendent of West Point and in 1855 received a permanent promotion to lieutenant colonel. Transferred to Texas, he served as second-in-command of a cavalry regiment until the outbreak of the Civil War.

Q What happened to Lee in April 1861?

A He was recalled to Washington, D.C., and on April 18 offered command of the United States' armies. However, when Virginia joined the Confederacy in the same month, he reached the agonizing, but for him unavoidable, decision to resign from the U.S. Army. Lee was immediately placed in command of Virginia's army and navy.

Q The original Union naval blockade of April 19, 1861, applied to which states?

A The Deep South states of Texas, Louisiana, Florida, Georgia, and South Carolina.

Q Which other states was the naval blockade applied to on April 27, 1861?

A Lincoln extended the proclamation to include North Carolina and Virginia.

> " THE MEN OF 1860–61 ALLOWED AN ACADEMIC
> ## ARGUMENT OVER A NEGRO
> ## TO END IN CIVIL WAR
> Peter J. Parish "

Q Which Confederate leader shot a fellow student while at the University of Virginia?

A While at the University of Virginia, John Mosby engaged in an argument with a fellow student, whom he then shot. After seven months in jail Mosby was pardoned in 1853 and began studying law.

Q When war broke out, who was professor of artillery tactics and natural philosophy at the Virginia Military Institute (VMI) in Lexington?

A Thomas Jonathan Jackson, who had been in the post since 1851. A Presbyterian, his faith had a profound influence on him for the rest of his life—he was sometimes called "Deacon Jackson".

Q Which clerk was given command of the 21st Illinois Volunteers in June 1861?

A Ulysses Simpson Grant. After several failed business ventures, in 1861 Grant was working as a clerk in the family store in Galena, Illinois. When war broke out in April 1861, Grant offered his services to the War Department. He was initially refused but, with the aid of a supportive senator, was given command of the 21st Illinois Volunteers in June.

Q What were the "Raccoon Roughs"?

A A company of Confederate volunteers raised in 1861. Part of the Sixth Alabama, one of the largest regiments in the Confederate army, they were known for their coon-skin caps, which they wore rather than the standard gray caps.

33

DID YOU KNOW

IN JANUARY 1860 VOLUNTEER MILITIA OFFICERS MET IN RICHMOND UNDER THE DIRECTION OF STATE MAJOR GENERAL WILLIAM B. TALIAFERRO, THE CONVENTION PRESIDENT. THE CONVENTION PASSED A NUMBER OF RESOLUTIONS DEALING WITH THE TRAINING AND GROWTH OF THE VOLUNTEER MILITIA CORPS, AND THESE APPARENTLY FORMED THE BASIS OF LEGISLATION LATER PASSED BY THE STATE GOVERNMENT. BY NOVEMBER 1860, SPURRED ON BY THE INCREASE IN TENSIONS AFTER THE JOHN BROWN RAID, AS WELL AS THE PRESIDENTIAL ELECTION RESULTS, THERE WERE THREE VOLUNTEER REGIMENTS AND SIX MORE BATTALIONS, STATE ADJUTANT GENERAL WILLIAM H. RICHARDSON REPORTED. THIS NUMBER GREW TO FIVE REGIMENTS AND SIX BATTALIONS BY THE FOLLOWING APRIL. STILL THERE WAS NO WAR. WHAT FINALLY TRIGGERED THE CONFLICT WAS THE ELECTION OF ABRAHAM LINCOLN, THE SECOND CANDIDATE OF THE NORTHERN-BASED REPUBLICAN PARTY.

Q Who was the highest-ranking officer to resign his commission in the U.S. Army on the outbreak of war?

A Joseph Eggleston Johnston. He entered Confederate service as a brigadier general—then the highest rank in the Confederate army.

Q What was Union strategy when war broke out in 1861?

A When war broke out on April 12, 1861, the Union had no overall strategy for defeating the Confederacy. The commander-in-chief of the U.S. Army, Winfield Scott, devised a plan that became known as the Anaconda Plan.

Q What were the main aims of the Anaconda Plan?

A Scott outlined his strategy in a letter to General George B. McClellan on May 3, 1861. He did not propose an invasion of the South but a campaign to surround and isolate the Confederate states to deprive them of supplies and force a peace deal.

DID YOU KNOW

THE POSSIBILITY OF SOUTHERN STATES ACTUALLY LEAVING THE UNION HAD BEEN UNDER DISCUSSION SINCE 1832, WHEN SOUTH CAROLINA'S LEGISLATURE DECLARED THE NATIONAL TARIFFS OF 1828 AND 1832 "NULL AND VOID" (TARIFFS TENDED TO PROTECT INDUSTRY, WHICH WAS FOUND IN THE NORTH, AT THE EXPENSE OF FARMERS WHO HAD TO IMPORT ALL THEIR MANUFACTURED GOODS). AT THAT TIME, THE U.S. CONGRESS AUTHORIZED THE PRESIDENT TO SEND TROOPS TO SOUTH CAROLINA TO ENFORCE ITS RULES, BUT THIS WAS AVOIDED BY CONGRESSMAN HENRY CLAY FROM KENTUCKY WHO ARRANGED A COMPROMISE TARIFF SO THAT SOUTH CAROLINA FELT FREE TO VOID HER PREVIOUS NULL AND VOID ACT.

Q What were the factors that made Winfield Scott decide on the Anaconda Plan?

A Scott decided on his plan for two reasons. First, he had a limited number of men. The U.S. Army he commanded was a tiny force of 16,000 professional soldiers, or "regulars." The other reason for Scott's strategy was that he hoped to win the South back without destroying it. The general understood the depth of hatred a civil war would create.

> " THE TRUTH IS, I AM MORE OF
> A FARMER THAN A SOLDIER.
> I TAKE LITTLE INTEREST
> IN MILITARY AFFAIRS "
> GENERAL GRANT, ON HIMSELF

Q What was the "Baltimore Riot" of April 1861?

A When the 6th Massachusetts Infantry Regiment changed trains in the city, it was attacked by a pro-Confederate mob. Bricks were thrown and shots exchanged between the two sides. Officials, including Baltimore's mayor, George Brown, vowed that no more Union troops would be allowed in the city. On May 13, however, Union troops occupied the city and rounded up and imprisoned Confederate supporters, including Brown.

Q When was the right of *habeas corpus* withdrawn by President Lincoln?

A April 27, 1861. This cornerstone of civil and constitutional law was not reinstated until 1866.

Q At the beginning of the war, why did the Union want to gain control of the Mississippi River?

A Mastery of the river would cut off the Confederate states of Texas, Arkansas, and most of Louisiana from the rest of the South. In Winfield Scott's words, "envelop the insurgent States and bring them to terms with less bloodshed than by any other plan." It was a cautious, long-term strategy that relied for success on squeezing the South economically.

Q What was the "Baltimore Bastille"?

A Baltimore's Fort McHenry became known as the "Baltimore Bastille." At one point during the war it housed 6,957 Confederate prisoners.

> ## THE VIRGINIA MILITARY INSTITUTE
> # WILL BE HEARD
> # FROM TODAY
> "STONEWALL" JACKSON AT FIRST BULL RUN

Q Who was appointed commander of land and naval forces in the state of Virginia on April 23, 1861?

A Major General Robert E. Lee.

Q What was the last state to secede from the Union?

A North Carolina, on May 20, 1861. When the secession was announced in the state capital, Raleigh, there was a 100-gun salute, and everybody congratulated everybody else.

Q Why were the Battles of Sewell's Point and Aquia Creek so similar?

A They both involved Union gunboats shelling Confederate positions. At Sewell's Point two Union gunboats, commanded by Lieutenant D.L. Braine, fired on Rebel positions in a small action at Sewell's Point in Norfolk Bay in an effort to reinforce the blockade of Hampton Roads. At Aquia Creek three gunboats led by Commander James H. Ward bombarded Confederate coastal batteries at the mouth of Aquia Creek for three days during the blockade of Chesapeake Bay.

Q Union Brigadier General Ebenezer Pierce was defeated in one of the first land battles of the war. Where?

A At the Battle of Big Bethel/Bethel Church in Virginia on June 10, 1861. Pierce, leading converging columns from Hampton and Newport News against advanced Confederate outposts at Little and Big Bethel, was repulsed.

37

DID YOU KNOW

THE REASON MOST QUOTED AFTER THE WAR BY SOUTHERN LEADERS FOR TRYING TO BREAK UP THE REPUBLIC WAS TO "DEFEND STATES' RIGHTS" (THE RIGHT OF A STATE'S POPULATION TO OVERRULE THE DECISIONS OF THE NATIONAL MAJORITY, AND TO PROTECT CERTAIN PRIVILEGES AND CUSTOMS, PARTICULARLY THE PRACTICE OF SLAVERY). THE POLITICIANS WHO MOST STRONGLY FELT THIS WAS NECESSARY SAW THEMSELVES AS DEFENDING THE STATUS QUO; INDEED, REVERTING TO THE ORIGINAL NATIONAL GOVERNMENT FOUNDED BY THE SOLDIERS OF THE REVOLUTION, AND ITS LEADERS, MEN SUCH AS THOMAS JEFFERSON.

Q Which state was admitted to the Union in June 1861?

A West Virginia. Its political leaders opposed Virginia's decision to leave the Union, and so broke away from the Confederacy. West Virginia was admitted to the Union as a separate state.

Q Which battle, fought on July 2, 1861, took place near Hainesville in what is now West Virginia?

A The Battle of Hoke's Run/Falling Waters/Hainesville. Union Major General Robert Patterson's division drove back the Confederate regiments of Brigadier General Thomas J. Jackson's brigade.

> **"** TWO MONTHS AFTER MARCHING
> # THROUGH BOSTON, HALF THE
> # REGIMENT WAS DEAD **"**
> ROBERT LOWELL, *FOR THE UNION DEAD*

Q Name the two opposing commanders at the Battle of First Manassas/First Bull Run.

A General Irvin McDowell, commander of the main Union force of 35,000 men, engaged the main Confederate army of 20,000, commanded by Pierre G.T. Beauregard (who had been McDowell's classmate at the military academy at West Point).

Q Why was Manassas so important?

A Manassas Junction, only 30 miles (48 km) from Washington, along a small stream called Bull Run Creek, was a key Confederate supply depot and a stop on the railroad linking northern Virginia with the Shenandoah Valley.

DID YOU KNOW

By 1860 THE UNITED STATES HAD SOME 30,600 MILES (48,960 KM) OF RAILROAD, THOUGH ONLY 8,500 MILES (13,600 KM) OF THIS WAS IN THE SOUTH. THERE WAS ONLY ONE DIRECT RAIL LINK FROM RICHMOND SOUTH TO THE MISSISSIPPI, WHICH RAN THROUGH CHATTANOOGA TO MEMPHIS. THE CIVIL WAR WOULD BE THE WORLD'S FIRST "RAILROAD WAR," WITH STRATEGICALLY IMPORTANT SOUTHERN RAIL JUNCTIONS SUCH AS PETERSBURG AND CHATTANOOGA BECOMING THE FOCUS OF UNION OFFENSIVES TO TAKE THEM.

Q Name two battles involving the Missouri State Guard in June and July 1861.

A The Battle of Boonville on June 17, when 1,700 Federals attacked Missouri State Guard troops at Boonville, forcing them out of the town and establishing Union control over a stretch of the Missouri River; and the Battle of Carthage, where Missouri State Guard divisions under Governor Claiborne Jackson forced a Union brigade into retreat around Carthage.

Q At First Bull Run, how did Johnston's Confederates reinforce Beauregard?

A By using the Manassas Gap Railroad.

Q Why was this a landmark in military history?

A It marked the first use of railroads for the purpose of battlefield maneuver in the history of warfare.

Q What were the rival battle plans at First Bull Run?

A Both McDowell and Beauregard determined on the same battle plan: a turning of the enemy's left flank. McDowell planned to cross Bull Run via the Sudley Ford and position his army between those of Beauregard and Johnston, forcing both the Confederates to retreat. Beauregard also planned to attack his opponent's left flank.

Q What saved the Confederates from defeat at First Bull Run?

A The timely arrival of reinforcements, many from Johnston's Shenandoah Valley force, turned the tide. The Confederates were rallied by Jackson's Virginia brigade. It made a counterattack on the slopes of Henry Hill that earned Jackson his famous nickname of "Stonewall."

Q Who commanded the Union Army of the West until his death in August 1861?

A Brigadier General Nathaniel Lyon.

> **" THE CONFEDERATE FLAG IS OFTEN**
> **JUST CONFETTI IN**
> **CARELESS HANDS NOW "**
> JONATHAN DANIELS, 1965

CIVIL WAR TRIVIA BOOK

DID YOU KNOW

THE OPENING OF THE MISSISSIPPI RIVER TO TRANSPORTATION WAS A MAJOR OBJECTIVE FOR THE UNION NAVY, AND THE MISSISSIPPI SQUADRON WAS ALSO CREATED IN MAY 1861. AN IRONCLAD-BUILDING PROGRAM ON THE UPPER REACHES OF THE MISSISSIPPI VERY RAPIDLY PRODUCED THE GUNBOATS FOR THIS SQUADRON—THE FIRST ONES WERE LAUNCHED IN OCTOBER 1861. SQUADRONS ALONG THE ATLANTIC COAST ALSO MAINTAINED IRONCLADS FOR WARFARE ON THE MANY RIVERS THAT OPENED INTO THE SEA. IRONCLADS WERE USED IN A NUMBER OF JOINT ARMY/NAVY OPERATIONS DURING THE WAR. THE POTOMAC FLOTILLA WAS ORGANIZED TO KEEP THE POTOMAC RIVER CLEAR AND TO DEFEND THE NATION'S CAPITAL. SQUADRONS OFF SOUTH AMERICA, EUROPE, AND AFRICA HAD THE DUTY OF DESTROYING CONFEDERATE COMMERCE RAIDERS, WHICH PREYED ON UNION MERCHANT SHIPS.

41

Q What was significant about the Battle of Wilson's Creek/Oak Hills, Missouri, fought on August 10, 1861?

A It was the first major battle west of the Mississippi River. It was bloody, with more than 2,500 dead, injured and missing. The Confederate victory gave the South control of the Springfield area.

Q Who was the first Union general to die in combat in the war?

A Nathaniel Lyon, at the Battle of Wilson's Creek, on August 10, 1861.

Q Stone Bridge and Henry Hill were features of which battlefield?

A Bull Run/Manassas.

DID YOU KNOW

LIKE THE INFANTRY, THE BASIC CAVALRY COMPONENT ON BOTH SIDES WAS
A REGIMENT COMMANDED BY A COLONEL. A CONFEDERATE CAVALRY
REGIMENT WAS MADE UP OF SOME 10 COMPANIES OF BETWEEN 60 TO 80
MEN. IN THE UNION ARMY A CAVALRY REGIMENT HAD ABOUT 1,000 MEN
DIVIDED INTO SIX SQUADRONS, EACH CONTAINING TWO TROOPS OF UP TO
100 MEN. THE ORGANIZATION WAS SIMPLIFIED IN 1863, AND THE
SQUADRON WAS REPLACED BY BATTALIONS OF FOUR TROOPS EACH.

Q Who was the only senator from a seceded state to remain at his
post in Washington, D.C.?

A Andrew Johnson from Tennessee. In the great debate of the 1850s
over whether or not slavery should be extended into the new territories, Johnson supported the Southern belief that it should. Although
Johnson upheld the institution of slavery, he remained pro-Union and
refused to support Southern secession even after Tennessee seceded in
May 1861.

Q Which Union commander said, "If I owned both Hell and Texas,
I'd rent out Texas and live in Hell"?

A Philip Sheridan, who hated the South with a passion.

" WE GO, WE CARE NOT WHERE OR WHEN.
OUR COUNTRY CALLS US,
WE ARE HERE!
HARPER'S WEEKLY, APRIL 1861 "

Q In February 1861 what steps did the Confederate government take to safeguard the security of the Southern states?

A Jailing potential enemies, and President Davis was authorized to suspend *habeas corpus* (the fundamental law that forbids arrest and imprisonment without trial) and was given the right to allow the army to impose martial law in Richmond and other towns in Virginia that were in danger of Union attack. Martial law gave the power of arrest to the army's provost marshal.

Q Who was the chief detective who foiled the Baltimore assassination plot against President Lincoln in March 1861?

A Allan Pinkerton, who had set up a successful detective agency in Chicago in 1852.

Q Who, on the outbreak of the Civil War, approached the Lincoln administration with a proposal to make a photographic record of the conflict?

A Mathew Brady. The idea was approved, but Brady had to finance the ambitious undertaking himself.

Q Who was Samuel Preston Moore?

A The founder of the Confederate Medical Department, who recruited doctors and nurses, set up procedures for treating the sick and wounded, founded hospitals, and eventually gave the Confederacy a medical service similar to that of the Union.

Q Which Union commander was born in Lancaster, Ohio, on February 8, 1820, one of 11 children?

A William Tecumseh Sherman.

Q Who built the first Union ironclad?

A In 1861 Union Secretary of the Navy Gideon Welles commissioned Swedish inventor John Ericsson to build the first Union ironclad. Ericsson completed his revolutionary ship, the USS *Monitor*, in January 1862.

> " IF WE ARE SURROUNDED, WE MUST CUT
> # OUR WAY OUT AS WE CUT
> # OUR WAY IN
> ULYSSES S. GRANT, NOVEMBER 1861 "

Q Why did Thomas "Stonewall" Jackson walk or ride with one arm raised?

A He imagined that one side of his body weighed more than the other and so often walked or rode with one arm raised to keep his balance.

Q Which famous unit was formed by New Yorker Hiram Berdan in November 1861?

A The 1st U.S. Sharpshooters, known as Berdan's Sharpshooters.

DID YOU KNOW

WHEN THE NORTHERN PRESS LEARNT OF WINFIELD SCOTT'S IDEA FOR STRANGLING THE SOUTH, THEY RIDICULED ITS CAUTION AND DUBBED IT "THE ANACONDA PLAN" FOR A RIVER SNAKE THAT COILS AROUND ITS PREY AND SQUEEZES IT TO DEATH. THE ANACONDA PLAN ALSO FOUND LITTLE FAVOR WITH UNION POLITICIANS AND ARMY OFFICERS EAGER FOR A QUICK VICTORY—THEY THOUGHT IT NOT AGGRESSIVE ENOUGH. SCOTT HAD FORESEEN THIS IN HIS LETTER TO MCCLELLAN: "THE GREATEST OBSTACLE IN THE WAY OF THIS PLAN [IS] THE IMPATIENCE OF OUR PATRIOTIC AND LOYAL UNION FRIENDS. THEY WILL URGE INSTANT AND VIGOROUS ACTION, REGARDLESS, I FEAR, OF THE CONSEQUENCES."

Q What were the entry requirements?

A Recruits had to pass a difficult shooting test in which they had to fire 10 bullets into a 10in (25 cm) circle 200 yards (180 m) away.

Q Who said he would not allow "millions of our people to perish to please the Northern states"?

A The British foreign secretary, Lord John Russell, commenting on the Union blockade of the South, which prevented cotton reaching British mills.

Q **What was the Trent Affair?**

A In November 1861, James M. Mason of Virginia and John Slidell of Louisiana slipped through the Union blockade at Charleston, South Carolina, and reached Havana in Cuba, where they boarded the British steamer *Trent* bound for Europe. Mason was on his way to take up the position of Confederate minister to Britain. Slidell was bound for Paris to fulfil the same diplomatic role in France. However, Captain Charles Wilkes of the 13-gun Union sloop *San Jacinto* intercepted the *Trent* and seized Mason and Slidell.

Q **Why did it cause outrage in Britain?**

A Wilkes' action was in breach of international law. Britain was a neutral country not at war with the Union.

Q **How was the affair resolved?**

A The Union accepted that Wilkes had acted without authority, and Mason and Slidell were released. By way of compromise, the British dropped their insistence on a formal apology.

Q Which victory gave the Union control over southeastern Missouri in October 1861?

A The Battle of Fredericktown. Missouri Guard troops under Brigadier General M. Jeff Thompson attempted to expel Union troops from Fredericktown but were repulsed.

Q What was the staple food of all Civil War troops?

A Hardbread, also known as hardtack, ship's biscuit, teeth-dullers, or pilot bread. It was made from flour, water, and salt.

Q Who was elected governor of Alabama in December 1861?

A John Gill Shorter. His support for President Davis' unpopular wartime measures cost him his position in 1863.

47

DID YOU KNOW

THE BASIC OBJECTIVE OF INFANTRY TACTICS WAS TO BE ABLE TO MANEUVER UNITS OF TROOPS INTO A POSITION WHERE THEY COULD DEPLOY ON THE BATTLEFIELD AS QUICKLY AND EFFICIENTLY AS POSSIBLE, SO AS TO BRING THE MAXIMUM AMOUNT OF MUSKET FIRE ON TO THE ENEMY AND THEN TO CHARGE WITH BAYONETS AND DRIVE THE ENEMY FROM THE FIELD. CONFEDERATE COMMANDER "STONEWALL" JACKSON'S BRIGADE BROKE THE UNION ATTACK ON HENRY HILL USING EXACTLY THESE TACTICS IN THE FIRST BATTLE OF BULL RUN (MANASSAS) IN JULY 1861.

Q What sort of action was the Battle of Hatteras Inlet Batteries/Fort Clark/Fort Hatteras, North Carolina, in August 1861?

A A Union amphibious raid against shore batteries around Hatteras Inlet.

Q At the start of the Civil War how did infantry fight on the battlefield?

A In a battle line two ranks deep facing the enemy.

Q What tactics did skirmishers use in battle?

A Skirmishers operated in "open order," each man spaced a few yards from the next, taking advantage of available cover to keep the enemy line under fire. They also maintained contact with the enemy and gave warning if they began to move forward for an attack.

DID YOU KNOW

NATHANIEL PRENTISS BANKS (1816–1894) WAS BORN IN WALTHAM, MASSACHUSETTS, ON JANUARY 30, 1816. HE CAME FROM A POOR FAMILY AND LEFT SCHOOL TO WORK IN A FACTORY. LATER BANKS STUDIED LAW AND BECAME A POLITICIAN, BEING ELECTED TO CONGRESS IN 1853 AS A DEMOCRAT. HE OPPOSED THE WESTERN EXPANSION OF SLAVERY, HOWEVER, AND SWITCHED TO THE REPUBLICAN PARTY IN 1855. IN 1858 HE WAS ELECTED GOVERNOR OF HIS HOME STATE. WHEN THE WAR BEGAN, LINCOLN NEEDED THE SUPPORT OF INFLUENTIAL MEN AND SO GAVE THEM KEY MILITARY OFFICES. IN MAY 1861 HE APPOINTED BANKS MAJOR GENERAL OF VOLUNTEERS DESPITE HIS LACK OF MILITARY EXPERIENCE.

> ## IF IT IS NECESSARY THAT I SHOULD FALL
> ## ON THE BATTLEFIELD FOR
> ## MY COUNTRY, I AM READY
> SULLIVAN BALLOU TO HIS WIFE SARAH, JULY 1861

Q At which battle was Robert E. Lee defeated in September 1861?

A The Battle of Cheat Mountain Summit in West Virginia. Lee was defeated by a trenchant Union defense on Cheat Mountain and in the Tygart Valley, despite the Confederates being in greater strength.

Q Which ship ran the Union blockade of the port of St. Pierre on Martinique in the West Indies in November 1861?

A The Confederate cruiser CSS *Sumter*.

49

Q Chief Opothleyahola led which Indian tribes?

A Creek and Seminole during the Indian Wars in Oklahoma in late 1861.

Q At the beginning of the war who headed the Union Army Medical Bureau?

A An 80-year-old veteran of the War of 1812, Surgeon General Thomas Lawson.

Q Name two other heads of the Army Medical Bureau.

A When Lawson died in May 1861, he was replaced by Clement A. Finley, who did little to improve the bureau. Finley held the surgeon general's job until April 1862, when 33-year-old William A. Hammond took his place. Hammond would bring much better leadership to the Medical Bureau, expanding its size and improving its professionalism.

> **❝** HE UNDERSTANDS NOTHING,
> **UNDERSTANDS NOTHING,**
> **AND IS EVER IN MY WAY ❞**
> McClellan, talking of Winfield Scott

Q Which Union commander asked to be relieved of his command in the autumn of 1861?

A William Tecumseh Sherman. In the autumn of 1861 Sherman was put in charge of the Department of the Cumberland, where his request for more troops led him to be labelled "crazy" in the press. He then became agitated and depressed, and asked to be relieved of his command.

DID YOU KNOW

In 1861, Union navy officials immediately began adding to the fleet by commissioning new vessels. In addition, they bought civilian vessels of all sorts to fit out for wartime use. By the end of 1861 the Union navy had nearly 200 vessels in service and 22,000 naval personnel. This number continued to grow until, by the end of the war, the navy had some 670 ships and 51,500 men.

Q Who, at the Battle of First Bull Run, said: "There is Jackson, standing like a stone wall!"?

A General Barnard Bee. A West Point graduate and Mexican War veteran, Bee was appointed brigadier general in the Confederate Army and assigned to command a brigade in General Beauregard's Army of Virginia at Manassas Junction. Bee was mortally wounded at First Bull Run.

51

Q At the beginning of the war what was the objective of infantry tactics?

A To bring the maximum amount of musket fire against the enemy and then to charge with bayonets fixed and drive the opposition from the field.

Q Which Confederate general fought in the Seminole Indian War in Florida (1835–1837) and the Mexican War (1846–1848)?

A Jubal Anderson Early. An 1837 graduate of the Military Academy at West Point, Early fought in the Seminole Indian War before resigning his commission to begin a career as an attorney and politician. He returned to serve in the Mexican War as a major of volunteers.

Q What was "Manifest Destiny"?

A The conviction, widely held in the early and mid-nineteenth century, that the entire North American continent must eventually belong to the United States.

Q Why was the Union commander John Charles Frémont known as "the Pathfinder"?

A He had led a series of expeditions to the West before the war, which had turned him into a national hero.

> " OH, THE MUSKETS THEY MAY RATTLE,
> AND THE CANNON THEY MAY ROAR,
> ### BUT WE'LL FIGHT FOR
> ### YOU, JEFF DAVIS, ALONG THE
> ### SOUTHERN SHORE "
> ANONYMOUS

Q On the outbreak of war, what percentage of Southerners lived in towns with a population greater than 2,500?

A Seven percent. Five Southern states had no city with 10,000 citizens.

1862

As the war increased in scope and ferocity,
the North captured New Orleans and
General Grant won the Battle of Shiloh.
But in the east Robert E. Lee fought larger
Union forces to a standstill, aided by the
superb generalship of "Stonewall" Jackson in
the Shenandoah Valley.

" YOU APPEAR MUCH CONCERNED AT MY ATTACKING ON A SUNDAY. I AM GREATLY CONCERNED, TOO "

"STONEWALL" JACKSON TO HIS WIFE, MARCH 1862

Q Which battle in January 1862 stopped the Confederates' 1861 Kentucky offensive?

A The Battle of Middle Creek. Union units commanded by Colonel James Garfield defeated Brigadier General Humphrey Marshall's troops at Middle Creek, eastern Kentucky.

Q What was the largest city in the Confederacy?

A New Orleans.

Q What were the Union Leagues?

A Nonofficial organizations that produced Union propaganda, which were maintained by middle-class enthusiasts. The first such league was formed in Philadelphia in 1862.

Q Which Union victory wrested control of eastern Kentucky from the Confederates in January 1861?

A The Battle of Mill Springs/Logan's Crossroads/Fishing Creek. Union Brigadier General George Thomas' forces, having arrived at Logan's Crossroads on January 17, were attacked by Confederates under Major General George Crittenden at dawn. The Confederate attack was initially successful but then ran into stiff resistance. A second Confederate attack was repulsed. Union counterattacks on the Confederate right and left eventually pushed the enemy back to Murfreesboro, Tennessee.

Q Who commanded the gunboats that bombarded Fort Henry from the Tennessee River on February 6, 1862?

A Commodore Andrew H. Foote. The fort was poorly sited, unfinished, and half-flooded.

Q What was the North's first major victory in the war?

A The capture of Fort Donelson, Tennessee, in February 1862.

Q Who was the "Young Napoleon of the West"?

A George B. McClellan. At the outbreak of the war McClellan joined the Ohio Volunteers and in May 1861 was appointed a major general in the regular army (he had left it four years earlier as a captain). As commander of Union forces in the Ohio Valley, his instructions were to hold on to western Virginia (later West Virginia) for the Union. He secured the region by mid-July, having encountered little resistance, and was soon being talked up in newspapers as the "Young Napoleon of the West."

DID YOU KNOW

Within a year the Union League movement had spread over 18 Northern states and even begun to make an appearance among Unionists in the South. The Loyal Publication Society, established by the Union League of New York, raised nearly $30,000 during the three years of its existence and published 900,000 copies of 90 different pamphlets. They were distributed to league organizations across the Union and to soldiers at the front.

DID YOU KNOW

By 1862 the British and French textile industries were suffering from the shortage of raw cotton, and there was considerable agitation to do something to alleviate the situation. On the surface this played into Southern hands. All Britain had to do was break the Union blockade. However, under international law, if a blockade was successful, then it had a firm legal standing. By contrast, if it was poorly enforced and easily evaded, then there was no obligation to respect it. Southerners were quick to point out that blockade-runners (many privately owned British merchant ships) managed to evade the blockade every day. However, this amounted to an admission that the Confederacy was wilfully holding back cotton. The last thing Confederate diplomats could do was admit to an embargo, since Russell had already declared that Britain would never submit to commercial blackmail. So the Confederacy was left unable to mount a convincing case against the legality of the blockade.

Q What was a corduroy road?

A Logs laid side by side to facilitate movement over mud.

Q When was the Confederate Territory of Arizona formed?

A Arizona became a Confederate Territory when it was annexed by the Confederate President Jefferson Davis, who was also the ex-Secretary of War under President Abraham Lincoln, in January 1862. It was created out of the southern half of what was the old Territory of New Mexico.

Q Which victory in February 1862 meant that the Tennessee River became a Union highway as far south as Muscle Shoals, Alabama?

A The loss of Fort Henry, which unhinged the Confederacy's western line. The overall Southern commander, Albert S. Johnston, was forced to evacuate his forces from Columbus and Bowling Green, Kentucky.

Q What was significant about the Battle of Pea Ridge in March 1862?

A The Battle of Pea Ridge/Elkhorn Tavern, March 6–8, was the biggest battle to take place on Arkansas soil.

Q Name the opposing commanders at Pea Ridge.

A Major General Sterling Price and his 8,000 Confederate troops from Missouri had been forced out of that state into northwestern Arkansas by the Union forces of Samuel R. Curtis early in 1862. Earl Van Dorn's Confederate Army of the West joined Price's troops in the Boston Mountains, and the combined force moved north again. Van Dorn resolved to attack. He decided to march around Curtis' Union Army of the Southwest on the night of March 6 and attack from the north.

> IT IS CALLED THE
> ARMY OF THE POTOMAC
> BUT IT IS
> ONLY MCCLELLAN'S
> BODYGUARD
> ABRAHAM LINCOLN, APRIL 1862

Q Who were the "Green Mountain Boys"?

A Union recruits from Vermont, the Green Mountain State. More than 28,100 Vermonters served in Vermont volunteer units, while 5,000 others served in other states' units, in the United States Army, or in the United States Navy.

Q What were the two principal missions of the Army of the Potomac?

A Offensively, its job was to threaten the Confederate capital of Richmond, Virginia, and, in the process, to destroy the rival army protecting it. Defensively, its job was to shield Washington, D.C. Often the latter task hampered efforts to accomplish the first. Moreover, the proximity of the army to the Union capital meant that Washington politics exerted an extensive and largely negative influence over its operations.

" IF MCCLELLAN IS NOT USING THE ARMY,
I SHOULD LIKE TO BORROW IT FOR A WHILE
ABRAHAM LINCOLN, APRIL 1862 "

Q What was the *Merrimack*?

A A Union frigate. The Confederates converted it into an ironclad, with 4 in (10 cm) of iron armor plating and an iron ram mounted on its bow, and renamed it CSS *Virginia*. They launched it on a trial cruise from Norfolk, Virginia, into Hampton Roads in March 1862.

Q Who were the main protagonists at the Battle of Hampton Roads in March 1862?

A The ironclads CSS *Virginia* and USS *Monitor*. On March 8 the former attacked Union ships blockading Chesapeake Bay. In just a few hours the *Virginia* destroyed two Union warships, USS *Cumberland* and *Congress*, and damaged USS *Minnesota*. On March 9 the *Virginia* returned to Hampton Roads to continue the battle. To the crew's great surprise, it was met by an enemy ironclad, the USS *Monitor*. Smaller than the *Virginia*, the *Monitor* featured a revolving gun turret, a shallower draft and a higher top speed, which enabled it to outmaneuver the *Virginia* in the running battle that developed. The two vessels pounded each other for almost four hours at close range, eventually fighting to a standstill. At nightfall the *Virginia* withdrew into the James River. It had been hit 97 times over the two days, and the *Monitor* 21 times, but neither was badly damaged.

Q Why did the Battle of Hampton Roads change naval warfare?

A The ironclad showed that wooden and sail-powered warships were obsolete. As a result, both sides accelerated their ironclad-building programs, though the Confederacy was unable to match the Union's ironclad production.

DID YOU KNOW

As the Civil War went on, troop movements by railroad became much bigger and took place over greater distances. In July 1862, for example, the Confederate Army of the Mississippi, under Braxton Bragg, was ordered north from Tupelo, Mississippi, to Chattanooga, Tennessee, a distance of 775 miles (1,250 km). The army traveled by no fewer than six different railroads, taking a complicated route through Alabama and Georgia, but arrived by the end of the month to allow Bragg to launch an invasion north into Kentucky.

Q What was significant about the CSS *Florida?*

A The CSS *Florida*, officially designated in August 1862, was the first foreign-built warship constructed for the Confederate States (it was manufactured in Liverpool, Britain).

Q Why did the Confederate commander of Fort Donelson, Tennessee, John B. Floyd, decide to flee from the fort during the night rather than defend it against Grant in February 1862?

A Floyd, fearing that as a former U.S. secretary of war he might be tried for treason, resolved to join part of the garrison that planned to escape from the fort under cover of night. He turned command over to Gideon J. Pillow, who immediately passed it to his subordinate, the fort's third-ranking officer, Simon Bolivar Buckner.

> " MY HEADQUARTERS WILL BE
> # IN THE SADDLE
> MAJOR GENERAL JOHN POPE, JUNE 1862 "

Q What was a "Quaker" gun?

A A simulated cannon made from a wooden log, sometimes painted black, used to deceive an enemy into believing an opponent possessed excess guns. During the Civil War such tactics were used at the siege of Petersburg, First Bull Run and the Battle of Corinth. The name derives from the Quaker religious opposition to war and violence.

Q Name at least two rivers that formed a natural line of defense for the Confederate army in Virginia?

A The Rappahannock, the Rapidan, North Anna, and Pamunkey. Most of the rivers in Virginia run west to east, while the Union armies generally advanced north to south.

DID YOU KNOW

AT FIRST THE UNION BLOCKADE OF THE SOUTH EXISTED MAINLY ON PAPER. THE UNION NAVY DID NOT HAVE NEARLY ENOUGH VESSELS TO SCREEN THE 187 PORTS AND NAVIGABLE INLETS ON THE LONG COASTLINE BETWEEN CHESAPEAKE BAY AND THE RIO GRANDE. HOWEVER, BY ARMING ALMOST ANY VESSEL THAT WOULD FLOAT, GIDEON WELLES, UNION SECRETARY OF THE NAVY, RAPIDLY BUILT UP A RESPECTABLE FORCE. THE BLOCKADE CONSISTED OF HUNDREDS OF WARSHIPS, EVENTUALLY NUMBERING SOME 600, THAT PATROLLED THE CONFEDERATE COAST. MOST STAYED CLOSE TO HARBORS, WATCHING FOR ANY VESSEL THAT VENTURED IN OR OUT. WHEN THEY SPOTTED ONE, THEY WOULD GIVE CHASE. FOR MUCH OF THE TIME, HOWEVER, BLOCKADE DUTY COULD BE VERY DULL.

61

Q What was the first Confederate state capital to fall to Union forces?

A Having lost the protective Forts Donelson and Henry, Nashville in Tennessee was the first Confederate state capital to fall to Union forces. It was surrendered by the town's mayor.

Q Who replaced General Joseph E. Johnston as the commander of the Confederacy's eastern army in June 1862?

A When General Johnston was wounded at Fair Oaks, Virginia, on May 31, 1862, President Davis replaced him with Robert E. Lee. Taking command on June 1, Lee renamed his force of around 70,000 men the Army of Northern Virginia.

Q Why was Virginia's Shenandoah Valley strategically important?

A As a source of crops and livestock (it was the breadbasket of the Confederacy) and as a route by which Confederate forces could invade the North.

Q Who was the husband of Varina Howell?

A Confederate President Jefferson Finis Davis. Jefferson married Varina Howell (1826–1905) in 1845 and, in the same year, was elected to Congress as a Democrat. Varina Howell Davis was a great influence on her husband and supported his politics. The couple had six children and a happy marriage.

Q Who issued the phrase: "No terms except unconditional and immediate surrender can be accepted"?

A General Ulysses S. Grant, in answer to Simon Bolivar Buckner when the latter sent a message to Grant asking for terms for the surrender of Fort Donelson, Tennessee. About 15,000 Southerners capitulated.

Q Name the three basic cavalry weapons used in the Civil War.

A The three basic cavalry weapons used in the war were the saber, the carbine, and the pistol.

DID YOU KNOW

FOR MUCH OF THE WAR THE POLICY OF BOTH SIDES WAS NOT TO KEEP PRISONERS BUT TO RELEASE THEM ON PAROLE—MEANING THEY HAD TO PROMISE NOT TO TAKE UP ARMS AGAIN UNTIL EXCHANGED FOR AN ENEMY SOLDIER. THE FIRST PRISONER EXCHANGE TOOK PLACE IN FEBRUARY 1862, AND IN JULY BOTH SIDES AGREED TO PAROLE PRISONERS WITHIN 10 DAYS AND TO EXCHANGE THEM AT AN AGREED RATE. ONE GENERAL, FOR EXAMPLE, COULD BE EXCHANGED FOR 60 ENLISTED MEN. HOWEVER, BY THE SUMMER OF 1863 THE EXCHANGE SYSTEM HAD BROKEN DOWN DUE TO A LACK OF TRUST ON BOTH SIDES. BY LATE 1864 THE NUMBER OF PRISONERS BEING HELD IN CAMPS HAD SOARED INTO THE HUNDREDS OF THOUSANDS. AND CONDITIONS IN MANY PRISON CAMPS BECAME MURDEROUS.

Q Name one of the most common types of carbine used by the Union cavalry in the war.

A The Sharps. The most advanced carbine was the Spencer breechloading repeater, which could fire seven rounds before reloading. By 1865 the Union Army had issued more than 80,000 Sharps and 90,000 Spencers to its cavalrymen.

> " NOT ONLY DOES ECONOMY, BUT NAVAL
> SUCCESS, DICTATE THE WISDOM
> ## OF FIGHTING WITH IRON
> ## AGAINST WOOD
> STEPHEN R. MALLORY, 1862 "

63

Q The river war in the West occurred roughly in three phases. What was the first phase?

A The first, from January to March 1862, saw Union forces concentrate on the Tennessee and Cumberland rivers. Commodore Andrew Foote and General Ulysses S. Grant carried out a model campaign of joint army-navy operations, capturing Forts Henry and Donelson, and opening up the Tennessee and Cumberland rivers all the way to Corinth, Mississippi, and Florence, Alabama.

Q What was the February 1862 Legal Tender Act?

A It issued $150 million in Treasury notes, popularly known as greenbacks. These notes were not directly backed by gold reserves.

Q What was at the center of the Legal Tender Act?

A The act compelled people to accept greenbacks for all debts, public or private, with two exceptions: customs duties and interest on government bonds. The system made government bonds a very attractive investment. The bonds sold briskly, and not just to banks and wealthy investors. Ordinary citizens could buy bonds in notes as low as $50, and a large-scale advertising campaign worked overtime to make sure that they did.

Q What was the fate of the CSS *Virginia*?

A In May 1862 the *Virginia* was sunk by its crew to prevent it falling into Union hands—the ironclad was trapped in the Norfolk shipyard when the Union retook it.

" NEVER TAKE COUNSEL OF YOUR FEARS "
"STONEWALL" JACKSON, JUNE 1862

Q Which battle, fought on March 23, 1862, resulted in Washington stationing nearly 60,000 troops to protect the Shenandoah Valley and the region around the Union capital?

A The Battle of Kernstown. General "Stonewall" Jackson, as part of his mission to divert as many Union troops as possible from the Peninsular Campaign in Virginia, attacked a Union division of 9,000 men at Kernstown (Jackson had 4,500 men). Jackson lost, but Washington assumed that he would only have attacked if he had outnumbered the Union force.

Q What was a rail gun?

A Siege artillery mounted on a flatbed rail truck.

Q What was the strategic aim of the Union's Peninsular Campaign in spring 1862?

A President Abraham Lincoln wanted an offensive straight through northern Virginia to capture Richmond, but the commander of the Army of the Potomac, George B. McClellan, suggested exploiting the Union navy's control of the coast by transporting troops from the Potomac River down Chesapeake Bay to the Union-held Fort Monroe on the tip of the Virginia peninsula between the James and York rivers. The Union army would then be only 75 miles (120 km) from Richmond, and could be kept supplied by sea.

Q What was "The Great Locomotive Chase"?

A In April 1862 Union agent James Ambrose and 22 soldier volunteers stole a Confederate train in an attempt to destroy sections of the Western & Atlantic Railroad, Georgia. The operation resulted in a prolonged railroad chase, but the Union insurgents were eventually captured, and James and seven others were hanged.

DID YOU KNOW

IN JULY 1862 THE CONFEDERATE CONGRESS AUTHORIZED THE FORMATION OF SHARPSHOOTER BATTALIONS WITHIN STANDARD INFANTRY BRIGADES. BRIGADE COMMANDERS COULD HANDPICK MEN FROM EACH REGIMENT FOR THIS DEMANDING AND RISKY DUTY. BECAUSE OF THE EXTRA TRAINING INVOLVED, THEY WERE OFTEN EXEMPTED FROM STANDARD CAMP DUTIES; IN COMBAT THEY SERVED AS ADVANCE AND REARGUARDS ON THE MARCH AND AS SKIRMISHERS ONCE FIGHTING BEGAN. CONFEDERATE SHARP-SHOOTERS HAD TO BE ABLE TO HIT A MAN-SIZED TARGET AT 600 YARDS (550 M). SHARPSHOOTERS IN BOTH ARMIES WERE USUALLY EQUIPPED WITH SPECIALIZED RIFLES, FREQUENTLY WITH TELESCOPIC SIGHTS.

Q Name the two opposing commanders at the Battle of Shiloh/Pittsburg Landing in April 1862.

A General Ulysses S. Grant with his Union army of 30,000 against General Albert S. Johnston's 45,000 Confederates, with General Pierre G.T. Beauregard as his second in command.

Q What was the Confederate plan at Shiloh?

A On April 3 Johnston advanced towards Pittsburg Landing. He planned a surprise attack; but disorganization and bad weather slowed the Confederates down, and they arrived south of Grant's position on the night of April 5. The delay did not jeopardize Johnston's plan, because Grant had not posted lookouts around his army. The Union soldiers had no idea they faced a Southern army until about 05:00 hours, when thousands of men in gray charged out of the woods.

> " I NEVER WENT INTO THE ARMY WITHOUT
> ## REGRET AND NEVER RETIRED
> ## WITHOUT PLEASURE
> ULYSSES S. GRANT "

Q What was the most famous exploit of the Confederate spy Belle Boyd?

A When she was staying at her father's hotel at Front Royal in Warren County, in May 1862, she discovered that a knothole in her bedroom floor allowed her to eavesdrop on Union officers in the parlor below. One night she overheard them discussing a plan to blow up key bridges around Front Royal in order to thwart an imminent attack by Confederates led by General Thomas "Stonewall" Jackson. Belle jumped on a horse and rode 15 miles (24 km) through Union positions to inform Jackson, who responded by beginning his attack early.

DID YOU KNOW

Q The Army of Northern Virginia incorporated leaders and units from all the states of the Confederacy, but where did the largest number come from?

A North Carolina.

Q What was "the Hornet's Nest"?

A At the Battle of Shiloh on April 6, 1862, the Confederates first struck the Union right, attacking William T. Sherman's division at Shiloh Church. They then attacked the Union center, pushing three divisions back across Purdy Road. Southern reinforcements forced Sherman's men back to the Savannah Road by 10:00 hours. The Union right retreated, but Generals Hurlburt and Prentiss held their ground on the center and left of the Union line in and around a peach orchard for nearly five hours. The buzzing noise of bullets gave Prentiss' position the name "the Hornet's Nest."

Q Why did General Beauregard assume command of the Confederate army at the Battle of Shiloh?

A By early afternoon on April 6 Johnston ordered forward his reserve corps. Soon afterwards he was wounded in the leg, and command passed to Beauregard. Johnston later bled to death.

> ❝ LEE IS THE ONLY MAN I KNOW WHOM I
> # WOULD FOLLOW BLINDFOLD
> JACKSON, OF LEE, MAY 1862 ❞

Q What happened on the second day of the Battle of Shiloh?

A Grant stabilized his army in the early hours on April 7, 1862. During the night Buell's divisions crossed the river, artillery was concentrated above Pittsburg Landing, and gunboats fired on Confederate positions. The Federals counterattacked. The Confederates lost all the ground they had won the day before and retreated to Corinth.

Q What were the casualties in the Battle of Shiloh?

A The battle, one of the bloodiest of the conflict, cost the South 10,700 killed and wounded for no gain at all, while the North narrowly avoided defeat at a cost of 13,000 casualties.

Q What was the objective of Jackson's campaign in the Shenandoah Valley in spring 1862?

A Tying down as many Union troops as possible, a strategic diversion to draw strength from McClellan's advance on Richmond (the Peninsular Campaign).

Q The Shenandoah Valley was more important to the Confederacy than the Union. Why?

A The Shenandoah Valley was important to the Confederacy as a source of provisions and as a route for invading the North. It was less important to the Union: the Valley was not a suitable invasion route. Nevertheless, it was important for Washington to deny its use to the enemy.

Q Who was the Confederate commander responsible for the defence of the Virginia peninsula in spring 1862?

A General John B. Magruder.

Q How did he prevent the Army of the Potomac advancing against Richmond?

A Magruder hastily built two defensive lines between the York and the James rivers, defended Yorktown, and fooled McClellan into believing that his force of 13,000 was much larger by carrying out a series of deceptive maneuvers. Faced with the Yorktown defenses, McClellan stalled his advance. He became convinced that he faced a Confederate army of at least 100,000; and instead of sweeping Magruder aside and racing for Richmond, he laid siege to Yorktown.

Q Who was the Union commander in the Shenandoah Valley in spring 1862?

A General Nathaniel P. Banks.

DID YOU KNOW

"JEB" STUART'S MOST FAMOUS EXPLOIT WAS HIS RAID IN JUNE 1862 AROUND UNION GENERAL GEORGE B. MCCLELLAN'S 100,000 TROOPS CAMPED OUTSIDE RICHMOND, VIRGINIA. ON THE THREE-DAY RAID HIS 1,200 MEN RODE 100 MILES (160 KM), CAPTURING 165 MEN AND 260 HORSES. FOLLOWING THIS RAID, STUART WAS PROMOTED, AT AGE 28, TO MAJOR GENERAL IN CHARGE OF ALL CAVALRY IN THE ARMY OF NORTHERN VIRGINIA. LATER THAT SUMMER STUART RAIDED THE HEADQUARTERS OF UNION GENERAL JOHN POPE DURING THE SECOND BULL RUN CAMPAIGN, MAKING OFF WITH ONE OF POPE'S UNIFORMS AND SOME IMPORTANT DOCUMENTS. IN OCTOBER OF THAT YEAR HE MADE A SECOND RAID AROUND MCCLELLAN AT CHAMBERSBURG, PENNSYLVANIA.

Q Why was the town of Winchester, Virginia, strategically important?

A Winchester lay directly on an invasion route that either the Confederacy or the Union might use for flanking movements around Washington, D.C., or Richmond, and it offered an entry into the Shenandoah Valley.

Q Name at least two neutral ports used by Confederate blockade-runners.

A Blockade-runners did not have to sail all the way to Europe. Instead, their usual destinations were the neutral ports of Nassau, Bahamas; St. George, Bermuda; Havana, Cuba; and St. Thomas in the Virgin Islands. There cotton was transferred to regular merchantmen for the voyage to Europe, while the blockade-runners loaded their cargoes for the dash back to the South through the Union blockade.

Q Which fort, near Paducah, helped the Union control western Kentucky?

A Fort Anderson, Kentucky.

DID YOU KNOW

WHEN MARTINSBURG, VIRGINIA, WAS OCCUPIED BY UNION FORCES IN 1861, THE 17-YEAR-OLD CONFEDERATE SPY BELLE BOYD CHARMED AND BEFRIENDED THE OFFICERS. POSING AS AN INNOCENT, SHE CAREFULLY NOTED DOWN UNGUARDED COMMENTS ABOUT TROOP MOVEMENTS AND PLANS, AND SMUGGLED THEM OUT BY MESSENGERS TO CONFEDERATES IN THE FIELD. SHOWING HER CONFEDERATE HEART AND METTLE, SHE SHOT DEAD A DRUNKEN UNION SOLDIER WHO BARGED INTO THE FAMILY HOME AND WAS ATTEMPTING TO RAISE THE STARS AND STRIPES OVER THE HOUSE. SHE WAS TRIED BUT ACQUITTED, AND THE VIVACIOUS YOUNG BELLE CONTINUED TO BE A FAVOURITE WITH THE UNION OFFICERS.

CIVIL WAR TRIVIA BOOK

> AN ADMIRABLE ENGINEER, BUT HE SEEMS TO HAVE A SPECIAL TALENT FOR THE STATIONARY ENGINE
>
> LINCOLN, TALKING OF McCLELLAN

Q What was the Confederate Partisan Ranger Act?

A Passed by the Confederate Congress on April 21, 1862, it recognized Southern guerrilla forces as legal military formations. The act essentially legalized Confederate partisan warfare.

Q In April 1862, why did the Confederate Louisiana authorities not retain many soldiers to protect the city of New Orleans?

A They believed that Forts Jackson and St. Philip on the Mississippi River, 75 miles (120 km) south of the city, would protect New Orleans from any Union invasion. However, a Union fleet sailed up the river to the forts, bombarded them, and then steamed on past, losing only four ships. The forts surrendered on April 29, and New Orleans fell the next day with little opposition.

Q What were the results of the fall of New Orleans to the Union in April 1862?

A It opened up the rest of Louisiana and the Mississippi Valley to Union invasion, and damaged Confederate morale.

Q What was the result of the First Battle of Winchester, May 25, 1862?

A Fought on the hills southwest of the town, General Thomas J. "Stonewall" Jackson's Confederates attacked Union General Nathaniel P. Banks' troops so fiercely that they broke ranks and fled north. Union losses were 2,019, compared with 400 Confederates. The latter had relieved the pressure on Richmond.

Q When was the first Confederate conscription act passed?

A April 16, 1862. The act enlisted Southern men between the ages of 18 and 50 and took them from their farms. Only planters who held public office or owned at least 20 slaves were exempt from military service. As Southern men left their farms, agricultural production declined. Production also suffered as slaves became increasingly reluctant to work. Slave men and women anticipated freedom.

Q Which Southern port did Fort Pulaski protect?

A Savannah. The port was also protected by Forts Walker and McAllister.

> " LAY ME DOWN AND
> ## SAVE THE FLAG!
> COLONEL JAMES A. MULLIGAN,
> BATTLE OF KERNSTOWN, MARCH 1862 "

Q Name at least two commanders of the Army of the Potomac.

A Four generals commanded the army during its career. They were McClellan (August 20, 1861, to November 9, 1862), Ambrose E. Burnside (November 9, 1862, to January 26, 1863), Joseph Hooker (January 26 to June 28, 1863), and George G. Meade (June 28, 1863, to September 1, 1865). To this list might be added Ulysses S. Grant, who habitually made his headquarters with the Army of the Potomac and gave detailed instructions to Meade, the nominal commander.

DID YOU KNOW

WHILE IRONCLADS FOUGHT FOR POSSESSION OF CONFEDERATE HARBORS, GUNBOATS FOUGHT FOR POSSESSION OF CONFEDERATE-HELD RIVERS. A FEW HAD LIGHT IRON ARMOR BUT MANY WERE ACTUALLY PROTECTED BY "ARMOR" MADE FROM COTTON BALES. THE ARMOR HAD TO BE LIGHT SO THAT THE VESSELS DID NOT DRAW TOO MUCH WATER TO NAVIGATE UP SHALLOW RIVERS AND INLETS. ALTHOUGH THE CONFEDERATES MANAGED TO CONSTRUCT A FEW GUNBOATS, THEY RELIED MAINLY ON SHORE-BASED ARTILLERY TO GUARD THEIR NAVIGABLE RIVERS.

Q What was phase two of the Western naval campaign, from March 1862 to July 1863?

A This involved attempts to open the length of the Mississippi River as a line of communication for Union forces. Foote and John Pope operated against Confederate forts north of Memphis, Tennessee, in 1862, completing the capture of most of Tennessee for Union forces. Grant, Foote, and David D. Porter cooperated in 1863 to besiege Vicksburg, Mississippi, which fell on July 4, 1863. With Vicksburg in Union hands the last fort on the Mississippi at Port Hudson surrendered, and Union naval forces had free access to the entire length of the river.

Q What was the result of the Siege of Corinth from April 29 to June 10, 1862, in Corinth, Mississippi?

A Union forces secured their positions in northern Mississippi by taking Corinth. The Union's capture of Corinth also cut the Confederacy's east–west railroad link.

Q Which Union general, after having executed a Southerner in June 1862 for tearing down the United States flag, was denounced by President Davis as a felon deserving capital punishment?

A General Benjamin Franklin Butler.

Q At which battle was Confederate leader Joseph E. Johnston wounded in May 1862?

A The Battle of Seven Pines/Fair Oaks Station, Virginia, on May 31–June 1. At about 19:00 hours on May 31 Johnston was seriously wounded, and command fell to General Gustavus W. Smith.

Q What was the only Confederate ship to escape the defeat at the Battle of Memphis, Tennessee, on June 6, 1862?

A *General Van Dorn*. Union Flag Officer Charles H. Davis and Colonel Charles Ellet launched a naval attack on Memphis after 04:00 hours on June 6. After 90 minutes the Union boats had sunk or captured all but one of the Confederate vessels; *General Van Dorn* escaped. Union casualties were one, Confederate losses were 180.

> ## A CASE OF SOUTHERN DASH AGAINST
> # NORTHERN PLUCK AND ENDURANCE
> ### ULYSSES S. GRANT, ON THE BATTLE OF SHILOH

Q What was the consequence of the fall of Memphis?

A Memphis was an important commercial and economic center on the Mississippi River. Its capture opened another section of the river to Union shipping.

Q What happened after the Seven Days' Battles, fought near Richmond between June 25 and July 1, 1862?

A The Union army was forced to retreat to Harrison's Landing on the James River, ending the Union's Peninsular Campaign.

DID YOU KNOW

AMBROSE BURNSIDE (1824–1881) GRADUATED FROM THE U.S. MILITARY ACADEMY AT WEST POINT IN 1847 AND SERVED ON THE WESTERN FRONTIER, WHERE HE WAS WOUNDED FIGHTING THE APACHES. IN MAY 1861, BURNSIDE BECAME COLONEL OF THE 1ST RHODE ISLAND INFANTRY AND WAS ASSIGNED TO DEFEND WASHINGTON, D.C. BY JUNE HE WAS COMMANDING A BRIGADE IN THE 2D DIVISION OF THE ARMY OF NORTHEASTERN VIRGINIA. IN AUGUST BURNSIDE WAS PROMOTED TO BRIGADIER GENERAL AND SENT TO COMMAND AN EXPEDITIONARY FORCE ALONG THE COAST OF NORTH CAROLINA. SUCCESSES AT ROANOKE ISLAND AND INLAND AT NEW BERN IN MID-FEBRUARY 1862 LED TO HIS PROMOTION TO MAJOR GENERAL. IN JULY BURNSIDE SAILED WITH REIN-FORCEMENTS TO HELP THE ARMY OF THE POTOMAC, WHICH WAS FIGHTING ALONG THE JAMES RIVER. TAKING COMMAND OF IX CORPS, HE TOOK PART IN THE LAST ACTIONS OF MCCLELLAN'S PENINSULAR CAMPAIGN.

Q What made Confederate leader Joseph E. Johnston attack the Union Army at Seven Pines in May–June 1862?

A McClellan's Union Army of the Potomac had reached the outskirts of Richmond. But McClellan had divided his army, positioning two corps south of the Chickahominy River and three corps to the north, where they could join with Union forces advancing from Fredericksburg. Johnston saw a chance to strike while the Union army was divided.

Q At Seven Pines why did President Davis replace General Gustavus W. Smith with Robert E. Lee?

A Smith renewed the Confederate attack on June 1 with a series of poorly orchestrated assaults, which were repulsed. Davis replaced Smith with Robert E. Lee, who immediately ordered a general withdrawal. The outcome of the battle was inconclusive. The Confederates suffered 6,150 casualties and the Union about 5,050 casualties.

Q Name the opposing commanders at the Battle of Cross Keys, Virginia, on June 8, 1862.

A Union General John C. Frémont (10,500 men), who was marching towards Jackson on the west side of the Massanutten mountain range, engaged General Richard S. Ewell's three Confederate brigades (5,000 men).

Q At Cross Keys, what maneuver could have proved disastrous for the Confederates.

A When a Union brigade attacked the Confederate right, General Isaac R. Trimble's Confederate brigade repulsed it with only a few volleys of rifle fire. Then Trimble decided to attack a Union battery half a mile away. The battery escaped, but Trimble's charge carried him a mile away from Ewell. Though the Confederates were now vulnerable, Frémont did not exploit their weakness.

Q Name at least two of the battles won by "Stonewall" Jackson during his campaign in the Shenandoah Valley in May–June 1862.

A During the campaign Jackson moved up and down the valley at great speed, confusing the Union command as to his strength and whereabouts. His army of 17,000 outmaneuvered three Union forces with a combined strength of 64,000. He won five battles—Front Royal, McDowell, First Winchester, Cross Keys, and Port Republic—between May 8 and June 9, 1862.

DID YOU KNOW

SHARPSHOOTERS PLAYED A VITAL ROLE IN THE CIVIL WAR. THE FEAR OF THEIR EXPERT MARKSMANSHIP HAD A STRONG PSYCHOLOGICAL EFFECT ON THEIR ENEMIES. THEY WERE ORGANIZED INTO SPECIAL UNITS THAT COULD OPERATE INDEPENDENTLY OF LARGE UNITS, PERFORMING SCOUTING AND SKIRMISHING DUTIES.

"
IT IS WELL THAT WAR IS SO TERRIBLE:
WE WOULD GROW TOO FOND OF IT
ROBERT E. LEE, DECEMBER 1862
"

Q What was the Confederate illustrated paper set up in 1862 to rival the North's illustrated papers?

A Richmond's *Southern Illustrated News*, which had some 20,000 subscribers.

Q What engagement was the first of the Seven Days' Campaign?

A The Battle of Oak Grove/ French's Field/King's School House, on June 25, 1862. General McClellan's Union advance in Henrico County, Virginia, was blunted.

Q Name the Confederate commander during the Seven Days' Campaign and the name of his army.

A Robert E. Lee. After an unsuccessful field command in western Virginia and an inspection tour of coastal fortifications in South Carolina and Georgia, Lee returned to Richmond to become chief military advisor to President Jefferson Davis. After Joseph E. Johnston was wounded in fighting against an advancing Union army, Lee assumed command of Confederate forces defending Richmond. He named his forces the Army of Northern Virginia.

Q Who was the Union commander at the Battle of Beaver Dam Creek/Mechanicsville/Ellerson's Mill, Virginia, on June 26, 1862?

A Fitz John Porter.

Q What was Robert E. Lee's first battlefield victory of the Civil War?

A The Battle of Gaines' Mill/First Cold Harbor, Virginia, on June 27, 1862.

Q Who commanded the Texas Brigade during the Seven Days' Campaign?

A John Bell Hood. At the Battle of Gaines' Mill it was Hood's brigade that made a bold frontal attack that succeeded in breaking through the Union position. The battle cemented the reputation of Hood's Texas Brigade as an accomplished and successful unit.

Q Who did Robert E. Lee refer to as "my bad old man"?

A Jubal Early, because of his temper and insulting behavior. At the outbreak of the Civil War Early entered Confederate service as colonel of the 24th Virginia Infantry. He was promoted to brigadier general after First Bull Run and served with the Army of Northern Virginia from 1862 to 1864. During this period he developed a reputation as a hard fighter and one of Robert E. Lee's best divisional commanders.

Q Which part of the Union army was engaged at the Battle of Savage's Station, Virginia, on June 29, 1862?

A The rearguard. The main body of the Union army, under Major General Edwin Sumner, was withdrawing towards the James River, being pursued along the railroad and the Williamsburg Road by Confederates under Major General John Magruder. The Confederates struck Sumner's Corps (the Union rearguard) with three brigades near Savage's Station.

Q What was the outcome of the battle?

A Union forces continued to withdraw across White Oak Swamp. As they did so they abandoned supplies and 2,500 wounded soldiers in a field hospital. Total battle casualties in this inconclusive battle were 4,700.

SHARPSBURG WAS
ARTILLERY HELL
STEPHEN D. LEE, DECEMBER 1862

Q Why was the Battle of Gaines' Mill, Virginia, on June 27, 1862, so called?

A The Union army's rearguard took up a strong position on high ground by a swampy tributary of the Chickahominy River named Boatswain's Creek. The troops were positioned between Cold Harbor and Mr. Gaines' farm and mill.

Q Where did the Battle of Glendale/Frayser's Farm/Riddell's Shop come in the sequence of the Seven Days' Campaign?

A Fifth.

Q Name the Confederate divisions involved in the battle.

A The Confederate divisions of Huger, Longstreet and A.P. Hill converged on the retreating Union army in the vicinity of Glendale or Frayser's Farm. Longstreet's and Hill's attacks routed McCall's division near Willis Church (McCall was captured).

Q What was the result of the battle?

A Union counterattacks by Hooker's and Kearny's divisions managed to restore the Union line of retreat along the Willis Church Road. Huger's advance was stopped on the Charles City Road. The forces of Jackson were delayed by Franklin at White Oak Swamp. Confederate Major General T.H. Holmes attempted to turn the Union left flank at Turkey Bridge but was driven back by Federal gunboats on the James River. It was a drawn battle, allowing McClellan to establish a strong position on Malvern Hill.

Q Who was "California Joe"?

A A famous marksman in the Union army unit known as Berdan's Sharpshooters.

> " SOME OF US MUST DIE.
> ## CROSS YOURSELVES AND MARCH FORWARD
> W.S. ROSECRANS,
> BATTLE OF MURFREESBORO, DECEMBER 1862 "

DID YOU KNOW

During The Seven Days' Campaign The Union Army of the Potomac was only a few miles outside the Confederate capital, Richmond, when Confederate General Robert E. Lee seized the initiative and attacked an isolated Union corps north of the Chickahominy River on June 26 at Mechanicsville. In the next few days Lee's Army of Northern Virginia fought McClellan's army at Gaines' Mill, Savage's Station, Frayser's Farm, and Malvern Hill, as well as in numerous skirmishes. McClellan, his army becoming more and more demoralized, gave up his attempt to besiege Richmond and retreated to Harrison's Landing on the James River. Richmond was safe for the moment, and away from the battlefield reports of Lee's and Jackson's achievements began to sway European opinion behind the Confederacy.

Q Which post was Andrew Johnson given in 1862?

A In March 1862, after Union forces had occupied central Tennessee, Lincoln appointed Johnson military governor of the state.

Q What were "infernal machines"?

A Concealed mines, also called torpedoes. They were first used by the Confederates during the Peninsular Campaign in 1862.

Q Who in his book *Tiger Lilies* described war as a "strange, enormous, terrible flower"?

A The poet and muscian Sidney Lanier (1842–1881).

> **"BOYS, HE'S NOT MUCH FOR LOOKS, BUT IF WE'D HAD HIM WE WOULDN'T BE CAUGHT IN THIS TRAP**
>
> CAPTURED UNION SOLDIER,
> OF "STONEWALL" JACKSON **"**

Q Who was Old Abe?

A An eagle presented to the 8th Wisconsin Regiment when it first mustered in Wisconsin. It accompanied the regiment into 42 battles and engagements through Tennessee and Georgia. The eagle became known as Old Abe after President Abraham Lincoln.

Q What other name did Old Abe have?

A The Confederates called him the "Yankee Buzzard" and made strenuous efforts to kill or capture him. All failed, and in September 1864 he was retired from active service. He was presented to the state of Wisconsin and housed in the state capital.

Q What was the Internal Revenue Act?

A Introduced by the Union on July 1, 1862, it placed a tax on the income of those earning more than $600 a year and also brought in a series of internal taxes on goods. The act was intended "to provide Internal Revenue to support the Government and to pay Interest on the Public Debt." As one of a rash of new taxes imposed to help fund the war, a Federal tax was placed on distilled spirits.

Q Who raided Paris, Kentucky, in July 1862?

A John Hunt Morgan's Confederate cavalry raided the town. This was one of a number of raids by Morgan beginning in July 1862.

Q What happened at the Battle of Malvern Hill/Poindexter's Farm, Virginia, on July 1, 1862?

A Despite facing a defensive position bolstered by more than 100 guns, Robert E. Lee's Confederates made a series of frontal assaults in an attempt to win a decisive victory. Infantry charges were met by barrages of Union artillery fire that Confederate artillery was unable to counter.

Q Why was Malvern Hill a defeat for both sides?

A The battle ended in defeat for Lee, who was unable to break the Union line, and left his army exhausted. Total casualties in the battle were 8,500, of which 5,300 were Confederate. It was also the last battle of the Peninsular Campaign, thus ending McClellan's attempt to capture Richmond.

DID YOU KNOW

THE FIRST CONFEDERATE DIPLOMATIC MISSION ARRIVED IN LONDON IN MAY 1861. THE THREE-MAN DELEGATION WAS LED BY WILLIAM L. YANCEY OF ALABAMA, AND IT WAS CORDIALLY RECEIVED BY RUSSELL. WHEN, ALMOST IMMEDIATELY AFTERWARDS, THE BRITISH GOVERNMENT DECLARED NEUTRALITY AND GRANTED THE CONFEDERACY THE STATUS OF A BELLIGERENT POWER, YANCEY'S HOPES WERE HIGH. FRANCE, THE SOUTH'S OTHER BIG COTTON CUSTOMER, SWIFTLY FOLLOWED BRITAIN'S LEAD, AND OTHER EUROPEAN POWERS FELL INTO LINE. TO BE RECOGNIZED AS A BELLIGERENT WAS NOT THE SAME THING AS TO BE RECOGNIZED AS AN INDEPENDENT NATION, BUT BY THE TERMS OF INTERNATIONAL LAW BELLIGERENT STATUS BROUGHT IMPORTANT PRACTICAL BENEFITS. IT MEANT THAT THE CONFEDERACY COULD RAISE LOANS AND ARMS ABROAD, WHICH IT SET ABOUT DOING. CONFEDERATE AGENT JAMES D. BULLOCH TRAVELED TO BRITAIN TO CONTRACT FOR WARSHIPS. THE SUBSEQUENT WORK OF PRIVATE BRITISH SHIPYARDS IN SUPPLYING WARSHIPS TO THE CONFEDERACY WAS A MATTER OF ONGOING FRICTION BETWEEN BRITAIN AND THE UNION DURING THE WAR.

Q When did President Lincoln read his initial draft of the Emancipation Proclamation to his cabinet?

A July 13, 1862.

Q The scene was recreated in a painting by which artist?

A F.B. Carpenter. In his painting, Secretary of State William H. Seward is seated in profile on the right, and Treasury Secretary Salmon P. Chase, who personally disliked Lincoln, stands on the left.

DID YOU KNOW

THE ABILITY QUICKLY TO MOVE ARMIES HUNDREDS OF MILES BY RAILROAD PRODUCED A REVOLUTIONARY CHANGE IN WARFARE. TROOPS NO LONGER NEEDED TO EXHAUST THEMSELVES MARCHING ACROSS COUNTRY, FOOD AND SUPPLIES COULD BE DELIVERED WHERE THEY WERE NEEDED, AND THE CAPTURE OF MAJOR RAIL JUNCTIONS COULD OPEN UP LARGE TRACTS OF ENEMY TERRITORY. THE NEGATIVE SIDE TO THIS WAS THAT ARMIES BECAME DEPENDENT ON THE RAILROAD AND HAD TO USE THOUSANDS OF MEN TO PROTECT AND MAINTAIN THE LINES. AN EXAMPLE OF THIS CAME IN JUNE 1862, AFTER UNION TROOPS HAD CAPTURED CORINTH, MISSISSIPPI, FOLLOWING THEIR VICTORY AT SHILOH. GENERAL ULYSSES S. GRANT'S ARMY COULD HAVE ADVANCED DEEPER INTO MISSISSIPPI BUT WAS PREVENTED FROM DOING SO BY THE NEED TO KEEP TROOPS IN TENNESSEE TO PROTECT THE HUNDREDS OF MILES OF RAILROAD THAT CARRIED ALL OF THE ARMY'S SUPPLIES.

> "
> ## A TYRANNICAL,
> ## HOT-HEADED VULGARIAN
> A SUBORDINATE DESCRIBING NATHAN BEDFORD FORREST
> "

Q **What was the CSS *Arkansas*?**

A A Confederate ironclad. On July 15, 1862, it attacked and damaged three Union ships at Vicksburg and swung naval power on the Mississippi back towards the Confederates.

Q **Which Confederate commander was a pallbearer at Ulysses S. Grant's funeral in 1885?**

A Simon Bolivar Buckner (1823–1914) was a friend of Ulysses S. Grant before the war. Joining the Confederate army in 1861, he fought at Perryville, Kentucky, and Chickamauga, Georgia.

Q **What was the Confiscation Act, which came into force on July 17, 1862?**

A The Confiscation Act stated that all escaped slaves who came under Union control would be freed, and that they could be employed by the Union to suppress the Confederate rebellion.

Q **What was the Militia Act, which came into force the same day?**

A The Militia Act gave the president the power to enrol "persons of African descent" for "any war service," including service as soldiers.

Q **What was the significance of these acts?**

A They brought black people officially into the Union war effort and opened the way for the formation of black units in the army.

Q **What was a Dahlgren gun?**

A A massive smoothbore iron cannon cast in a distinctive "soda
bottle" shape that provided extra-thick walls at the breech of the
gun. The revolutionary design allowed for the production of larger, more
potent guns that were less likely to explode at the breech when fired.
The first Dahlgren-designed cannon was the 9 in gun produced in 1850,
followed by an 11 in version in 1851. Designed to fire shells against
wooden ships, they proved to be strong enough also to fire massive
170 lb solid shot, which were used against ironclad ships in the Civil War.

Q **What was the most populous city of the Northern states?**

A New York, with a population of more than 3,880,000.

Q The Union Irish Brigade was initially composed of three New York Regiments. What were they?

A The 63rd, 69th, and 88th Volunteer Infantry Regiments.

Q What was distinctive about the brigade's recruits?

A The Irish Brigade was composed largely of Irish Catholic immigrants, many of whom left their ships in New York Harbor and marched directly into service.

Q At the Battle of Cedar Mountain, Virginia, on August 9, 1862, what events before the battle put the Confederates at a serious disadvantage?

A Jackson's (the Confederate commander) secretiveness over his orders caused confusion, and the Confederate forces arrived on the battlefield in a piecemeal condition. Jackson himself added to the confusion by spending hours placing artillery pieces on the right side of his line. Charles S. Winder was left to deploy his division on the Confederate left flank in some trees.

❝ I CAN ONLY SAY THAT I AM NOTHING BUT A POOR SINNER, TRUSTING IN CHRIST ALONE FOR SALVATION ❞
ROBERT E. LEE

Q What happened to Jackson's sword at the Battle of Cedar Mountain?

A He tried to pull it from its scabbard, only to find that it had rusted in place. He thus removed his sword and its scabbard from his belt and waved it in the air.

Q At the Battle of Cedar Mountain, what did "Stonewall" Jackson shout to rally his men?

A He took a battle flag from a soldier and waved it, shouting, "Jackson is with you!" His example, combined with arriving reinforcements, turned temporary Union success into defeat. The attacking Union forces, tired and disorganized from marching and fighting on a hot day, gave way before the Confederate attack and left the field by nightfall. At a cost of 1,400 casualties Jackson's force had defeated Banks, inflicting 2,500 Union casualties in the process.

Q Who was the first reporter lost in action in the Civil War?

A Irving Carson of the *Chicago Times*, who was decapitated by a cannon ball at the Battle of Shiloh on April 6, 1862.

Q Who was appointed "to command the whole land forces of the United States as general-in-chief" in July 1862?

A Major General Henry Halleck. Halleck had the reputation of being the most unpopular man in Washington (on one occasion Lincoln said that he was Halleck's friend because nobody else was).

Q Who were the Shakers?

A The Shakers, properly known as the United Society of Believers, were pacifist Christians who objected to the war. There were around 6,000 Shakers in the United States in 1860.

> **❝** SEND FOR A CLERGYMAN, I WISH TO BE
> # BAPTISED. I HAVE BEEN
> ## BASELY MURDERED
> UNION GENERAL WILLIAM NELSON,
> AFTER BEING WOUNDED IN A DUEL **❞**

DID YOU KNOW

To support the blockade of the South, the Union navy captured bases on the Southern coast to serve as stations where its vessels could put in for coal and repairs. It also captured the forts that guarded Confederate ports or seized the ports outright. The first major port to fall was also the South's largest city: New Orleans, Louisiana, which capitulated to a Union fleet under David G. Farragut in April 1862. Union forces systematically neutralized or captured other Southern ports, so that by the end of December 1864 the only major port still open was Wilmington, North Carolina. When it, too, was sealed off on January 15, 1865, the Confederacy lost its last significant access to the outside world.

Q What was the largest city in the state of Pennsylvania?

A Philadelphia. It had a population of 565,529 in 1860.

Q What happened at Fort Ridgely, Minnesota, in August 1862?

A Rebellious Santee Sioux in Minnesota forced Union soldiers and civilians into Fort Ridgely, from where they repelled many Indian attacks.

Q Which minor action on August 28 allowed Confederate forces to unite for victory at the Second Battle of Manassas.

A The Battle of Thoroughfare Gap/Chapman's Mill in Virginia. Brigadier General James Ricketts's Union division was flanked by a Confederate column passing through Hopewell Gap several miles to the north and by troops securing the high ground at Thoroughfare Gap.

> ## " GENERAL, WE LITTLE THOUGHT THAT THE
> # ENEMY WOULD TURN HIS BACK
> # UPON US SO EARLY "
> ### LEE TO LONGSTREET, AUGUST 1862

Q What was the plan of the Union commander, John Pope, at the Battle of Second Manassas/Second Bull Run in August 1862?

A He planned to use his new Army of Virginia, combined with reinforcements from the Army of the Potomac, to attack the Confederate capital, Richmond, from the north.

Q What was Pope's boast before the battle?

A Pope, a brash general from the Western theater, promised his troops that they would soon see the backs of their retreating enemies.

Q What was the situation faced by Robert E. Lee before Second Manassas/Second Bull Run?

A Confederate General Robert E. Lee had recently completed his defeat of the Army of the Potomac in the Seven Days' Campaign of June 1862. However, Lee found himself in a strategically dangerous position. His army was positioned between the two much larger forces of McClellan and Pope. McClellan's forces were not yet ready to advance, however. Lee used the chance to confront Pope.

Q Name at least two design features of a Confederate blockade-runner.

A They typically had shallow drafts so they could navigate small inlets and low silhouettes and gray paint to make them difficult to spot. Their engines burned anthracite, a form of coal that produced little smoke, and they had pipes to expel steam underwater to make them less visible. Above all, they were fast.

Q **What was Lee's plan at Second Bull Run?**

A Lee devised a risky plan to deal with Pope, whom he personally disliked. In direct contradiction to accepted military strategy, he divided his forces, leaving a small detachment of his army outside Richmond to contain the Army of the Potomac. He sent "Stonewall" Jackson with 24,000 men to advance into central Virginia to confront Pope. Jackson defeated part of Pope's army at Cedar Mountain on August 9. Lee then rejoined Jackson with the rest of the army along the Rappahannock River.

Q **At Second Bull Run what action did Confederate soldiers take when they ran out of ammunition?**

A They resorted to throwing rocks at their adversaries. Their line held, however, because the Union attacks were poorly coordinated.

Q **What was the decisive moment at the Battle of Second Bull Run on August 30, 1862?**

A Confederate General Longstreet launched a massive attack at 16:00 hours, and the result was decisive. The Union left flank was crushed. Pope's army began withdrawing from the field.

DID YOU KNOW

SECOND BULL RUN IN AUGUST 1862 WAS THE MOST COMPLETE OF LEE'S VICTORIES. AT THE COST OF 9,500 CASUALTIES HE INFLICTED 14,500 CASUALTIES ON POPE'S ARMY AND ENDED ANOTHER UNION ATTEMPT TO CAPTURE RICHMOND. IT WAS THE HIGH POINT OF A SUMMER THAT HAD SEEN LEE TAKE COMMAND OF THE ARMY OF NORTHERN VIRGINIA AND DEFEAT TWO UNION ARMIES. THE INITIATIVE NOW IN HIS HANDS, LEE DECIDED TO INVADE THE NORTH IN HOPES OF ANOTHER DECISIVE BATTLEFIELD VICTORY.

> **RESULTS ARE NOT FOR US TO CONSIDER**
> ## AND ORDERS ARE RECEIVED
> ## TO BE OBEYED
> NATHANIEL BANKS, MAY 1862

Q In early September 1862 Confederate General Robert E. Lee's Army of Northern Virginia crossed the Potomac River and entered which Northern state?

A Maryland.

Q How did Union General George B. McClellan get to know that Lee had split his army into four parts on September 9, 1862?

A McClellan moved out of the Washington defences in pursuit of Lee. Lee split his army into four parts, three of which were sent to capture the Union garrison at Harpers Ferry. A lost copy of Lee's orders came into McClellan's possession on September 13, putting the fragmented Army of Northern Virginia in great peril.

Q McClellan planned to force his way through three passes in South Mountain in September 1862 both to engage Lee's army and also to relieve Harpers Ferry. Name at least two of these passes.

A Crampton's Gap, Fox's Gap, and Turner's Gap.

Q Who was the "Butcher of Palmyra"?

A General John McNeil, who became infamous when he ordered 10 Confederate prisoners to be shot in retaliation for the presumed murder of a local Union man in September 1862. McNeil became known as the "Butcher of Palmyra." He led Union forces in Missouri until he resigned his command in April 1865.

DID YOU KNOW

EVEN AFTER IT CURTAILED THE EMBARGO, THE CONFEDERATE GOVERN-
MENT WAS SLOW TO MAKE BLOCKADE-RUNNERS GIVE CARGO SPACE TO
MILITARY SUPPLIES. MOST BLOCKADE-RUNNERS OPERATED ENTIRELY FOR
PROFIT, TRANSPORTING LUXURY GOODS. RIGHT TO THE END OF THE WAR
BLOCKADE-RUNNERS SATISFIED THE DESIRE OF SOUTHERNERS FOR LUXURY
GOODS. THE BLOCKADE AFFECTED BOTH SIDES' RELATIONS WITH OTHER
COUNTRIES. UNION WARSHIPS SOMETIMES HARASSED OR EVEN FIRED ON
NEUTRAL SHIPPING, OR WAITED JUST BEYOND THE 3-MILE (5-KM) LIMIT OF
BLOCKADE-RUNNER DESTINATIONS, SUCH AS NASSAU OR HAVANA,
ESTABLISHING WHAT WAS IN EFFECT AN ILLEGAL BLOCKADE OF A FOREIGN
PORT. OTHER COUNTRIES, ESPECIALLY BRITAIN, PROTESTED SUCH ACTIONS.

Q What was the main Confederate field gun in the first year of the war?

A The six-pounder cannon. It did not have the range or power of the Napoleon 12-pounder. By July 1862 it was being withdrawn from service, and the main Confederate gun foundry, the Tredegar Works in Richmond, Virginia, had begun casting the 12-pounder. By the end of the war the Confederacy had produced more than 450 Napoleons, a figure outstripped by the 1,127 produced in the Union.

Q Why was A.P. Hill's Confederate division known as the "Light Division"?

A Hill's division earned the nickname the "Light Division" for its fast marching and aggressive attacks. During the Confederate invasion of the North in 1862, Hill's men made a forced march on September 17 to Antietam, arriving in time to deliver a devastating counterattack.

Q Who wrote the Civil War novel *The Red Badge of Courage*?

A Stephen Crane.

Q The novel was turned into a film in 1951. Which actor played the hero of the story.

A World War II hero Audie Murphy.

Q Which 1862 act of Congress established 14 cemeteries for the burial of war dead.

A On July 17, 1862, Congress gave the President the authority, "whenever in his opinion it shall be expedient, to purchase cemetery grounds and cause them to be securely enclosed, to be used as a national cemetery for the soldiers who shall die in the service of the country." By the end of the Civil War, 14 national cemeteries had been established pursuant to this act.

Q What was the "Crescent City"?

A New Orleans.

Q What was a Zouave?

A Originally the *Zouaoua*, this fiercely independent Kabyli tribe lived in the rocky hills of Algeria and Morocco. In the summer of 1830 a number of *Zouaoua* tendered their services to the French colonial army, and in October of that year were organized into two battalions of auxiliaries, called Zouaves. In the 1850s "Zouave fever" spread to America, especially after Colonel Elmer Ellsworth took his Chicago Zouave Cadets on a tour of North America, challenging militia units to drill competition.

Q Name at least two items of Zouave uniform.

A Uniforms usually consisted of a fez and turban, very baggy pants, leggings, a vest, a short jacket that was cut away from the top with only one button or clasp at the throat, and a sash.

95

DID YOU KNOW

THE CONFEDERACY HAD ONLY ONE MAJOR SHIPYARD IN NEW ORLEANS AND ONE IRONWORKS: TREDEGAR IRONWORKS IN RICHMOND, VIRGINIA. HOWEVER, WHEN VIRGINIA SECEDED FROM THE UNION IN 1861, CONFEDERATE FORCES TOOK OVER THE U.S. NAVY'S NORFOLK SHIPYARD IN THE STATE. WITH THIS ACTION THE CONFEDERATES GAINED THE U.S. NAVY'S NEW STEAMSHIP, THE *MERRIMACK*, WHICH UNION TROOPS HAD PARTLY BURNED AND SUNK BEFORE LEAVING. ENGINEERS RAISED THE *MERRIMACK* AND BUILT ON ITS HULL A LARGE ARMORED CASEMATE. AN IRON RAM WAS MOUNTED ON ITS BOW. THE CONFEDERACY NAMED ITS NEW CASEMATE IRONCLAD THE CSS *VIRGINIA*, AND IT SET SAIL IN MARCH 1862. THE *VIRGINIA* WAS DESIGNED TO OPERATE BOTH IN COASTAL WATERS AND ON RIVERS. ON MARCH 9, 1862, THE FIRST-EVER BATTLE BETWEEN IRONCLADS TOOK PLACE IN HAMPTON ROADS, VIRGINIA, WHEN THE USS *MONITOR* AND CSS *VIRGINIA* POUNDED EACH OTHER IN A FOUR-HOUR DUEL THAT ENDED INCONCLUSIVELY.

Q Who was nicknamed "Dragon Dix"?

A Dorothea Dix, appointed by President Lincoln to be superintendent of nurses. The nickname was given to her by women whom Dix had rejected as nurses.

Q What was the "Bucktail Regiment"?

A The Union 42nd Pennsylvania Volunteer Infantry Regiment raised in Pennsylvania, because many of the men were lumberjacks, raftsmen, and farmers accustomed to living in the rugged mountainous areas of the "Wildcat" district (Elk, McKean, Tioga, and Cameron counties). The men adopted the tail of a buck as their "regimental badge of honour." The deer tails were placed on each recruit's cap and they became known as the Bucktail Regiment.

DID YOU KNOW

CIVIL WAR COMMANDERS WOULD HAVE FACED A TOUGH JOB EVEN IF THEY HAD STARTED THE WAR WITH HEALTHY TROOPS. BUT MANY OF THE MEN WHO JOINED BOTH ARMIES WERE PHYSICALLY UNFIT. EARLY IN THE WAR MEN EAGER FOR MILITARY GLORY OFTEN TRIED TO HIDE ANY ILLNESSES OR DISABILITIES THAT MIGHT DISQUALIFY THEM FROM MILITARY SERVICE. AS THE WAR WENT ON, AND BOTH SIDES BECAME DESPERATE FOR MANPOWER, RECRUITING OFFICERS WOULD OVERLOOK ALL BUT THE MOST OBVIOUS PHYSICAL HANDICAPS. HOWEVER, COMMANDERS SOON LEARNT THAT PHYSICALLY UNFIT TROOPS WERE NOT MERELY USELESS IN COMBAT; CARING FOR THEM TOOK AWAY VALUABLE MANPOWER AND RESOURCES FROM THE MILITARY EFFORT. IN 1862 AN INVESTIGATION IN THE UNION ARMY FOUND THAT 25 PERCENT OF THE SOLDIERS WERE UNFIT FOR MILITARY DUTY.

" MY PARAMOUNT OBJECT IN THIS STRUGGLE
IS TO SAVE THE UNION
ABRAHAM LINCOLN
"

Q Give at least two reasons why Lee's position at the Battle of Antietam was weak.

A He had only 18,000 men stretched along a 3-mile (4.8-km) line on high ground above Sharpsburg, with his back to a bend of the Potomac River. The far left of the line lay along the Hagerstown Pike about 2 miles (3.2 km) north of the village at an area called the West, East, and North Woods. His far right lay barely a mile south of the village on the Harpers Ferry Road. The center was split by the Boonsboro Pike. It was an exposed position, mostly running through cornfields and fruit orchards with little natural cover.

Q Which Confederate law of October 1862 gave rise to the popular cry that the war was a "rich man's war but a poor man's fight"?

A The Twenty-Negro Law, which exempted the owner or overseer of a plantation with twenty or more slaves, was particularly resented—as was the substitution system, whereby a man could pay another, not otherwise liable for the draft, to serve in his stead.

Q Who was Zebulon B. Vance?

A The governor of North Carolina. He took office in September 1862 and was reelected in 1864. Unfortunately for Richmond, he was a North Carolinian first and a staunch believer in states' rights.

Q Which was the only Confederate state to equip and clothe its own regiments?

A North Carolina, which had a policy of exporting North Carolina cotton abroad using blockade-runners and using the material received in exchange for the benefit of North Carolinians, both civilian and military.

Q What was the first action of the Battle of Antietam?

A Fighting began at dusk on September 16 when Joseph Hooker's Union I Corps attacked from the north down the Hagerstown Pike toward the North Woods. "Stonewall" Jackson and the first of his units began to arrive, and by nightfall the Confederates had repulsed Hooker's advance.

Q What was the sequence of attacks and counterattacks in and around the West Woods at the Battle of Antietam?

A Ten brigades hit the Confederate left and pushed their line back to the West Woods. Jackson counterattacked at 07:00 hours and threw the Union forces back, but Hooker received reinforcements from Mansfield's XII Corps. The battle now centered on the struggle for the possession of the Dunker Church, in the West Woods. Three divisions of Sumner's II Corps advanced from the Union right to help Mansfield. Attacking into the West Woods, one of the divisions advanced straight into a line of Confederates and suffered more than 2,500 casualties in 20 minutes, including General John Sedgwick, the division's commander. Falling back nearly a mile, the Union troops took up defensive positions. The fighting for the West Woods was at a stalemate.

" ALL WE ASK IS TO BE LEFT ALONE
JEFFERSON DAVIS **"**

DID YOU KNOW

THE MOST VERSATILE AND WIDELY USED ARTILLERY PIECE OF THE CIVIL WAR WAS THE MODEL 1857 12-POUNDER NAPOLEON. THIS FIELD GUN WAS DEVELOPED FROM A FRENCH DESIGN NAMED FOR THE EMPEROR NAPOLEON III. IT WAS DESIGNED TO REPLACE THE MODEL 1841 SIX-POUNDER CANNON; BUT AS THE CIVIL WAR BROKE OUT, ONLY FIVE NAPOLEONS WERE IN SERVICE. U.S. ARSENALS WERE STILL STOCKED WITH THE OLD SIX-POUNDERS, AND IT WAS THEY THAT THE CONFEDERATES SEIZED WHEN THEY CAPTURED FEDERAL ARSENALS IN 1861. THE NAPOLEON WAS A MUZZLELOADED SMOOTHBORE CANNON WITH A BRONZE BARREL 5FT 6IN (168 CM) LONG. IT HAD A RANGE OF UP TO 1,600 YARDS (1,463 M) AND COULD FIRE FOUR DIFFERENT TYPES OF SHOT FOR USE AGAINST DIFFERENT TARGETS.

Q After the Union capture of New Orleans in April 1862, what was the only significant Confederate port left on the Gulf of Mexico?

A Mobile, Alabama.

Q At the Battle of Antietam why was "Bloody Lane" so called?

A A sunken road between the Boonsboro and Hagerstown Pikes, it was defended by two brigades of D.H. Hill's division, and soon the men began stacking fence rails on the north side of the road to provide additional protection from the Union forces approaching them (General William H. French's division of Sumner's Union corps). At 09:30 hours the division attacked the sunken road between the pikes. Fighting continued there for four hours as first one Union division and then a second (General Israel B. Richardson's division) made repeated charges. By 13:00 hours about 5,600 killed and wounded troops from both sides lay along and in front of the lane.

Q Which partisan fought as a private in the 1st Virginia Cavalry Regiment, commanded by Lieutenant Colonel J.E.B. Stuart?

A John Singleton Mosby. Stuart and Mosby got along well, and Stuart made it a practice to assign the young private difficult scouting missions. After soldiering with Stuart in 1862, in March 1863 Mosby was commissioned a captain and formed a unit of partisan rangers in northern Virginia.

Q What converted warehouse became a Confederate prison?

A Libby Prison, Richmond. The prisoners, mostly Union officers, were housed on the upper two floors, while the ground floor was used for offices, guardrooms, and the kitchen. Cells in the basement held spies, dangerous prisoners, and those sentenced to death.

" MY RELIGIOUS BELIEF TEACHES ME TO FEEL
AS SAFE IN BATTLE
AS IN BED
"STONEWALL" JACKSON **"**

Q What was the Morrill Act passed by Congress in 1862?

A Also known as the Land Grant College Act, it established institutions in each state that would educate people in agriculture, home economics, mechanical arts, and other professions. It gave each state 30,000 acres of public land for each Senator and Representative. The land was then to be sold and the money from the sale of the land was to be put in an endowment fund which would provide support for the colleges in each of the states.

DID YOU KNOW

During July and August 1862, Confederate General Robert E. Lee's Army of Northern Virginia picked up 55,000 new rifles after beating the Army of the Potomac during the Seven Days' Campaign and the Second Battle of Bull Run, when Union soldiers threw away their weapons in retreat.

Q At Antietam what is Rohrbach Bridge better known as?

A Burnside Bridge. On September 17, 1862, at Antietam, IX Corps under Ambrose E. Burnside began attacking across the creek at the Rohrbach Bridge, later renamed Burnside Bridge. Burnside sent in brigade after brigade but was held off by a Confederate force of just 400 Georgians. They held the bridge until 13:00 hours, when one of Burnside's division commanders had the good sense to use a nearby ford and flank the Confederate position.

Q What was the Pacific Railroad Act of 1862?

A An act passed by Congress that designated the 32nd parallel as the initial transcontinental railroad route and gave huge grants of lands for rights-of-way. The legislation authorized two railroad companies, the Union Pacific and the Central Pacific, to construct the lines. Beginning in 1863, the Union Pacific, employing more than 8,000 Irish, German, and Italian immigrants, laid the line westward from Omaha, Nebraska. The Central Pacific, whose workforce included more than 10,000 Chinese laborers, constructed eastward from Sacramento, California.

Q Which Confederate commander had a deep and ongoing quarrel with "Stonewall Jackson"?

A Ambrose Powell Hill. Their quarrel at one time led to Hill being briefly arrested.

Q What was the bloodiest day of the war?

A The Battle of Antietam, September 17, 1862. McClellan had lost a total of 12,400 dead, wounded, or missing, while Lee had suffered more than 10,000 casualties. Although the battle was a draw in tactical terms, it was a strategic victory for the Union because the Confederate invasion of the North had been halted.

Q What were Jayhawkers?

A Pro-Union guerrilla bands that operated along the Kansas-Missouri border.

> " SENDING ARMIES TO MCCLELLAN IS LIKE
> ## HOVELING FLEAS ACROSS
> ## A BARNYARD
> ABRAHAM LINCOLN, 1862 "

Q Charles Hart was an alias used by which Civil War commander?

A The Confederate guerrilla leader William Quantrill. Before the war he traveled to Utah with an army wagon train and there made his living as a gambler, using the alias of Charles Hart.

Q Which Union division commander was wounded three times and lost half his men at the Battle of Antietam?

A Major General John Sedgwick. He returned to active service in early 1863 as a corps commander, first leading II Corps, then IX, and finally VI Corps of the Army of the Potomac.

Q What action did President Lincoln take a month after the Union "victory" at Antietam?

A He issued the preliminary version of his Emancipation Proclamation, which specified that the final document would take effect on January 1, 1863.

Q What was the Erlanger loan?

A The Confederate government struck a deal with the French banking house of Emile Erlanger & Company (signed on October 28, 1862, and modified on January 3, 1863). The bank agreed to sell $15 million worth of Confederate bonds (paper money) to private investors. The loan was unusual because the bonds were guaranteed not by gold but by "white gold:" cotton. Investors could exchange the bonds for cotton after the war at a good rate. The loan was hugely popular, attracting a host of high-profile investors in England, including the future prime minister, William Ewart Gladstone. The Confederate government used the money to buy vitally needed armaments and supplies for the troops.

DID YOU KNOW

CONFEDERATE IMPRESSMENT OFFICERS WERE APPOINTED BY STATE GOVERNORS TO SEIZE CATTLE, CLOTHING, FOOD, HORSES, IRON, RAILROADS, DOMESTIC AND INDUSTRIAL PROPERTY, SLAVES, AND EVEN FREEDMEN. COMPENSATION FOR THE IMPRESSED PROPERTY WAS SET BY A PRICE SCHEDULE AND BY TWO INDEPENDENT PARTIES, ONE CHOSEN BY THE IMPRESSMENT OFFICER, THE OTHER APPOINTED BY THE PROPERTY OWNER. IMPRESSMENT OF FREEDMEN WAS LIKE A DRAFT—THE LABORERS WERE COMPENSATED PERSONALLY WITH AN ESTABLISHED MINIMUM WAGE.

Q What were Civil War "camps of instruction"?

A Often located in or near state capitals, they were camps where newly formed regiments received their initial training.

Q What did soldiers mean when they referred to "seeing the elephant"?

A It was a term used when referring to combat.

Q What was "Salt Horse"?

A Union army beef that was so saturated with salt that troops had to soak it for days before it could be eaten.

DID YOU KNOW

IN MID-SEPTEMBER 1862, AMBROSE BURNSIDE WAS IN COMMAND OF BOTH IX AND I CORPS. ON SEPTEMBER 14, THIS WING OF THE ARMY OPPOSED THE CONFEDERATE INVASION OF MARYLAND AT THE BATTLE OF SOUTH MOUNTAIN AND ON SEPTEMBER 17 AT THE BATTLE OF ANTIETAM. AT ANTIETAM, BURNSIDE, COMMANDING IX CORPS, WAS ORDERED TO ADVANCE AT 08:00 HOURS BUT TOOK MOST OF THE DAY TO FORCE HIS WAY OVER A BRIDGE AT ANTIETAM CREEK—LATER CALLED BURNSIDE BRIDGE. AFTER ANTIETAM, BURNSIDE WAS OFFERED COMMAND OF THE ARMY OF THE POTOMAC. HE FELT UNEQUAL TO THE POST, BUT HE TOOK CONTROL ON NOVEMBER 9, 1862. HE REORGANIZED THE ARMY'S SIX CORPS AND CAVALRY INTO THREE GRAND DIVISIONS, RIGHT, CENTER AND LEFT, AND ORDERED A MARCH ON RICHMOND. BURNSIDE WAS STOPPED AT FREDERICKSBURG. THE BATTLE WAS A FAILURE, AND ON JANUARY 25, 1863, HE WAS REPLACED BY JOSEPH HOOKER.

Q What was The Harpers Ferry Rifle?

A The popular name for the U.S. Rifle, Model 1855, a shorter version of the Rifle Musket of the same year.

Q Who replaced Simon Cameron as Secretary of War in Washington after Cameron's resignation in January 1862?

A Edwin M. Stanton.

"

RETREAT? NO! I PROPOSE
TO ATTACK AT DAYLIGHT AND WHIP THEM
GENERAL GRANT TO COLONEL McPHERSON
AT SHILOH, 1862

"

105

Q Which battle, fought on October 3–4, 1862, spoiled plans for a Confederate drive into mid-Tennessee?

A The Battle of Corinth, Mississippi. A combined Confederate army of 22,000 men was defeated attempting to crush heavily defended Corinth.

Q What happened at the Battle of Hatchie's Bridge/Davis Bridge/Matamora, Tennessee, on October 5, 1862?

A Following their defeat at Corinth, elements of Major General Earl Van Dorn's Confederate Army of West Tennessee were pushed back across the Davis Bridge over the Hatchie River.

Q Which Southerner, the victor of the Battle of Mill Springs in January 1862, chose to fight for the Union?

A George H. Thomas from Virginia. His decision alienated him from the members of his family and generated mistrust in Union quarters.

Q Who was Daniel Webster?

A One of General George McClellan's favorite horses.

Q In October 1862, which two Confederate generals launched an invasion of Kentucky from Tennessee?

A Braxton Bragg and Kirby Smith. By October 4 Bragg had secured the state capital of Frankfort and set up a new Confederate state government. It was shortlived, though.

" THE VALLEY WAS FILLED WITH AN
IMPENETRABLE SMOKE
AND NOTHING COULD
BE SEEN
UNION PRIVATE AT GAINES'S MILL, JUNE 1862 **"**

Q The Confederate invasion of Kentucky was stopped at which battle?

A The Battle of Perryville on October 8. The Union Army of the Ohio led by Don Carlos Buell met Bragg's Army of the Mississippi and defeated it. Bragg retreated into East Tennessee. Union losses were 4,211; Confederate 3,196.

DID YOU KNOW

As late as September 1862, the two key Confederate diplomats, James Mason in London and John Slidell in Paris, were confidently looking forward to a breakthrough on the Confederacy being recognized as an independent nation. The reason for their confidence was a series of Confederate victories that summer that had culminated in General Robert E. Lee's long-anticipated invasion of the North. By now it was plain that Britain and France would only climb off the fence when the war's outcome was assured. Lee's imminent victory would surely, therefore, be rewarded by recognition. But Lee's invasion was halted at the Battle of Antietam (Sharpsburg) on September 17.

Q How many cannon were there in a Union artillery battery?

A Six.

Q How many cannon were there in a Confederate artillery battery?

A Four.

Q After Antietam, who were the Army of Northern Virginia's corps commanders?

A Generals Thomas Jackson and James Longstreet.

DID YOU KNOW

THE NORTH BUILT OR CONVERTED DOZENS OF GUNBOATS. THEY PLAYED A VITAL ROLE IN THE WAR IN THE WESTERN THEATER. UNION GUNBOATS ASSISTED IN THE CAPTURE OF FORTS HENRY AND DONELSON IN FEBRUARY 1862, THEN EXPLOITED THESE VICTORIES BY RAIDING FAR UP THE TENNESSEE AND CUMBERLAND RIVERS, WHICH THE FORTS HAD BEEN BUILT TO DEFEND. THEY WERE CRUCIAL TO THE UNION ARMY'S CAMPAIGN AGAINST VICKSBURG, MISSISSIPPI, IN 1863.

Q Who said of his troops: "There were never such men in an army before. They will go anywhere and do anything if properly led."?

A Robert E. Lee, of the Army of Northern Virginia.

Q Which woman was made an honorary member of "Stonewall" Jackson's staff?

A Belle Boyd.

Q The melody of Elvis Presley's "Love me Tender" was derived from which Civil War ballad?

A The ballad "Aura Lee" by George R. Poulton and W.W. Fosdick.

Q What was the nickname of Major General William L. Jackson, the cousin of "Stonewall" Jackson?

A "Mudwall."

Q **What was the most famous sharpshooter regiment of the Civil War?**

A The most famous was the 1st U.S. Sharpshooters, formed by New Yorker Hiram Berdan in November 1861. Recruits had to pass a difficult shooting test in which they had to fire 10 bullets into a 10 in (25 cm) circle 200 yards (180 m) away. Berdan's Sharpshooters took part in all the campaigns of the Army of the Potomac, exhibiting both bravery and skill.

Q **Who was the only Jewish member of the cabinet of Confederate President Jefferson Davis?**

A Secretary of War Judah P. Benjamin.

Q **Who was General Grant's chief engineer during the battles at Shiloh, Tennessee, and Iuka.**

A James McPherson, who was given command of the Army of Tennessee in March 1864, and was killed in the Battle of Atlanta four months later.

“ HAVE HAD A TERRIBLE CONTEST. ATTACKED
BY GREATLY SUPERIOR NUMBERS
IN ALL DIRECTIONS
MAJOR GENERAL GEORGE B. MCCLELLAN,
HEADQUARTERS, ARMY OF THE POTOMAC, JUNE 27, 1862 ”

Q **Who became commander of the Army of the Potomac in November 1862?**

A President Abraham Lincoln appointed Ambrose E. Burnside commander of the Union Army of the Potomac in place of George B. McClellan, who he felt was not aggressive enough.

Q Which Confederate commander took charge of the Department of the West in November 1862?

A President Jefferson Davis placed the recuperating Joseph Johnston in command of the Department of the West. Johnston oversaw two Confederate armies, one based at Chattanooga, Tennessee, and the other at Vicksburg, Mississippi.

Q Which female Rebel spy was deported to the Confederacy in June 1862?

A Rose O'Neal Greenhow. She was an attractive widow who moved in the highest circles of Washington society. She used her contacts to gain valuable military intelligence. She is credited with providing General Pierre G.T. Beauregard with information on Union troop movements that helped the Confederate victory at the First Battle of Bull Run.

> " LEE HAS ARRIVED, AND OUR HOPES
> ARE HIGH THAT WE WILL
> ## WIPE THEM CLEAN OUT
> ## THIS TIME
> LIEUTENANT JOHN H. CHAMBERLAYNE,
> VIRGINIA ARTILLERY, AUGUST 1862 "

Q How was this spy caught?

A In August 1861, Allan Pinkerton, head of the Union intelligence service, caught up with Greenhow. Posing as an army major, Pinkerton gained entry to her home and arrested her, while his agents carried out a thorough search for evidence. She was placed under house arrest for some months, then moved to prison in Washington. In June 1862 she was deported to the Confederacy.

DID YOU KNOW

PHILIP HENRY SHERIDAN BEGAN THE CIVIL WAR AS A UNION QUARTER-
MASTER BUT LOBBIED FOR MORE RESPONSIBILITY. IN MAY 1862 HE WAS
PROMOTED TO COLONEL OF THE 2ND MICHIGAN CAVALRY. IMMEDIATELY,
HE PROVED HIMSELF WORTHY OF HIS PROMOTION. HE WENT BACK TO THE
INFANTRY AS A BRIGADIER GENERAL IN THE ARMY OF THE OHIO IN
KENTUCKY, WHERE HE PLAYED A VITAL ROLE IN THE VICTORY AT
PERRYVILLE ON OCTOBER 8, 1862. BY THE AGE OF 32 HE WAS
MAJOR GENERAL OF VOLUNTEERS.

Q What was unique about the military record of Alfred Thomas
Archmedes Torbert?

A He held commissions in both the Union and Confederate armies
simultaneously.

Q What was a coehorn?

A A small bronze mortar, used in sieges. It weighed about 290lb (131
kg) and could be carried by four men. The coehorn was used in the
trenches around Petersburg, Virginia, in the fighting and siege of 1864
and 1865.

Q Who was Henry Hotze?

A Chief Confederate propaganda agent. Hotze employed writers to
publicize the Confederate cause in newspapers abroad. Favorable
books and pamphlets were printed and freely distributed to politicians
and others in positions of influence. Most importantly, Hotze was
responsible for *The Index*, a newspaper published in London to present
Southern views. It provided copy for many other papers in Britain and
elsewhere.

Q Which battle, fought on December 7, 1862, gave Federal forces control over northwest Arkansas?

A The Battle of Prairie Grove/Fayetteville. Confederate forces were forced to retreat after a bloody engagement in Washington County.

Q What was General Burnside's plan as the new commander of the Army of the Potomac in December 1862?

A Eager to prove his aggressiveness as the commander of the Army of the Potomac, Burnside planned a winter offensive toward Richmond, Virginia, aiming to cross the Rappahannock River at Fredericksburg.

> " NO TONGUE CAN TELL, NO MIND
> CONCEIVE, NO PEN PORTRAY THE
> ## HORRIBLE SIGHTS I WITNESSED
> ## THIS MORNING
> UNION CAPTAIN JOHN TAGGERT ON ANTIETAM "

Q What was the 43rd Battalion Virginia Cavalry better known as?

A Most people knew the unit as "Mosby's Rangers." Mosby planned and executed raids on Union outposts in the northern Virginia counties around Washington, D.C. He used the area around Warrenton as his base, but continually moved his headquarters to avoid Union retaliatory attacks. His rangers frequently served in raiding parties and melted back into the local populace afterward.

Q What is an "abatis"?

A An obstacle formed of felled trees with sharpened branches toward the enemy.

DID YOU KNOW

ONE OF THE MOST WIDELY ISSUED RIFLES OF THE CIVIL WAR WAS THE U.S. MODEL 1861 RIFLE MUSKET, OF WHICH MORE THAN A MILLION WERE PRODUCED, MOST OF THEM AT THE UNION ARSENAL AT SPRINGFIELD, MASSACHUSETTS. THEY WERE ISSUED TO THE UNION ARMY, BUT THE CONFEDERATES GOT HOLD OF HUGE NUMBERS OF THEM AFTER SOME OF THE UNION'S WORST DEFEATS.

Q Name the Army of the Potomac's Grand Divisions in December 1862.

A Right, Center and Left.

Q Which Confederate corps occupied Marye's Heights prior to the Battle of Fredericksburg?

A On November 19, General James Longstreet's corps (41,000 men) arrived on Marye's Heights, a ridge overlooking the city, and began digging in.

Q What was the name of James Longstreet's horse?

A Hero.

Q Why was the Confederate position so formidable at the Battle of Fredericksburg in December 1862?

A As well as Longstreet's corps on Marye's Heights, "Stonewall" Jackson's corps of 39,000 was posted south to Prospect Hill. Lee assembled an army of 90,000 men entrenched on heights from which they could fire on almost every inch of ground to the Rappahannock River.

Q What was Burnside's second great assault at the Battle of Fredericksburg in December 1862?

A Burnside's second attack was toward Longstreet. From 12:00 hours on December 13, brigade after brigade of Edwin V. Sumner's Grand Division advanced out of the city, trying to cover the 800 yards (730 m) of open ground to the Confederate guns on Marye's Heights positioned behind a stone wall. There were 14 successive charges, but not one Union soldier got to within 100 ft (30 m) of the wall. By evening 6,500 Union troops lay dead and dying.

Q Name the two armies that clashed at the Battle of Murfreesboro/Stones River, Tennessee, in December 1862.

A The Union Army of Cumberland and the Confederate Army of Tennessee.

> " WE WERE LAVISH OF BLOOD IN THOSE
> DAYS, AND IT WAS THOUGHT TO BE
> ## A GREAT THING TO
> ## CHARGE A BATTERY
> MAJOR GENERAL D.H. HILL
> ON THE SEVEN DAYS' CAMPAIGN, JUNE–JULY 1862 "

Q Why did the Confederate commander at the Battle of Murfreesboro/Stones River, Braxton Bragg, order a retreat on the morning of January 3, 1863?

A He was swayed by the false impression that the Union army had been reinforced. The battle was among the hardest fought of the Civil War. Of Bragg's 35,000 troops, 27 percent were killed or wounded. The Union forces lost 23 percent of their 41,400 men. The battle was a strategic victory for the Union forces, which secured control of Kentucky while increasing their hold on Tennessee.

1863

President Lincoln's Emancipation Proclamation turned the Civil War into a moral crusade to end slavery, thus making European military or diplomatic support for the South impossible. And, on the battlefield, Lee's defeat at Gettysburg meant the South would face ultimate defeat in the war.

Q Why was Lincoln's Emancipation Proclamation a disaster for the Confederacy diplomatically?

A In neither France nor Britain was there any support for the institution of slavery. The British were very proud of having outlawed it across their vast empire in 1834 and of having used the power of their navy to suppress the African slave trade. Southerners had portrayed the struggle as a fight for freedom against an enemy that would not let them secede peacefully. The Union's original position backed up this claim. Lincoln had made it clear that the war was about preserving the Union, not about ending slavery. Before Lincoln's proclamation, therefore, Europeans had seen the war as being almost entirely an issue of Southern independence. With the Emancipation Proclamation the nature of the war changed, and the tide of opinion began to move against the slaveholding South.

> **" BEWARE OF RASHNESS, BUT WITH ENERGY AND SLEEPLESS VIGILANCE GO FORWARD"**
> LINCOLN TO JOSEPH HOOKER, JANUARY 1863

Q What was the Homestead Act of January 1863?

A The first Federal law to encourage enterprise, it granted a farmer 160 acres of Federal land in the West after he or she had lived on the land for five years and made improvements to it. A total of 80 million acres were allocated in this way, and the Homestead Act gave a major push to western migration.

Q What was Panada?

A A hot gruel made of corn meal, army crackers mashed in boiling water, ginger, or bully soup.

DID YOU KNOW

ALTHOUGH THERE ARE NO AUTHORITATIVE FIGURES FOR THE NUMBER OF UNION DESERTERS, THE CONSENSUS AMONG MODERN HISTORIANS IS THAT THERE WERE MORE THAN 200,000 DESERTERS FROM THE UNION ARMY, INCLUDING NEARLY 45,000 FROM NEW YORK, MORE THAN 24,000 FROM PENNSYLVANIA, AND 18,000 FROM OHIO. THE CHIEF METHOD OF DESERTION WAS TO TAKE THE OPPORTUNITY OF SICK LEAVE OR A FURLOUGH (LEAVE OF ABSENCE) TO GO AWAY AND NEVER RETURN. OTHERS DESERTED BY STRAGGLING (SLIPPING TO THE REAR DURING A MARCH OR IN BATTLE) OR BY OFFERING THEMSELVES FOR CAPTURE TO THE ENEMY, WHO TREATED THEM HONORABLY. VERY FEW DESERTERS CHANGED SIDES.

Q How did President Lincoln's Emancipation Proclamation of January 1863 change the nature of the war?

A It ensured that the Civil War became a war of black liberation in addition to a struggle to save the Union. Lincoln had repeatedly asserted that his responsibility as president was to suppress the South's rebellion, not to free its slaves. However, the issue of slavery lay at the heart of the conflict and had to be addressed sooner or later. Lincoln judged that there was enough public support for emancipation to incorporate it into national policy.

Q What was Lincoln's ultimatum to the rebellious states in his preliminary Emancipation Proclamation of September 1862?

A If they did not stop fighting and reaffirm their allegiance to the United States by the end of the year, their slaves would be declared free. When Lincoln's deadline came and went and not a single Confederate state had surrendered, emancipation of the South's slaves became a major war aim.

Q Where was the headquarters of the Confederate spy service?

A The Confederate spy service was run out of an anonymous office in Richmond next to the offices of President Jefferson Davis and the secretary of state.

" THERE IS NO BETTER WAY OF
DEFENDING A LONG LINE THAN BY
MOVING INTO THE
ENEMY'S TERRITORY
ROBERT E. LEE, MARCH 1863 **"**

Q Why were Northern newspapers very helpful to the Confederacy?

A The Confederacy could gain huge amounts of information from simply reading war reports in Northern newspapers, which were not censored. Similarly, the Union gained information from the Southern papers. The Confederate spy service was receiving packets of Northern newspapers every week, which were then assessed and passed on to the various Confederate army commands. General Braxton Bragg is said to have changed his tactics at Chickamauga, Tennessee, in 1863 because he read the Union battle plan printed in the *New York Times*.

Q Who was Pauline Cushman?

A An actress and spy. Cushman gained the confidence of Southern officers by toasting Confederate President Jefferson Davis on stage, for which she was fired. She then stayed with the Confederate army and gathered information to send to the Union authorities.

Q Name the two types of officers in the Union navy.

A The first, known as executive officers, were actually in charge of vessels. From August 1863 they wore a star over their gold sleeve rank stripes. The second type of officers were specialists. They included surgeons, who were stationed onboard ships and in naval hospitals set up in ports; naval constructors, who designed and built vessels; paymasters, who handled ships' funds and supplies, as well as pay; engineers, who maintained onboard machinery; chaplains; and maths and chemistry professors, who taught midshipmen and cadets chemistry, geometry, and calculus. The specialized officers, who did not wear the executive star, held "relative rank" with executive officers. Thus, a fleet surgeon was ranked equal to a captain, although he only commanded individuals in his field, rather than a ship.

Q What was the task of the Union Cavalry Bureau?

A The War Department established the Cavalry Bureau to buy mounts for the cavalry. Within a year, 150,000 horses had been purchased and supplied through two depots, one in Washington, D.C., and one in St. Louis, Missouri.

DID YOU KNOW

THE TRADITIONAL METHOD OF TRAINING NAVAL OFFICERS THROUGH YEARS OF SEA SERVICE WAS UNABLE TO PRODUCE ALL THE OFFICERS NEEDED FOR SUCH A RAPIDLY ENLARGING UNION NAVY, SO SENIOR MIDSHIPMEN WERE COMMISSIONED IMMEDIATELY IN 1861 BEFORE THEIR SCHOOLING WAS FINISHED. THIS MEASURE ALONE DID NOT MANAGE TO MAKE UP THE SHORTAGE OF OFFICERS, SO ON JULY 24, 1861 THE SECRETARY OF THE NAVY WAS AUTHORIZED TO APPOINT ACTING, VOLUNTEER OFFICERS BELOW THE RANK OR RELATIVE RANK OF LIEUTENANT. AT ITS GREATEST EXTENT THE UNION NAVY HAD SOME 7,500 VOLUNTEER OFFICERS, AND 84,500 MEN ENLISTED IN THE NAVY DURING THE WAR.

Q What was Jackson's "Foot Cavalry"?

A In early 1862 "Stonewall" Jackson led a campaign in the Shenandoah Valley, during which he defeated Union generals whose combined strength was several times his own. His orders were to keep Union General Nathaniel P. Banks from joining forces with General George B. McClellan, who was fighting the Peninsular Campaign. During the six-week campaign his diversionary tactics succeeded brilliantly. The speed with which Jackson's troops were able to march earned them the nickname of Jackson's "Foot Cavalry."

Q What happened at the Boa Ogoi camp, Idaho, in January 1863?

A Union retaliation against the Shoshoni tribe resulted in more than 380 Native Americans being killed at their Boa Ogoi camp.

Q Who was nicknamed the "Gray Ghost"?

A John Singleton Mosby.

DID YOU KNOW

IN THE FALL OF 1862 THE CONFEDERACY BEGAN CONSTRUCTING A REMARKABLE 18 IRONCLADS. THE CONFEDERACY ALSO PLANNED TO DEFEAT THE UNION WITH MORE TECHNICALLY ADVANCED SHIPS BUILT IN EUROPE. AT THE END OF THE WAR TWO LARGE RAMS WERE ACTUALLY UNDER CONSTRUCTION IN ENGLAND. HOWEVER, THEY NEVER REACHED THE CONFEDERACY. ENTHUSIASM IN THE SOUTH HAD WANED BY EARLY 1863. IN ALL, THE CONFEDERACY COMPLETED 22 IRONCLADS DURING THE WAR WHILE THE UNION BUILT MORE THAN 40. THE UNION WAS ABLE TO CAPITALIZE ON ITS STRENGTHS IN INDUSTRY, SKILLED LABOR, AND ACCESS TO IRON TO FAR OUTSTRIP THE SOUTH IN IRONCLAD PRODUCTION.

Q **What was the "Mud March" of January 1863?**

A In late January 1863, the Union Army of the Potomac began its march to cross quickly the Rappahannock River, Virginia, above Robert E. Lee's left and attack that flank of the Confederate position. However, it began to rain relentlessly, turning the whole area into a sea of mud. The "Mud March" ended with Burnside ordering his army to return to their camps across the river from Fredericksburg.

WE MUST MAKE THIS CAMPAIGN
AN EXTREMELY
ACTIVE ONE
"STONEWALL" JACKSON, APRIL 1863

Q **Who was "Commissary Banks"?**

A Nathaniel Prentiss Banks. In the summer of 1861 Banks and his men were routed by Thomas "Stonewall" Jackson in the Shenandoah Valley. As the Union troops fled, they left behind valuable provisions. The grateful Confederates dubbed the Union general "Commissary Banks."

Q **Who said, "I consider General A.P. Hill the best commander with me. He fights his troops well and takes good care of them"?**

A Robert E. Lee.

DID YOU KNOW

DENIED THEIR TRADITIONAL ROLE AS SHOCK-TROOPS AND BATTLE-WINNERS, BY 1862 THE CAVALRIES OF BOTH ARMIES WERE STRUGGLING TO FIND A NEW CONTRIBUTION TO MAKE. THE UNION CAVALRY WAS STILL A YOUNG AND INEXPERIENCED FORCE AND WAS MAINLY USED TO GUARD SUPPLY LINES AND ENCAMPMENTS. THE CONFEDERATE CAVALRY, WHICH HAD BETTER LEADERSHIP AND FINER HORSEMEN, BEGAN TO SPECIALIZE IN LARGE-SCALE RAIDS AND RECONNAISSANCE OPERATIONS, SUCH AS J.E.B. STUART'S RIDE AROUND GEORGE B. McCLELLAN'S UNION ARMY. AS THE WAR WENT ON, THE CONFEDERATES GOVERNMENT AUTHORIZED THE RAISING OF UNITS OF "PARTISAN RANGERS."

Q Which Confederate commander is believed to have killed 30 men in single combat, had 29 horses killed under him and been wounded three times?

A Nathan Bedford Forrest.

Q What Northern state first called for the enlistment of black troops in the Civil War.

A Rhode Island.

Q Why was the Union's National Conscription Act of March 1863 so unpopular?

A Opposition to the draft grew out of racial tensions in Union cities. The war's deprivations had hit hard the poor working classes, in particular the Irish Catholic immigrant community. After the announcement of the Emancipation Proclamation in January 1863, some questioned waging a war for black freedom.

Q How could one avoid the Union draft?

A Hire a substitute or pay a $300 fee to avoid military service.

Q What happened to the Union General Edwin Stoughton on March 8, 1863?

A Confederate partisan leader John Mosby and 29 of his men mounted a raid behind enemy lines to Fairfax Court House, Maryland, only a few miles from the Union capital, Washington, D.C. Mosby found and captured Stoughton, commander of the division garrisoning the Fairfax area. Mosby plus his men, the general, 33 other prisoners, and 58 captured horses were back in Warrenton by dawn.

Q What caused the bread riots in the South in April 1863?

A Despite the Confederate government's best efforts, increasing desperation was leading to civilian protests across the South. The crops from 1862's drought-ravaged season were running out. Prices were spiralling out of control. A family's weekly grocery bill for staples such as flour and butter had risen from a prewar $6.55 to $68.25. Civilians suspected that storekeepers and the government were hoarding supplies, and so in a dozen or more places starving women staged bread riots.

" A RICH MAN'S WAR AND A POOR MAN'S FIGHT
DRAFT RIOTEERS' SLOGAN, JULY 1863 **"**

Q Where did the worst bread riot take place?

A Richmond on April 2, 1863. Several hundred women, later joined by men and boys, began to smash store windows and seize food and clothing. Confederate President Jefferson Davis himself arrived on the scene to calm the rioters.

Q How was the Richmond riot brought to an end?

A Despite Davis's appeal to Southern patriotism, the crowd refused to leave. Eventually he warned them to go home or he would order the militia to fire, and the crowd dispersed.

124

> " MY OPINION IS THAT
> THE NORTHERN STATES
> ## WILL MANAGE SOMEHOW
> ## TO MUDDLE THROUGH
> JOHN BRIGHT
> "

Q What was the nickname of the Irish Brigade?

A The Sons of Erin.

Q What happened on March 5, 1863, that aided the Federal government's finances?

A Gold was discovered in Montana territory.

Q Who launched an assault on the city of Charleston, South Carolina, on April 7, 1863?

A Union Rear Admiral Samuel F. Du Pont launched a major assault on the city with a flotilla of seven monitor warships and two other ironclads. However, the ships were driven back by 77 Confederate cannon on Fort Sumter and ran into the harbor's mines and obstructions. Du Pont was forced to withdraw.

Q What was the fate of the ironclad USS *Keokuk*?

A It sank during the evening of April 7, 1863, the date of the Battle of Charleston Harbor.

Q The Arkansas state flag featured a white and blue diamond. Why?

A To show that the state had the country's only diamond mine.

DID YOU KNOW

THE BRITISH GOVERNMENT WAS DETERMINED NOT TO BE MANEUVERED INTO A CONFRONTATION WITH THE UNION. BRITISH PRIME MINISTER LORD PALMERSTON, IN HIS MID-70S, HAD BEEN IN AND OUT OF GOVERNMENT FOR MORE THAN HALF A CENTURY. FAR FROM BEING IN HIS DOTAGE, HOWEVER, "OLD PAM" WAS FAMED FOR THE CUNNING WAY HE PROMOTED HIS COUNTRY'S INTERESTS. LORD JOHN RUSSELL, A PAST AND FUTURE PRIME MINISTER, WAS AS WILY AS PALMERSTON. THEY MAY HAVE BEEN SYMPATHETIC TO THE SOUTHERN CAUSE AND AS CONCERNED AS THEY CLAIMED TO BE ABOUT UNEMPLOYED MILL WORKERS, BUT THEY CARED FAR MORE ABOUT SAFEGUARDING BRITAIN'S INTERNATIONAL POSITION. THE SUREST WAY TO DO THIS, AS RUSSELL SAID IN MAY 1861, WAS TO "KEEP OUT OF IT!"

Q Which Confederate commander said he trusted Lee so much he would follow him blindfolded?

A "Stonewall" Jackson.

Q What was Grierson's Raid?

A Union Colonel Benjamin H. Grierson led the 2d Iowa, 6th Illinois, and 7th Illinois Cavalry, and several artillery batteries out of La Grange, Tennessee, south into Mississippi. This raid was part of General Ulysses S. Grant's plan for the cavalry raiders to divert the attention of Confederate forces protecting Vicksburg so that he could move his army south of the vital river city.

Q Which railroad did Grierson's men cut?

A The Southern Mississippi Railroad, the only rail link between the eastern and western parts of the Confederacy.

Q How did Grierson and his men get back to Union lines?

A After ravaging 600 miles (960 km) of Confederate territory, Grierson did the unexpected and escaped back behind Union lines by riding south to Union-held Baton Rouge, Louisiana, rather than north.

> MAJOR, TELL MY FATHER THAT I DIED
> # WITH MY FACE TO THE ENEMY
> COLONEL I.E. AVERY,
> BATTLE OF GETTYSBURG, JULY 1863

DID YOU KNOW

DURING 1863 THE CONFEDERATE CAVALRY BEGAN TO DECLINE, AS ITS NUMBERS AND FIGHTING QUALITY SUFFERED THROUGH A LACK OF NEW RECRUITS, HORSES, AND WEAPONS. THE UNION CAVALRY, ON THE OTHER HAND, WAS GROWING IN NUMBER, CONFIDENCE, AND EXPERIENCE, AND WAS TAKING A MORE OFFENSIVE ROLE BY ADOPTING THE TACTICS OF MOUNTED INFANTRY. THEIR HORSES GAVE THE TROOPERS MOBILITY ON THE BATTLEFIELD, WHILE THE CARBINE, ESPECIALLY THE SPENCER, GAVE THEM THE FIREPOWER TO HOLD POSITIONS AGAINST CONFEDERATE INFANTRY WHEN FIGHTING ON FOOT.

Q Who captured the Union Colonel Abel Streight in May 1863?

A Nathan Bedford Forrest. In April 1863 Forrest and a small force of cavalry pursued a Union column of 1,500 mounted infantry under Abel Streight, which was raiding out of Nashville. At Cedar Bluff, Alabama, Forrest called for Streight's surrender. Fooled by the Confederate's self-confident demand, Streight surrendered his entire force to Forrest's cavalry, which by that time numbered barely 600 men.

Q In what state was the song "I Wish I Was In Dixie Land," composed?

A New York City, NY.

Q What were Galvanized Yankees?

A Confederate soldiers who deserted the Confederate cause and joined the Union army to fight Indians.

Q Why was the March 1863 Confederate impressment law so unpopular?

A The Confederate law of March 1863 simply legalized established practice and was an attempt to regulate the behavior of army units. Confederate armies already used impressment in emergencies and paid for the goods later when the owner brought compensation claims. Nevertheless, the law was widely unpopular. Many Southern governors complained to the War Department, taking the view that the power of impressment violated state and individual rights.

Q What was "The Child of the Storm"?

A West Virginia.

" THE FATHER OF WATERS AGAIN GOES
UNVEXED TO THE SEA
LINCOLN, ON HEARING OF THE SURRENDER OF
VICKSBURG, JULY 1863
"

Q Who wrote *The History of the United States' Secret Service*, published in 1867?

A Lafayette Curry Baker. When McClellan was fired as commander of the Army of the Potomac in November 1862, Allan Pinkerton's work as Union spymaster also ended. He returned to Chicago and his detective agency. After Pinkerton left, a new secret service was set up under Lafayette Curry Baker.

Q Who said: "War means fighting and fighting means killing"?

A Nathan Bedford Forrest.

DID YOU KNOW

NATHAN BEDFORD FORREST HAD VERY LITTLE FORMAL EDUCATION AND
NO MILITARY TRAINING AT ALL BEFORE THE CIVIL WAR BROKE OUT IN
1861, BY WHICH TIME HE WAS ONE OF THE RICHEST MEN IN TENNESSEE.
THE STATE GOVERNOR SOON PERSUADED HIM PERSONALLY TO FINANCE A
NEW CAVALRY UNIT, AND IN OCTOBER HE BECAME LIEUTENANT COLONEL
OF FORREST'S TENNESSEE CAVALRY BATTALION. FORREST FIRST SAW
ACTION DURING THE DEFENSE OF FORT DONELSON, TENNESSEE, IN
FEBRUARY 1862. WHEN THE FORT SURRENDERED, HE LED HIS MEN TO
SAFETY THROUGH UNION LINES. FORREST WAS PROMOTED TO FULL
COLONEL IN MARCH AND TOOK COMMAND OF THE 3RD TENNESSEE
CAVALRY. AFTER THE BATTLE OF SHILOH IN APRIL HE FOUGHT AS PART OF
THE REARGUARD. DURING THE RETREAT TO CORINTH, MISSISSIPPI, HE WAS
SERIOUSLY WOUNDED FOR THE FIRST TIME.

Q **What happened at the Battle of Grand Bluff, Mississippi, on April 29, 1863?**

A Seven Union ironclads were unable to subdue Confederate shore batteries at Grand Gulf, Claiborne County, despite a five-and-a-half-hour bombardment.

Q **What was the plan of Joseph Hooker, commander of the Army of the Potomac, at the Battle of Chancellorsville, in May 1863?**

A Instead of attempting a frontal attack on the Confederate positions overlooking Fredericksburg, Hooker divided his army and took half of it—three corps totalling 75,000 men—to cross the river at fords upstream and come around in a wide sweep to hit Lee from behind. John Sedgwick stayed at Fredericksburg with 40,000 men to pin the Confederates.

Q Why did Hooker's plan fail at the Battle of Chancellorsville in May 1863?

A Lee realized that Hooker was trying a flanking march. On April 29 he sent two brigades toward Chancellorsville to discover the size of the threat. Once they confirmed the Union army was at Chancellorsville, he went on the attack. Like Hooker, Lee divided his forces, leaving 10,000 men under Jubal A. Early to hold Fredericksburg and marching his remaining 50,000 men west to meet Hooker. Hooker was taken by surprise on May 1 when the Confederates started an attack on his lead divisions at noon. He lost his nerve, halted the advance, and ordered his forces back to Chancellorsville to take up defensive positions.

Q Who said of Jackson, "I know not how to replace him"?

A Robert E. Lee.

DID YOU KNOW

MANY OF THE REASONS FOR DESERTION WERE COMMON TO BOTH UNION AND CONFEDERATE ARMIES. COWARDICE WAS ALWAYS A MAJOR CONSIDERATION, BUT IT WAS BY NO MEANS THE MAIN ONE. MORE INFLUENTIAL WAS THE LACK OF SUCH NECESSITIES AS FOOD, CLOTHING, AND EQUIPMENT. OTHER IMPORTANT CONTRIBUTORY FACTORS INCLUDED BATTLE FATIGUE AND GENERAL DESPONDENCY AT THE COURSE AND DURATION OF THE WAR. IN ADDITION, A SIGNIFICANT NUMBER OF SOLDIERS DESERTED BECAUSE THEY DID NOT BELIEVE IN THE CAUSE. OTHERS RESENTED THE COERCION, BOTH OF THEMSELVES AND OTHERS. FOR EXAMPLE, MANY NORTHERN TROOPS OBJECTED TO THE FEDERAL GOVERNMENT'S ATTEMPTS TO BRING THE SECESSIONIST STATES BACK INTO THE UNION BY FORCE. YET MORE SOLDIERS WERE OVERWHELMED BY CONCERN FOR THEIR LOVED ONES BACK HOME.

Q How was "Stonewall" Jackson mortally wounded at the Battle of Chancellorsville?

A Scouting between two frontline Confederate regiments on the evening of May 2, Jackson's party was mistaken for enemy troops, and he was shot by his own men. The wound was not fatal, but his arm had to be amputated. He contracted pneumonia and died eight days later, on May 10, 1863.

" THEY WILL ATTACK YOU IN THE MORNING AND THEY WILL COME BOOMING

UNION BRIGADIER GENERAL JOHN BUFORD,
JUNE 1863
"

131

Q What was "Bragg's Body Guard"?

A Body lice.

Q At the Battle of Chancellorsville, what corps did Jackson rout on May 2?

A The Union XI Corps.

Q Who was the only Civil War Confederate soldier to be pictured on Confederate currency?

A "Stonewall" Jackson.

Q Why did Darius Couch take command of the Union army at the Battle of Chancellorsville?

A On May 2 Hooker was stunned when a shell exploded near him, and he handed over command to Darius Couch.

Q Which Union cavalry commander fought the Sioux and participated in the 1858 Mormon War in Utah?

A John Buford. After serving in the defense of Washington, D.C., in July 1862, he assumed command of a cavalry brigade in John Pope's Army of Virginia. Although wounded in the Second Battle of Bull Run, he recovered to serve as chief of cavalry of the Army of the Potomac during the Antietam and Fredericksburg campaigns in late 1862.

> **❝ MY DEAD AND WOUNDED WERE NEARLY AS GREAT IN NUMBER AS THOSE STILL ON DUTY**
> CONFEDERATE COLONEL WILLIAM C. OATES,
> GETTYSBURG, JULY 1863 **❞**

Q What was the problem with Robert E. Lee's strategy in 1862 and 1863?

A Lee dealt the Union stinging defeats at Fredericksburg (December 1862) and Chancellorsville (May 1863). His aggressive methods continued to result in victories, but at a high cost in casualties the army could ill afford.

Q Why was Jackson, Mississippi, important to the Confederacy?

A Jackson, the state capital, was an important transportation hub 38 miles (60 km) east of Vicksburg.

DID YOU KNOW

DESPITE JOSEPH HOOKER'S PROWESS IN BATTLE, HIS PRIVATE LIFE WAS LESS CONTROLLED. HE COULD BE DISAGREEABLE AND CRITICAL OF HIS SUPERIORS. IN DECEMBER 1862, PRESIDENT LINCOLN PROMOTED HOOKER TO COMMAND OF THE ARMY OF THE POTOMAC FOLLOWING THE ARMY'S DEFEAT AT FREDERICKSBURG UNDER GENERAL AMBROSE E. BURNSIDE. AT THE BATTLE OF CHANCELLORSVILLE IN MAY 1863 HOOKER PROVED BADLY INDECISIVE. HE WAS OUTGENERALED BY ROBERT E. LEE AND HIS CONFEDERATE ARMY OF NORTHERN VIRGINIA, WHO DEFEATED THE UNION FORCES DESPITE BEING OUTNUMBERED TWO TO ONE. HOOKER STAYED IN COMMAND FOR A SHORT WHILE BUT RESIGNED ON JUNE 28 WHEN HE WAS REFUSED REINFORCEMENTS. HE WAS REPLACED BY GENERAL GEORGE G. MEADE. HOOKER WENT ON TO SERVE ABLY IN THE BATTLE OF LOOKOUT MOUNTAIN IN NOVEMBER AND UNDER WILLIAM T. SHERMAN IN GEORGIA.

Q Who was the provost marshal of the Army of the Potomac?

A General Marsena R. Patrick.

Q Who were the opponents at the Battle of Jackson on May 14, 1863?

A Union General Ulysses S. Grant, commander of the Army of the Tennessee, and the Confederate commander, John C. Pemberton.

Q What were the results of the battle?

A Union forces entered Jackson, the fourth Southern state capital to fall. The victory had two important results. First, it allowed Grant's troops to destroy much of Jackson's railroads and war factories. Second, it meant that Pemberton's army, outnumbered and outgeneraled, had to face Grant alone.

Q Who defended Port Hudson in the spring of 1863?

A Confederate General Franklin Gardner, who turned the town into a system of fortified positions facing both over the river and toward the landward approaches.

Q Who attacked Port Hudson in May 1863?

A Union General Nathaniel P. Banks. Land and naval forces under Banks moved out of Baton Rouge in a concerted attack. Gardner had only 7,500 men against more than 30,000 Union troops, but he used them skillfully, and for two weeks held off a series of assaults.

> **COME ON BOYS!**
> **GIVE THEM THE COLD STEEL!**
> # WHO WILL FOLLOW ME?
> CONFEDERATE BRIGADIER GENERAL LEWIS ARMISTEAD,
> PICKETT'S CHARGE, GETTYSBURG, JULY 1863

Q What was gagging and bucking?

A A form of military punishment in which the victim was gagged with a stick tied in his mouth, and seated on the ground with his hands tied together in front of him. Then his knees were forced up between his elbows and another stick was forced between his arms and knees. In this uncomfortable position he would be forced to sit for hours.

Q How was the Army of Northern Virginia reorganized after the Battle of Chancellorsville in May 1863?

A Lee made the second major reorganization of the army, this time into three army corps, commanded initially by Longstreet, Richard S. Ewell, and Ambrose P. Hill.

DID YOU KNOW

AFTER THE FALL OF NEW ORLEANS IN APRIL 1862, PORT HUDSON WAS THE LOGICAL NEXT STEP IN A PROGRESSIVE UNION ATTEMPT TO MOVE UPRIVER IN THE DIRECTION OF VICKSBURG, MISSISSIPPI. AS UNION GENERAL ULYSSES S. GRANT CONTINUED HIS EFFORTS TO CAPTURE VICKSBURG IN EARLY 1863, UNION GENERAL NATHANIEL P. BANKS FORMED A PLAN TO MOVE AGAINST PORT HUDSON. IT WOULD BE A DIFFICULT TARGET. CONFEDERATE GENERAL FRANKLIN GARDNER HAD BEEN STEADILY RECEIVING REINFORCEMENTS AND HAD TURNED THE TOWN INTO A SYSTEM OF FORTIFIED POSITIONS FACING BOTH OVER THE RIVER AND TOWARD THE LANDWARD APPROACHES. THE FIRST ATTEMPT TO CAPTURE PORT HUDSON WAS A NAVAL ATTACK BY GUNBOATS UNDER DAVID G. FARRAGUT, BUT IT ENDED IN FAILURE. ON MAY 11, 1863, LAND AND NAVAL FORCES UNDER BANKS MOVED OUT OF BATON ROUGE IN A MORE CONCERTED ATTACK. GARDNER HAD ONLY 3,500 MEN AGAINST MORE THAN 30,000 UNION TROOPS, BUT HE USED THEM SKILLFULLY, AND FOR TWO WEEKS HELD OFF A SERIES OF BLOODY AND UNCOORDINATED ASSAULTS.

135

Q What rank of officer commanded a Union corps?

A A major general or lieutenant general.

Q When were soldiers in the Union army due to be paid?

A Every two months in the field, though they were lucky if they were paid every four months.

Q Who became commander of the Army of the Potomac in June 1863?

A George Meade.

Q Which Civil War commander said: "Abstinence from spirituous liquors is the best safeguard of morals and health"?

A Robert E. Lee.

Q What was case shot?

A Also called shrapnel or shrapnel shell after its inventor, British artilleryman Henry Shrapnel, case shot was a hollow projectile filled with black powder and up to 70 musket balls. Case shot was designed to explode in the air, so nearly always used time fuses.

DID YOU KNOW

ACCORDING TO U.S. ARMY LIEUTENANT WILLIAM HARDEE'S *INSTRUCTION FOR SKIRMISHERS*, "THE INTERVALS BETWEEN SKIRMISHERS DEPENDS ON THE EXTENT OF GROUND TO BE COVERED; BUT, IN GENERAL, IT IS NOT PROPER THAT THE GROUPS OF FOUR MEN SHOULD BE REMOVED MORE THAN FORTY PACES FROM EACH OTHER. THE HABITUAL DISTANCE BETWEEN MEN OF THE SAME GROUP IN OPEN GROUNDS WILL BE FIVE PACES; IN NO CASE WILL THEY LOSE SIGHT OF EACH OTHER." MOREOVER, HARDEE WROTE, "SKIRMISHERS SHOULD TAKE ADVANTAGE PROMPTLY, AND WITH INTELLIGENCE, OF ALL SHELTER, AND OF ALL ACCIDENTS OF THE GROUND, TO CONCEAL THEMSELVES FROM THE VIEW OF THE ENEMY, AND TO PRO-TECT THEMSELVES FROM HIS FIRE. IT MAY OFTEN HAPPEN THAT INTERVALS ARE MOMENTARILY LOST WHEN SEVERAL MEN NEAR EACH OTHER FIND A COMMON SHELTER; BUT WHEN THEY QUIT THIS POSITION THEY SHOULD IMMEDIATELY RESUME THEIR INTERVALS AND THEIR PLACES IN LINE, SO THAT THEY MAY NOT BY CROWDING NEEDLESSLY EXPOSE THEMSELVES TO THE FIRE OF THE ENEMY." SKIRMISHERS GENERALLY MOVED OUT SO THAT THEY WERE 400–500 YARDS (365–457 M) IN FRONT OF THE MAIN BODY.

Q What was the "Indian Rush"?

A A form of battlefield infantry tactic. To reduce the number of casualties suffered in frontal infantry attacks, assault tactics began to change. Greater emphasis was placed on skirmishers, and more sophisticated maneuvers were developed. One of these was the "Indian Rush" in which two lines advanced side by side, one providing cover while the other moved forward. This divided enemy fire and allowed at least half the assault force to return fire at any one time.

> **IT'S JUST LIKE SHOOTING SQUIRRELS, ONLY THESE SQUIRRELS HAVE GUNS**
> UNION INSTRUCTOR TO NEW RECRUITS

137

Q What was "Whistling Dick"?

A A banded and rifled 18-pounder Confederate siege and garrison weapon. "Whistling Dick" began life as an iron smoothbore Model 1839 which had been rifled. Because of poor rifling, all shells fired from the gun made a peculiar whistling sound, hence its name. The gun was part of the river defenses at Vicksburg, Mississippi, in 1863, and is credited with the sinking of the Union gunboat *Cincinnati*.

Q What was the primary unit of Civil War cavalry?

A The primary unit of the cavalry was the troop or company of some 90–100 officers and men, which would also include wagoners, teamsters, farriers, and saddlers, to keep the unit operational.

Q What was the "Stars and Bars"?

A The Confederate national flag, first pattern. Adopted by the Confederate Congress on March 4, 1861 and in use until 1863, it was originally designed with seven stars, but by the end of 1861 it would bear 13 as the number of seceded states grew. The "Stars and Bars" was carried as the Confederate battle flag at First Manassas in July 1861 and continued in that role in Virginia until September, when the first pattern battle flag was introduced.

> ## THAT OLD MAN HAD MY DIVISION
> # MASSACRED AT GETTYSBURG
> ### GEORGE PICKETT TO JOHN S. MOSBY,
> ### ABOUT ROBERT E. LEE, 1863

Q Which general lost an arm at Gettysburg and a leg at the Battle of Chickamauga in Georgia?

A John Bell Hood of Kentucky.

Q Who was the chief of Lee's artillery during the Chancellorsville Campaign?

A Brigadier General William N. Pendleton. It was the swift and efficient movement of gun batteries between Chancellorsville and Fredericksburg—in support of the rapidly marching infantry—that was one of the key elements of the Confederate victory.

DID YOU KNOW

In September 1863 Lee was taken ill, suffering from acute rheumatic pains and other pains that are now believed to be symptoms of angina pectoris. He was probably also suffering from hypertension, the rosy glow in his cheeks being one symptom of this. On September 4 he wrote to his wife: "I have been suffering ever since my last visit to Richmond from a heavy cold taken in the hot & badly ventilated rooms in the various departments which resulted in an attack of rheumatism in my back, which has given me a great pain & anxiety, for if I cannot get relief I do not see what is to become of me. I had at one time to go about a great deal & the motion of my horse was extremely painful, so much so that I took a spring wagon, but the stony roads I had to traverse made the motion of the wagon almost as bad. I think today I am better. I rode to church this morning on horse back & was surprised to experience so little pain & mounted & dismounted with comparative ease. The doctor gave me some lotion, which I applied faithfully a week to the almost excoriation of the back without apparent benefit. I hope though it is passing away."

Q Which Civil War commander liked to suck lemons?

A "Stonewall" Jackson, it being a question among his staff where he managed to get them in a South cut off from much of the world by a blockade.

Q What was a Vivandière?

A The term "Vivandière" came from a mixture of French and Latin meaning "hospitality giver." In the Civil War it was a term applied to women who traveled with soldiers for little or no pay as sutlers, mascots, or nurses, while others fought alongside their male counterparts.

Q What was a shebang?

A The Confederates were short of all resources, including tents. Most Southerners on campaign improvised brushwood shelters called shebangs, often topped with half a pup tent captured from a Union soldier.

Q What were "Copperheads"?

A Northern Democrats sympathetic towards their Southern brethren. They were also called "Peace Democrats" by their friends and "Copperheads" by their opponents, identifying themselves by copper pennies worn on their lapels.

140

DID YOU KNOW

WHEN THE CIVIL WAR BROKE OUT, GEORGE MEADE WAS APPOINTED BRIGADIER GENERAL OF VOLUNTEERS AND GIVEN COMMAND OF A PENNSYLVANIA BRIGADE. HE PARTICIPATED IN GENERAL GEORGE B. MCCLELLAN'S PENINSULAR CAMPAIGN IN SPRING 1862 AND THE SEVEN DAYS' CAMPAIGN AT THE END OF JUNE, WHERE HE WAS SERIOUSLY WOUNDED. HE WAS NOT FULLY RECOVERED WHEN HE RETURNED TO COMMAND HIS BRIGADE AT THE SECOND BATTLE OF BULL RUN (AUGUST 1862). IN RECOGNITION OF HIS SERVICE THERE, AND AT ANTIETAM A MONTH LATER, MEADE WAS PROMOTED TO MAJOR GENERAL OF VOLUNTEERS. IN THAT CAPACITY HE COMMANDED A DIVISION IN THE DISASTROUS UNION DEFEAT AT FREDERICKSBURG (DECEMBER 1862) AND V CORPS IN A FURTHER UNION DEFEAT AT THE BATTLE OF CHANCELLORSVILLE (MAY 1863). DESPITE THESE DEFEATS, MEADE'S OVERALL COMBAT RECORD WAS GOOD. PRESIDENT LINCOLN APPOINTED HIM COMMANDER OF THE ARMY OF THE POTOMAC IN JUNE 1863, REPLACING GENERAL JOSEPH HOOKER.

Q What was a "Bull Pup"?

A A smaller piece of artillery compared with the 3in Ordnance Rifle or the 12-pounder Napoleon. Employed in special terrain and short-range situations, this weapon was very effective. The Confederates affectionately called it the "Bull Pup."

> **LET US PASS OVER THE RIVER AND REST UNDER THE SHADE OF THE TREES**
> "STONEWALL" JACKSON ON HIS DEATHBED, MAY 1863

Q What were Contrabands?

A Fugitive slaves who sought protection behind Union lines. The term was first coined by the Union general and abolitionist, Benjamin F. Butler, who declared the slaves to be "contrabands of war."

Q Why were Civil War nurses forbidden to wear hooped skirts?

A They needed to walk between rows of cots and could not have a boned sweep of skirt hitting the wounded as they passed.

Q Give at least three alternative names for the Civil War.

A The War Between the States, War for Southern Independence, War of Northern Aggression, War in Defense of Virginia, Mr. Lincoln's War, War of Secession, War of the Insurrection, The Slaveholders' War, The Great Rebellion, The War to Save the Union.

Q **In the Union navy what were receiving ships?**

A New volunteers were first sent aboard receiving ships. They were old ships that had been converted into floating barracks and training facilities. Here they received their uniforms, which they had to pay for, and were given basic training in seamanship and gunnery. Sailors were sent from the receiving ships to their duty stations as soon as they were needed, regardless of how much training they had had. In fact, training was fairly rare; most new sailors learnt their jobs once they reached their duty station.

Q **Who was Charles Francis Adams?**

A President Lincoln's Minister to England, serving from March 20, 1861, to May 13, 1868.

" ALL THIS HAS BEEN MY FAULT
ROBERT E. LEE TO THE SURVIVORS OF
PICKETT'S CHARGE, JULY 1863 "

Q **What was the main difference between the Union and Confederate cavalry?**

A Southern troopers had to supply their own horses. The system worked well enough in the first years of war, because the South was largely rural, and most volunteers could supply their own mounts. As the war went on and losses of horses through battle, sickness, and sheer exhaustion took their toll, the numbers of Confederate cavalry dwindled as cavalrymen who had no horses to ride had to leave their companies to find new mounts. Attempts by the army to make these men fight on foot as infantry usually failed—most cavalrymen would sooner desert than become infantrymen.

Q What were *chevaux-de-frise*?

A An obstacle consisting of a horizontal beam pierced by two diagonal rows of sharpened lances. Since it was freestanding and could be moved about, it was considered suitable for blocking roadways and closing the entrances to temporary fortifications.

Q What naval weapon did the Confederates use to defend their ports?

A Sea mines (then called torpedoes), which were explosive charges anchored in shipping channels. A torpedo could also be deployed by being attached to a long spar mounted on a small, fast, unarmored vessel. The spar would strike an enemy vessel, and the torpedo would explode, but the torpedo boat itself usually survived with little or no damage.

DID YOU KNOW

BLACK SAILORS HAD WORKED ON NAVAL VESSELS FOR YEARS AND WERE ACCEPTED INTO THE UNSEGREGATED UNION NAVY FROM THE BEGINNING OF THE WAR. THEY MADE UP BETWEEN 8 AND 25 PERCENT OF ALL UNION NAVY PERSONNEL. THERE WERE SEVERAL CELEBRATED INCIDENTS OF NAVAL DARING BY BLACK SAILORS. THE MOST FAMOUS WAS THE ACTION OF ROBERT SMALLS, A SLAVE WHO WORKED ON THE CONFEDERATE TRANS-PORT STEAMER, THE CSS *PLANTER*. ON MAY 13, 1862, SMALLS SAILED THE *PLANTER* OUT OF CHARLESTON HARBOR WITH THE HELP OF 12 OTHER SLAVES WHILE THE SHIP'S WHITE OFFICERS WERE ASLEEP ONSHORE. ONCE PAST THE CONFEDERATE GUNS, HE HANDED OVER THE SHIP TO THE UNION NAVY. AS A RESULT OF THIS HEROIC ACTION, SMALLS WAS FETED IN THE NORTH. HE LATER SERVED WITH DISTINCTION IN THE UNION NAVY.

Q What was a bomb-proof?

A Any structure constructed with a roof designed to resist or absorb the impact and explosion of shells. Bomb-proofing in field fortifications required a heavy post and beam framework sunk below the natural level of the ground with a roof covering consisting of one or more courses of large-diameter timbers covering tamped soil. Powder magazines were generally made bomb-proof; fortifications exposed to enemy shell fire often included bomb-proof dugouts and shelters where troops occupying works could retire when under enemy bombardment. Bomb-proofing in permanent fortifications was considered to require masonry vaulted enclosures with arches.

> **"** YOU JUST TELL ME THE BRAND OF WHISKEY GRANT DRINKS: I WOULD LIKE TO **SEND A BARREL OF IT TO MY OTHER GENERALS** **"**
> ABRAHAM LIINCOLN, NOVEMBER 1863

Q Who was the governor of South Carolina between December 1862 and December 1864?

A Milledge Luke Bonham. He was appointed major general and commander of the Army of South Carolina in February 1861; then brigadier general in the Confederate army in April 1861. He resigned his commission on January 27, 1862, to enter the Confederate Congress. He was appointed brigadier general of cavalry in the Confederate army in February 1865.

Q Two sons of the abolitionist Frederick Douglass fought in which Union regiment?

A The 54th Massachusetts.

DID YOU KNOW

MANY OF THE PRIVATIONS THAT DROVE MEN AWAY FROM THE UNION ARMIES WERE THE SAME AS THOSE THAT INSPIRED DESERTIONS FROM THE SOUTH'S ARMIES. IN ADDITION, THE CONFEDERATE ARMY HAD NUMEROUS CONSCRIPTS—AMONG THEM NORTHERNERS AND MEXICANS—WHO HAD NO INTEREST IN THE SOUTHERN CAUSE AND NO SYMPATHY FOR SLAVERY. WHEN CONDITIONS BECAME INTOLERABLE, THESE DRAFTEES WERE AMONG THE FIRST TO DESERT. CONFEDERATE WAGES WERE SOMETIMES AS MANY AS 14 MONTHS LATE IN PAYMENT, AND ARMY CAMPS WERE NOTORIOUS FOR THEIR LACK OF SANITATION. MANY MEN DECIDED THAT THEY WERE MORE USE AT HOME PROTECTING THEIR FAMILIES THAN IN THE ARMY (ESPECIALLY AFTER THEIR HOMES FELL BEHIND UNION LINES AND FAMILIES WERE PLEADING FOR HELP). IN SOME PARTS OF THE SOUTH THE FEAR OF NATIVE AMERICANS ON SCALPING TOURS WAS EVEN GREATER THAN THAT OF UNION SOLDIERS. EVEN A MERE RUMOR IN CAMP THAT INDIANS WERE IN THE AREA WAS OFTEN ENOUGH TO PROVOKE LARGE-SCALE DESERTIONS.

Q Who was Frederick Augustus Washington Bailey better known as?

A The slave, and later famous abolitionist, Frederick Douglass. The son of a slave woman and an unknown white man, Frederick Augustus Washington Bailey was born in February 1818 on Maryland's eastern shore. He spent his early years with his grandparents and with an aunt, seeing his mother only four or five times before her death when he was seven (he knew nothing of his father).

Q Where was the biggest Union horse depot in the Civil War?

A In the summer of 1863 a vast cavalry depot was established at Giesboro Point, within the District of Columbia across the eastern branch of the Potomac (Anacostia River). Giesboro was the powerhouse behind the great Union cavalry operations of the last two years of the war.

Q Which famous American author served in the war as a nurse?

A Louisa May Alcott, author of *Little Women*.

Q What congressional bill was introduced in the Confederate Congress, but failed to pass after the Emancipation Proclamation was to take effect on January 1, 1863?

A "Take no Federal officers alive as prisoners!"

Q Which soldier was the only person in the Civil War to win two Congressional Medals of Honor?

A Thomas Custer, brother of George Armstrong Custer.

146

DID YOU KNOW

ONE OF PRESIDENT LINCOLN'S GREATEST AND MOST IMPORTANT ASSETS WAS THE WAY HE INTERPRETED HIS POWER, MAKING EXTENSIVE USE OF EXECUTIVE ORDERS. THE GREATEST OF THESE WAS THE EMANCIPATION PROCLAMATION, WHICH CAME INTO EFFECT ON JANUARY 1, 1863. LINCOLN ACCEPTED THAT SLAVERY COULD ONLY BE ABOLISHED BY STATE-LEVEL ACTION OR BY AN AMENDMENT TO THE CONSTITUTION—NEITHER OF WHICH WERE POLITICALLY POSSIBLE AT THAT TIME. WHEN HE DECIDED TO STRIKE A BLOW AGAINST SLAVERY, HE THEREFORE DID IT BY ISSUING A PRESIDENTIAL PROCLAMATION. HE JUSTIFIED THE MEASURE ON THE GROUNDS OF "MILITARY NECESSITY," WHICH IS WHY IT WAS LIMITED TO STATES IN REBELLION RATHER THAN APPLYING TO THE WHOLE COUNTRY. FOR THIS REASON THE PROCLAMATION DID NOT FREE SLAVES IN UNION TERRITORY.

> YOU ARE BETTER OFF THAN I AM,
> FOR WHILE YOU HAVE LOST
> ## YOUR LEFT, I HAVE
> ## LOST MY RIGHT ARM
> LEE TO JACKSON, MAY 1863

Q Who were the "Young Lions" of the South?

A Students of the Virginia Military Institute, the South Carolina Military Academy, the Georgia Military Academy, and the University of Alabama Corps of Cadets.

Q What was field artillery?

A Batteries assigned to operate in the field with either infantry or cavalry. Field artillery was itself subdivided into two functional groups called mounted and horse artillery. Again, a given unit could be assigned to either.

Q What was peculiar about the term "mounted artillery"?

A Mounted artillery was *not* mounted. The drivers rode, but generally, like the infantrymen with whom they worked, the "mounted" artillerymen walked (thus resulting in the added confusion of having them referred to as "foot" artillery). This strange usage originated with the structure of the artillery in the 1830s. Before then, the men of an artillery company were divided into distinct groups of drivers and cannoneers. These men wore different uniforms, received different rates of pay, and did not undertake each other's duties. In 1838, however, these distinctions were eliminated. Henceforth, the men were cross-trained and each would ride whenever assigned to be a driver. Thus, all of the men occasionally were "mounted."

Q Why was Vicksburg, Mississippi, such a formidable fortress?

A Vicksburg controlled the middle stretch of the Mississippi River. It was located on high, unscalable bluffs from which its heavy artillery could control the river below. It was also very difficult to approach overland. Directly to the north was the vast Yazoo Delta, impassable to any large body of troops. Federal gunboats could not sail past the city without risking destruction.

Q What were Robert E. Lee's plans after the Battle of Chancellorsville?

" I DO NOT WANT TO MAKE THIS CHARGE.
I DO NOT SEE HOW IT CAN SUCCEED
JAMES LONGSTREET ABOUT
PICKETT'S CHARGE, JULY 1863 **"**

A Although Chancellorsville had been a decisive victory for the Confederacy, Lee knew that all he had really done was bought time. The battle had repelled the Federals from much of Virginia, thus protecting Richmond. But Lee knew it would only be a matter of time before the Army of the Potomac moved south again. He thus decided to launch another invasion of the North.

Q In which state did the Battle of Big Black River on May 17, 1863, take place?

A Mississippi.

DID YOU KNOW

THE MISSISSIPPI IS THE SECOND LONGEST U.S. RIVER, AFTER THE
MISSOURI, AND THE LARGEST—A THIRD OF ALL AMERICAN STREAMS EMPTY
INTO IT. THE MISSISSIPPI WAS USED BY NATIVE AMERICANS FOR TRADE AND
TRANSPORTATION FOR CENTURIES BEFORE EUROPEAN COLONIZATION
BEGAN. IN THE SEVENTEENTH CENTURY FRENCH SETTLERS USED IT IN THE
FUR TRADE. BY THE 1800S THE RIVER WAS THE PRINCIPAL OUTLET TO THE
SEA FOR THE NEWLY SETTLED AREAS OF THE CENTRAL UNITED STATES.
GOODS WERE FLOATED DOWNSTREAM TO NEW ORLEANS AND THEN
SHIPPED ABROAD. IMPORTS WERE DRAGGED UPSTREAM ON RAFTS. THE
INTRODUCTION OF STEAMBOATS IN 1811 MEANT THAT GOODS COULD BE
TRANSPORTED AGAINST THE CURRENT MUCH FASTER AND LED TO A BOOM
IN RIVER TRADE. THIS ERA WAS DESCRIBED IN MARK TWAIN'S *LIFE ON THE
MISSISSIPPI* (1883). BEFORE ENGINEERS TAMED THE RIVER IN THE
DECADES AFTER THE CIVIL WAR, SAILING ON THE MISSISSIPPI COULD BE
HAZARDOUS. THE RIVER WAS CONTINUALLY SHIFTING ITS COURSE, THROW-
ING UP NEW SANDBARS AND SNAGS. THE WATER LEVEL ROSE AND FELL AT
DIFFERENT TIMES OF THE YEAR. SUBMERGED TREES AND OTHER OBSTACLES
COULD TEAR A HOLE IN THE BOTTOM OF A BOAT.

149

Q Which battle in May 1863 closed the last Confederate escape
routes from Port Hudson, Louisiana?

A The Battle of Plains Store/Springfield Road on May 21. As part of
the Port Hudson Campaign, Union troops secured a landing base
on the Baton Rouge, despite Confederate counterattacks.

Q Who commanded Union forces at the Battle of Brandy Station,
Virginia, on June 9, 1863?

A General Alfred Pleasanton.

Q At the Battle of Brandy Station what happened at Fleetwood Hill?

A Fleetwood Hill became the scene of a remarkable battle, as thousands of cavalrymen participated in massed charges and counercharges, with neither side able to gain an immediate advantage. As the afternoon of June 9 wore on, however, casualties mounted, and the northernmost Union forces under Buford and Pleasanton began to withdraw across the Rappahannock, pushed on by a series of Confederate counterattacks. Union forces near Fleetwood Hill also began to withdraw, leaving Stuart's cavalrymen in possession of the field.

Q Why was "Jeb" Stuart ridiculed in the South after the battle?

A "Jeb" Stuart could legitimately claim victory in the Battle of Brandy Station. His troopers had held their positions and inflicted almost twice as many casualties (866) as they suffered themselves (485). This was not the whole story, however. Stuart had carried out a grand review of his cavalry on the day before the raid and was taken by surprise by the bold Union attack.

Q What were Robert E. Lee's strategic options in mid-1863?

A Either to dig in and fight another defensive battle for Richmond, or to assume the initiative and attack.

Q What were the results of the Battle of Brandy Station in 1863?

A This battle, and a skirmish at Kelly's Ford along the Rappahannock the previous March, signaled the great improvement of the fighting spirit and skill of the Union cavalry. It also led "Jeb" Stuart to take extra risks during the coming Gettysburg campaign to redeem his reputation.

Q What other factors influenced Lee's decision to invade the North in 1863?

A His army was short of supplies; a thrust into Pennsylvania would provide an opportunity to correct those deficiencies. A victory might gain foreign recognition for the Confederacy, and would strengthen the Northern Democrats, who favored making peace with the South.

DID YOU KNOW

THE PHOTOGRAPHER MATHEW BRADY'S EFFORT TO CREATE AN ENDURING RECORD OF THE CIVIL WAR BROUGHT HIM NOTHING BUT MISERY. HIS PROFESSIONAL ETHICS WERE CRITICIZED BY SOME OF HIS PHOTOGRAPHERS, WHO FELT IT WAS UNFAIR TO HAVE "PHOTOGRAPH BY BRADY" STAMPED ON EVERY PHOTOGRAPH THEY TOOK. THAT WAS ALWAYS THE BRADY WAY, HOWEVER. NO MATTER WHO TOOK A PHOTOGRAPH—AND HE TOOK VERY FEW HIMSELF DURING THE CIVIL WAR—IF BRADY OWNED IT, IT WAS A "PHOTOGRAPH BY BRADY." THIS PRACTICE WENT BEYOND PUTTING HIS FAMOUS NAME TO THE WORK OF HIS COLLEAGUES AND EMPLOYEES. IN HIS DESIRE TO CREATE A TOTAL RECORD OF THE WAR HE TRACKED DOWN AND BOUGHT THOUSANDS OF PHOTOGRAPHS TAKEN BY OTHER STUDIOS AND PHOTOGRAPHERS. EVERY TIME SUCH PHOTOGRAPHS WERE REPRINTED, THEY ALSO BORE THE CREDIT "PHOTOGRAPH BY BRADY."

Q What date marked the start of Lee's 1863 invasion of the North?

A June 15, when the leading divisions of Ewell's Corps crossed the Potomac river near Sheperdstown and entered Maryland. Officially still loyal to the Union, the state had provided several excellent combat units to Lee's army. On June 19, the Maryland-Pennsylvania border was crossed by the Army of Northern Virginia, threatening the cities of Baltimore and Washington and ensuring that Meade, commander of the Army of the Potomac, would have to respond.

Q What battle had cleared the way for Lee's invasion of the North?

A The Second Battle of Winchester on June 14. Confederate General Richard S. Ewell's II Corps attacked a Union garrison from the Army of the Potomac led by General Robert H. Milroy, which was blocking the Confederate advance and endangering the army's communications and supply lines. The Confederates' victory at Winchester cleared a path for their invasion.

152

Q List the Army of Northern Virginia's corps in June 1863.

A The army had four corps: II Corps under Richard S. Ewell, I Corps under James Longstreet, and III Corps under Ambrose P. Hill. Together with J.E.B. Stuart's cavalry corps, Lee's army numbered about 75,000 men.

> **"**
> ANY VICTORY WOULD BE DEAR
> ## AT SUCH A PRICE
> ROBERT E. LEE
> ON THE DEATH OF "STONEWALL" JACKSON
>

DID YOU KNOW

FOR THE FIRST TWO YEARS OF THE CONFLICT UNION CAVALRY UNITS HAD SUFFERED FROM POOR LEADERSHIP AND TRAINING AND WERE COMPLETELY OUTCLASSED BY REBEL CAVALRY. MANY UNION CAVALRYMEN, BORN AND RAISED IN TOWNS AND CITIES, KNEW LITTLE ABOUT HORSES. INDEED, MANY HAD TO LEARN TO RIDE ONCE THEY ENLISTED. IN CONTRAST, CAVALRYMEN FROM THE MORE RURAL SOUTH HAD MORE EXPERIENCE WITH CARING FOR AND RIDING HORSES. ALSO, MANY CONFEDERATE CAVALRYMEN FOUGHT IN THEIR OWN LOCALITIES, GIVING THEM A GREAT ADVANTAGE IN AN AGE WHEN FEW DETAILED MAPS OF THE UNITED STATES EXISTED. OVER TIME THE GAP IN QUALITY BETWEEN UNION AND CONFEDERATE CAVALRY UNITS NARROWED. BY THE TIME OF THE BATTLE OF BRANDY STATION, NORTHERN SUPERIORITY IN RESOURCES AND MANUFACTURED GOODS ALLOWED UNION CAVALRY TO BE BETTER ARMED AND BETTER SUPPLIED WITH MOUNTS. THE FIGHTING SPIRIT OF THE INDIVIDUAL UNION CAVALRYMAN WAS NEVER IN DOUBT, EITHER, AND LEADERS SUCH AS BUFORD TURNED THEIR UNITS INTO SUCCESSFUL COMBAT FORCES. AFTER JUNE 1863 THE CAVALRY PLAYED AN INCREASINGLY EFFECTIVE ROLE IN THE UNION WAR EFFORT.

153

Q What was Lee's aim in June 1863?

A The plan was to march through Maryland and into Pennsylvania and win a decisive battle there, and perhaps even take Washington, D.C.

Q Give the corps organization of the Army of the Potomac in June 1863.

A I Army Corps under Major General John F. Reynolds, II Army Corps under Major General Winfield S. Hancock, III Army Corps under Major General Daniel E. Sickles, V Army Corps under Major General George Sykes, VI Army Corps under Major-General John Sedgwick, XI Army Corps under Major General Oliver O. Howard, XII Army Corps under Major General Henry W. Slocum, and the Cavalry Corps under Major General Alfred Pleasonton.

Q When was West Virginia admitted to the Union?

A On June 20, 1863, following a presidential proclamation.

Q When did George Meade become the Army of the Potomac's commander?

A June 28, 1863.

Q What was the main Union force in Tennessee between November 1862 and November 1863?

A The Army of the Cumberland.

Q What happened at the Battle of Hanover, Pennsylvania, on June 30, 1863?

A J.E.B. Stuart's cavalry, attempting to circle around Union forces and link up with Lee's army, was diverted and delayed by Union General Farnsworth's cavalry brigade at Hanover.

DID YOU KNOW

SOME RIVER GUNBOATS HAD ARMOUR THAT WASN'T REALLY ARMOR AT ALL. MANY HAD "ARMOR" MADE FROM COTTON BALES. BALES COULD STOP RIFLE BULLETS AND SMALL-CALIBER ARTILLERY ROUNDS. BALES WERE ALSO LIGHT, WHICH ALLOWED VESSELS TO NAVIGATE SHALLOW RIVERS.

BULLETS HISSING, HUMMING, AND
WHISTLING, EVERYWHERE: CANNON ROARING
UNION CANNONEER AUGUSTUS BUELL,
GETTYSBURG, JULY 1, 1863

Q What was "Buck and Ball"?

A A musket load, usually used in a defensive situation. It was made up of three large buckshot bound on top of a .69-caliber, smooth-bore musket ball and was encased in a paper cartridge like those used with the Minie bullet. The .69-caliber musket was an inaccurate weapon that could be converted to good use at close range with this load. The use of the buck and ball was not common.

Q What was the clash that began the Battle of Gettysburg?

A The encounter that developed into the largest battle of the Civil War began almost by chance. On June 29, 1863, one of A.P. Hill's divisions under Harry Heth went foraging toward Gettysburg, Pennsylvania. On July 1 it ran into a Union cavalry brigade from John Buford's 1st Cavalry Division, posted about 4 miles (6.5 km) west of the town across the Chambersburg Pike.

Q Why was the town of Gettysburg so important?

A Gettysburg was strategically important because it lay at the junction of roads running out to Washington and Baltimore to the south and east and to Harrisburg, the capital of Pennsylvania, to the north.

Q Why was Union General John Buford's role at the Battle of Gettysburg so critical?

A The evening of June 30, 1863, found Buford's 1st Division, Cavalry Corps, posted north and west of the market town of Gettysburg. Buford correctly deduced that the Confederate army was concentrating in his direction. Although outnumbered, he prepared to hold the town until reinforcements could arrive. Fighting dismounted, his troopers fended off the Confederates for over three hours. Buford's correct pinpointing of the location of the invading Confederate army, coupled with his skillful defense of the ridges west of the town on July 1, 1863, helped ensure that the battle was fought on terms favorable to the Union.

> **THERE ARE THOSE DAMN BLACK-HATTED FELLOWS AGAIN, T'AINT NO MILITIA.**
> **IT'S THE ARMY OF THE POTOMAC**
> CONFEDERATE SOLDIER
> AT GETTYSBURG, JULY 1, 1863

Q What was a camouflet?

A A French term describing a whiff of smoke puffed into someone's face. Confederates and Federals sometimes used a simple explosive device called a camouflet to combat enemy miners tunnelling under their siege works or trenches. The explosive charge was planted in front of the defenses so that as enemy miners tunneled forward the camouflet would lie in their way. When the enemy struck the device with a pick or shovel he would have to retreat hastily or the shaft would collapse on him. If planted skilfully, the camouflet would explode downward, leaving the earth above intact so as not to reveal the mine's location.

DID YOU KNOW

GIVEN COMMAND OF THE ARMY OF THE TENNESSEE IN OCTOBER 1862, ULYSSES S. GRANT'S NEXT OBJECTIVE WAS VICKSBURG, THE KEY TO CONFEDERATE CONTROL OF THE LOWER MISSISSIPPI RIVER. IN A COMBINED OPERATION WITH UNION NAVY GUNBOATS, GRANT ADVANCED ON VICKSBURG AND LAID SIEGE TO IT. THE CITY SURRENDERED ON JULY 4, 1863, TO HUGE REJOICING IN THE NORTH. THE VICTORY WAS A TURNING POINT IN GRANT'S CAREER. HE WAS REWARDED WITH A PROMOTION TO MAJOR GENERAL. ON OCTOBER 16, 1863, HE TOOK COMMAND OF ALL UNION FORCES FROM THE MISSISSIPPI RIVER TO THE APPALACHIAN MOUNTAINS. HE AT ONCE WENT TO ASSIST THE UNION ARMY BESIEGED AT CHATTANOOGA, TENNESSEE. VICTORY THERE DURING THE BATTLES OF NOVEMBER 23–25 SECURED GRANT THE THANKS OF HIS PRESIDENT AND A MOVE BY CONGRESS TO AWARD HIM THE SPECIALLY REVIVED RANK OF LIEUTENANT GENERAL. HE WENT TO WASHINGTON, D.C., IN MARCH 1864 TO RECEIVE BOTH HIS PROMOTION AND THE POST OF GENERAL-IN-CHIEF OF ALL UNION ARMIES.

157

Q Define furlough.

A A furlough was an enlisted man's leave from the Union or Confederate army, granted at his superior's discretion. Rules in both armies specified that furlough be granted by a commander actually quartered with the soldier's company or regiment. A furloughed soldier's weapons and equipment remained behind, and he carried furlough papers giving a detailed description of his physical appearance, return and departure dates, unit designation, and pay and subsistence allowances. Furlough papers warned that the soldier must rejoin his unit by the date specified "or be considered a deserter." Officers were granted leaves, whose rules and stipulations were more extensive. Both leaves and furloughs were freely abused, and both armies had occasion to cancel all leaves and furloughs to account for deserters.

Q What saved Union forces from defeat at the Battle of Gettysburg on the afternoon of July 1, 1863?

A Fighting developed north of the town with the arrival of Oliver O. Howard's Union XI Corps in the afternoon. It was pushed back through the town by two divisions of Ewell's corps led by Jubal A. Early and Robert E. Rodes. The retreating Union forces were on the verge of defeat, but were rallied south of the town on Cemetery Hill by the arrival of Winfield Scott Hancock and the lead unit of his II Corps.

Q What was a cotton-clad?

A A gunboat that used cotton bales stacked on its deck as a shield against enemy fire.

> ## THE REBEL ARMY IS NOW THE LEGITIMATE PROPERTY OF THE ARMY OF THE POTOMAC
> JOSEPH HOOKER
> BEFORE THE BATTLE OF CHANCELLORSVILLE, 1863

Q Which Union corps commander was killed at Gettysburg on July 1, 1863?

A John F. Reynolds, commander of the Union I Corps. On July 1 Lee's Confederates began arriving from the north and northwest, while Meade's lead corps began arriving from the south. By midmorning A.P. Hill was reinforcing Heth, while John F. Reynolds established a defensive line across the Chambersburg Pike at McPherson's Ridge. Reynolds was killed, and Abner Doubleday took over his command.

Q Which Union officer was promoted to major general on his deathbed?

A John Buford. In the autumn of 1863 he fell mortally ill with typhoid fever. On his deathbed he was promoted to major general, a rare honor. It was backdated to July 1, 1863, in recognition of his great day at the Battle of Gettysburg.

Q At Gettysburg where was Culp's Hill?

A Culp's Hill lay on the extreme right of the Federal line and was the scene of heavy fighting.

DID YOU KNOW

RAIDS BEHIND ENEMY LINES, DISTRACTING AND CONFUSING THE ENEMY, DID WONDERS FOR THE CAVALRY'S REPUTATION AND RAISED MORALE. HOWEVER, WHILE THE CAVALRY WAS RAIDING, IT COULD NOT CONCENTRATE ON ITS OTHER VITAL BUT LESS GLAMOROUS TASK OF KEEPING A WATCH ON THE ENEMY'S MOVEMENTS. THIS FAILURE HAD SERIOUS CONSEQUENCES IN LATER BATTLES. AT CHANCELLORSVILLE IN MAY 1863, UNION GENERAL JOSEPH HOOKER SENT HIS CAVALRY AWAY ON A RAID AND, AS A RESULT, WAS NOT WARNED OF THE ARRIVAL OF LEE'S ARMY FROM FREDERICKSBURG. TWO MONTHS LATER IN PENNSYLVANIA LEE HIMSELF WAS LET DOWN BY J.E.B. STUART, WHO, IN AN ATTEMPT TO REPEAT HIS EXPLOIT ON THE PENINSULA WAS NOT IN A POSITION TO WARN HIS COMMANDER THAT THE UNION ARMY WAS CONCENTRATING AT GETTYSBURG. THESE FAILURES WERE PARTLY RESPONSIBLE FOR THE CAVALRY'S POOR REPUTATION AMONG THE INFANTRY OF BOTH SIDES, WHO WERE DOING MOST OF THE FIGHTING AND DYING. "WHOEVER SAW A DEAD CAVALRYMAN?" WAS A COMMON INFANTRY JIBE, WHILE IN 1864 ONE DISGRUNTLED CONFEDERATE SOLDIER WROTE: "I DO WISH THE YANKEES WOULD CAPTURE ALL THE CAVALRY … THEY NEVER WILL FIGHT SO I THINK IT IS USELESS TO HAVE THEM IN THE ARMY EATING RATIONS."

Q What were sutlers?

A Civilians officially appointed to supply soldiers with a long list of approved items. In both the Union and Confederate armies each regiment was allowed one sutler. From these camp vendors soldiers could purchase items such as as food, newspapers, books, tobacco, razors cups, cutlery, and even illegal alcohol.

Q What was created under the Union General Orders No. 147?

A In August 1862 General McClellan issued General Orders No. 147 creating the Ambulance Corps for the Army of the Potomac under the control of the Medical Director.

Q On which Civil War battlefield was Cemetery Hill?

A Gettysburg.

Q What was the Letterman Ambulance Plan?

A The Army of the Potomac, under its medical director Jonathan Letterman, developed the Letterman Ambulance Plan. In this system the ambulances of a division moved together, under a mounted line sergeant, with two stretcher-bearers and one driver per ambulance, to collect the wounded from the field, bring them to the dressing stations and then take them to the field hospital.

" HELLO, MASSA;
BOTTOM RAIL ON TOP
DIS TIME
BLACK UNION SOLDIER TO HIS FORMER MASTER "

DID YOU KNOW

In December 1862 Grant ordered William Sherman to assault Chickasaw Bluff just north of the fortress of Vicksburg on the Mississippi. Grant himself was supposed to support the assault but failed to show up. Sherman attacked anyway. Although the attempt failed, Sherman played a key role in the Union victory at Vicksburg on July 4, 1863. After the fall of Vicksburg Sherman replaced Grant as commander of the Army of the Tennessee. Just over two months later the Union Army of the Cumberland was surrounded at Chattanooga, Tennessee. Grant, Sherman, and much of the Army of the Tennessee went to its rescue. The ensuing Battle of Chattanooga was a dramatic Union success. When Grant became Union general-in-chief in March 1864, Sherman once more replaced him, this time becoming head of the Military Division of the Mississippi.

161

Q Who was the "Drummer Boy of Chickamauga"?

A John Lincoln Clem, born in 1851. He became a drummer boy in the Union army, and at the Battle Of Chickamauga he rode an artillery caisson to the front and carried a musket trimmed down to size. While retreating, a Confederate officer ran after the cannon Clem rode with, and before the drummer killed him, said, "Surrender, you damned little Yankee!" This act won Clem national acclaim and the name "Drummer Boy of Chickamauga." He retired from the army as a major general in 1916 and died on May 13, 1937.

Q Of the hundreds of African-American women to serve with the Union army's colored regiments, who was the only one who left a published memoir of her experiences.

A Susie King Taylor.

Q Describe the situation at the beginning of the second day of the Battle of Gettysburg, July 2, 1863.

A Meade had more than 90,000 men consolidating their position on the high ground, which extended in a fishhook-shaped line from Culp's Hill around Cemetery Hill and south along Cemetery Ridge. On the Confederate side Hill and Ewell had been joined by Longstreet, whom Lee ordered to deploy along Seminary Ridge next to Hill's corps on the Confederate right.

Q What was Lee's plan at Gettysburg on July 2?

A Lee planned to attack both of Meade's flanks. Longstreet would begin the attack by a strike at the Union left.

Q Who received a congressional message of thanks for his success at the Battle of Gettysburg?

A George Meade, commander of the Army of the Potomac.

DID YOU KNOW

THE WAR WAS FOUGHT MAINLY ON CONFEDERATE SOIL. THE CONFEDERACY COULD ONLY MAINTAIN THE WAR EFFORT WITH THE SUPPORT OF ITS POPULATION, AND IT COULD NOT DRAW ON THE TRADITIONS OF LOYALTY AND PATRIOTISM THAT WERE OPEN TO THE UNIONISTS. YET, DESPITE THE OBVIOUS NEED TO ENLIST PUBLIC OPINION IN SUPPORT OF THE CONFEDERACY, PRESIDENT JEFFERSON DAVIS SEEMS TO HAVE GIVEN LITTLE ATTENTION TO PROPAGANDA. UNOFFICIAL PROPAGANDA IN THE SOUTH WAS HARDLY MORE EFFECTIVE. THE PRESS WAS SUBJECT TO VERY LITTLE REGULATION OR CENSORSHIP, TO THE EXTENT THAT MILITARY INFORMATION USEFUL TO THE ENEMY OFTEN APPEARED IN THE COLUMNS OF SOUTHERN NEWSPAPERS. SOME NEWSPAPERMEN DID GIVE THE DAVIS ADMINISTRATION STEADY SUPPORT, BUT THEY WERE OUTNUMBERED BY CRITICS WHO WROTE WITH LITTLE RESTRAINT.

Q Estimate the number of deserters from the Army of the Potomac in 1863?

A In 1863 Union General Joseph E. Hooker reckoned that no fewer than 85,000 officers and men had deserted from his Army of the Potomac. In December 1862, 180,000 Union soldiers were absent, either with or without leave.

> **I HAVE STOOD YOUR MEANNESS**
> # AS LONG AS
> # I INTEND TO
> NATHAN BEDFORD FORREST TO BRAXTON BRAGG

Q What Union disaster began the second day of fighting at the Battle of Gettysburg?

A The fighting began in the afternoon. Daniel E. Sickles, leading III Corps, advanced without orders from Cemetery Ridge toward the Emmitsburg Road. Caught in open ground by Longstreet's troops, III Corps was cut to pieces around the Peach Orchard and Devil's Den. The Union left flank was now exposed, and a Confederate division under John Bell Hood advanced toward the hill position of Little Round Top, which dominated the south of Cemetery Ridge.

Q Which Union commander rectified the situation around Little Round Top?

A Gouverneur K. Warren, who spotted the importance of Little Round Top and ordered its occupation. Hood's attacks on the hill reached the lower slopes but failed to break through to the top.

Q What was the most violent civil disorder in American history?

A The New York draft riot of July 1863.

Q What was Lee's plan at the Battle of Gettysburg on July 3, 1863?

A An all-out bid to break the Union center on Cemetery Ridge. He concentrated his artillery—some 150 guns—on Seminary Ridge and ordered three infantry divisions, totaling 15,000 men, to make a frontal assault across nearly 1 mile (1.6 km) of open ground toward the Union positions ranged above them behind a stone wall.

> ## WAR SHOULD BE PURE AND SIMPLE
> # AS APPLIED TO THE
> # BELLIGERENTS
> WILLIAM SHERMAN, SEPTEMBER 1863

Q What measures did Lee take to weaken the Union line along Cemetery Ridge?

A To weaken the Union line, Lee brought up all his 150 guns to his position on Seminary Ridge, and at 13:00 hours they opened fire and began a two-hour bombardment. At about 15:00 hours the guns fell silent, and the Confederates advanced over the tract of open land that separated the two armies. However, the bombardment had not done its job. Union infantry were still in position behind a long stone wall, and the Union artillery was waiting behind the ridge.

DID YOU KNOW

On July 3, 1863, the third day of the Battle of Gettysburg, Confederate General Robert E. Lee ordered a frontal assault on the center of the Union position along Cemetery Ridge. This attack would be Lee's final chance to get on that high ground and win the battle. The attack was spearheaded by George E. Pickett's division. Supported by just under 15,000 Confederate troops, Pickett was to break the Union hold on the ridge, which lay about 1 mile (1.6 km) from Southern lines.

Q Who said, after Pickett's Charge, "It's all my fault. It is I who have lost this fight"?

A Robert E. Lee, in admission of his own gross tactical error. At about 15:00 hours the guns fell silent, and the Confederates advanced over the tract of open land that separated the two armies. However, the bombardment had not done its job. Union artillery opened up on the Confederates until the survivors were within 200 yards (180 m) of the Union frontline. Then the infantry opened up with volleys of musket fire. Only a handful of men reached the stone wall.

Q Name the two regiments that defended Cemetery Ridge against Pickett's Charge at Gettysburg on 3 July.

A The 69th and 71st Pennsylvania Infantry. The Confederate troops were within 200 yards (180 m) of the wall when the Pennsylvanians opened fire, mowing down the Confederate line. Barely 100 Southerners reached the wall before the attack finally broke.

Q Why was Pickett's Charge known as the high tide of the Confederacy?

A After this defeat the Confederacy was never again able to mount a large-scale invasion of the North.

Q What did the Union Corps of Topographical Engineers do?

A Conducted explorations, surveys, and the reconnaissance of uncharted areas and sites for defenses. First commanded by Colonel John J. Abert then Colonel Stephen H. Long, the unit was absorbed by the Corps of Engineers in 1863.

Q Who were Wheat's Tigers?

A A Confederate unit from New Orleans which adopted the style of the French Zouave uniform.

Q What was a "butternut"?

A A Confederate army volunteer. Due to equipment shortages, Confederate soldiers actually wore combinations of uniform pieces and items of personal clothing. Infantrymen sometimes went without shoes altogether; and broad felt hats were as common as kepis. From 1863 many uniforms were homespun and dyed a yellow-brown with coloring from butternuts, hence the name butternut

DID YOU KNOW

IN THE 1860S, DOCTORS KNEW LITTLE MORE ABOUT THE CAUSES OF INFECTION AND DISEASE THAN THEY HAD HUNDREDS OF YEARS EARLIER. THE EXISTENCE OF BACTERIA AND VIRUSES WAS STILL UNDISCOVERED. SURGEONS OPERATED WITH DIRTY INSTRUMENTS IN FILTHY CONDITIONS, SO EVEN WHEN INJURED SOLDIERS HAD BULLETS REMOVED OR WOUNDS SEWED UP, THEY WERE LIKELY TO FACE DEADLY INFECTIONS. COMBAT WOUNDS WERE NOT THE GREATEST KILLERS OF CIVIL WAR SOLDIERS, HOWEVER. DISEASE TOOK FAR MORE LIVES, AND IT CREATED A HUGE PROBLEM THAT NEITHER SIDE IN THE WAR WAS ABLE TO SOLVE.

" HIS VIRGINIA WAS
TO HIM THE WORLD
WILLIAM SHERMAN, OF ROBERT E. LEE "

Q In the Army of the Potomac what was "heavy marching-order"?

A The troops carried all they possessed with them on the march.

Q In the Army of the Potomac what was "light marching-order"?

A The men marched with only the musket, ammunition, haversack, and canteen.

Q Why was the fall of Vicksburg to General Grant in July 1863 a disaster for the Confederacy?

A Vicksburg, located on well-defended high bluffs on a loop in the Mississippi River, dominated the trade of a vast area between New Orleans and Memphis. By June 1862 both New Orleans and Memphis had fallen to the Union, leaving Vicksburg as the city linking the two halves of the Confederacy. If Vicksburg fell, the South would be split in two. Confederate President Jefferson Davis had ordered it to be held at all costs.

Q During the siege of Vicksburg where did the civilian population take refuge?

A Many took refuge in caves dug out of the hillsides behind the city. The Union army dug 15 miles (24 km) of trenches and brought up 220 heavy guns to bombard the city day and night. Inside Vicksburg the civilian population suffered as badly from the shelling as the soldiers. Food began to run out, and by late June mule and rat meat was all that was left.

Q Why was control of the Mississippi River so important to the Confederacy?

A The Confederacy needed to defend the vital transportation route and the rich agricultural lands of the lower Mississippi Valley. Although the South had fewer vessels than the North, it only needed to hold one strong-point on the river to prevent any Northern commerce with the outside world. The Confederates fortified strategic points on the Mississippi with forts and gun emplacements and laid mines, then known as torpedoes, along the river.

Q What were "Pook Turtles"?

A Union ironclads, named after their designer James Pook, designed specifically to do battle on the lower Mississippi.

> **SUCH AN EXECUTIVE OFFICER THE SUN**
> # NEVER SHONE ON
> ROBERT E. LEE
> ABOUT "STONEWALL" JACKSON

Q What were Grant's surrender terms as his Union army lay siege to Vicksburg in the summer of 1863?

A Grant initially demanded unconditional surrender, but modified his terms and agreed to let the Confederates sign paroles agreeing not to fight again until they had been exchanged for captured Union soldiers.

Q What role did the Union commander David D. Porter play during the siege of Vicksburg?

A Porter was a daring naval commander who helped Grant to victory at Vicksburg. His boats ran past the Vicksburg batteries at night so that they could ferry the Union army across the river.

Q Why did General Franklin Gardner surrender Port Hudson, Louisiana, on July 9, 1863?

A Under siege since late May, Gardner had no hope of relief; Confederate forces in Vicksburg had been under siege themselves. Medicine, ammunition, and food had run out. When word reached Gardner that Vicksburg had surrendered, he saw no point in continuing to resist.

Q What was the most common disease among Southern soldiers?

A Measles.

Q Who was the first colonel of the Union 54th Massachusetts Infantry Regiment in 1863?

A Robert Gould Shaw.

DID YOU KNOW

THE CHURCH PROVED A SUCCESSFUL CONDUIT FOR UNOFFICIAL PROPAGANDA IN THE SOUTH. SOUTHERN SOCIETY WAS DEEPLY RELIGIOUS, AND RELIGION PROVED TO BE A KEY FACTOR IN STIRRING AND MAINTAINING ENTHUSIASM FOR THE WAR. THE CLERGY OFFERED SOLACE TO THE BEREAVED AND INJURED, WHILE DESERTERS AND SPECULATORS WERE CONDEMNED AS BOTH OFFENSIVE TO GOD AND DETRIMENTAL TO THE WAR EFFORT. CONFEDERATE VICTORIES WERE SEEN TO CONFIRM SOUTHERNERS' STATUS AS GOD'S CHOSEN PEOPLE. IN THE UNION, PROPAGANDA ACTIVITIES WERE SCARCELY BETTER ORGANIZED. THERE WAS NO OFFICIAL PROGRAMME AIMED TO MAINTAIN ENTHUSIASM FOR THE CONFLICT. PRESIDENT ABRAHAM LINCOLN'S FINELY CRAFTED SPEECHES WERE IMPORTANT IN RALLYING PUBLIC OPINION TO THE UNION CAUSE, BUT LINCOLN HIMSELF SHOWED LITTLE INTEREST IN THE POTENTIAL OF PROPAGANDA.

Q What did the U.S. Christian Commission do?

A The commission distributed food and aid and cared for wounded Union soldiers.

Q What was the significance of the abortive Union attack on Fort Wagner, South Carolina, on July 18, 1863?

A The Union 54th Massachusetts charged the Confederate stronghold at Fort Wagner. Although the assault failed, the regiment's courage under fire proved to whites the fighting quality of black soldiers.

> **SHERMAN MUST RANK AS THE FIRST OF THE MODERN TOTALITARIAN GENERALS**
> J.F.C. FULLER ON WILLIAM SHERMAN

Q In 1863 were white Union soldiers paid the same as black Union soldiers?

A No. Black soldiers were not paid equally for their service. A white Union soldier received on average $13 a month plus a $3.50 clothing allowance; a black soldier received $10 a month less a $3 clothing deduction. In addition, black soldiers received no financial bounty on enlistment as white volunteers did.

Q After the Battle of Gettysburg which Confederate commander criticized his superior officer?

A Jubal Early criticized Richard S. Ewell for failing to attack the Union position on Cemetery Hill.

DID YOU KNOW

THROUGHOUT MOST OF THE WAR CONDITIONS IN THE UNION ARMY WERE BAD. SOME OF THE ADVERSITIES—THE FEAR OF DYING, THE LOW MORALE THAT FOLLOWED DEFEAT, THE BOREDOM OF MILITARY ROUTINE—WERE FORESEEABLE CONSEQUENCES OF WAR, BUT OTHERS WERE PARTICULAR TO THE CIVIL WAR. THIRST, STARVATION, EXTREME HEAT, AND DISEASE WERE RIFE. THE MEN WERE OFTEN FURTHER DEMORALIZED BY LACK OF CONFIDENCE IN THEIR OFFICERS AND BY THE HABITUAL DELAYS IN PAYMENT. FORCED MARCHES WERE OFTEN SO LONG AND HARD THAT ONLY THE FITTEST COULD KEEP UP. MANY SOLDIERS WHO FELT OPPRESSED BY ONE OR MORE OF THESE HARDSHIPS MADE ACTIVE DECISIONS TO DESERT. OTHERS SIMPLY GOT LOST AS AN ARMY MOVED ACROSS COUNTRY, AND THEY WERE NEITHER WELL TRAINED NOR MOTIVATED ENOUGH TO FIND THEIR WAY BACK. A SMALL BUT SIGNIFICANT MINORITY SIMPLY LACKED THE SELF-DISCIPLINE NEEDED FOR LIFE IN THE ARMED FORCES.

Q What happened to Union General George Meade after the Battle of Gettysburg?

A Meade remained in command of the Army of the Potomac for the rest of the war. But when General Ulysses S. Grant was made general-in-chief of all Union forces in March 1864, Meade found himself effectively demoted and subject to Grant's orders. In August 1864, Meade was promoted to major general in the regular army and after the war remained in charge of various military departments until his death from pneumonia in 1872.

Q Despite being forced to surrender Port Hudson in July 1863, what had Confederate General Franklin Gardner, the garrison commander, succeeded in doing?

A Tying down more than 30,000 Union troops who could have been used to assist in the siege of Vicksburg.

Q When did the New York antidraft riots erupt?

A July 13, 1863. On July 11, days after word reached the city of the Union victory at Gettysburg, New York held its first draft lottery (the drawing of draftees' names) without incident. However, public meetings on July 12 raised antidraft feeling, and the following day a crowd of angry workers burned the city draft offices.

Q What sparked the riots?

A Poverty, ethnic discrimination (by the second day of the riots the crowd was made up largely of Irish immigrants), and an unfair draft.

> **" HIS HORSE FURNITURE AND EQUIPMENT WERE POLISHED LEATHER AND BRIGHT METAL "**
> JOHN W. THOMASON ON "JEB" STUART

Q List the targets of the antidraft riots.

A The homes of leading Republicans, the offices of antislavery newspapers, and the élite Brooks Brothers department store. However, the rioters soon targeted New York's African-Americans, who were blamed as a cause of the war. Rioters lynched at least 11 people, burned the city's Colored Orphan Asylum, and forced hundreds of blacks to flee New York.

Q Did antidraft riots take place only in New York?

A No, they erupted across the North, from small towns in Vermont and New Hampshire to Port Washington, Wisconsin.

Q At the Battle of Gettysburg, which Union commander led a bayonet charge when his men ran out of ammunition?

A Joshua Lawrence Chamberlain. At Gettysburg Chamberlain led his regiment in defense of Little Round Top, a small wooded hill on the far left of the Union line. For holding this key position in the face of repeated enemy attacks, and for leading a bayonet charge when his men ran out of ammunition, Chamberlain was awarded the Congressional Medal of Honor in 1893.

DID YOU KNOW

AFTER THE BATTLE OF GETTYSBURG, REFUSING TO BELIEVE THAT A YANKEE ARMY COULD HAVE BESTED THE ARMY OF NORTHERN VIRGINIA, CONFEDERATES BEGAN LOOKING FOR SCAPEGOATS AMONG THEIR OWN. "JEB" STUART, WHOSE CAVALRY WAS MISSING FOR ALL THE IMPORTANT EARLY HOURS IN THE GETTYSBURG BATTLE, CAME IN FOR THE FIRST AND HARSH-EST CRITICISM. LEE HIMSELF WAS QUOTED AS SAYING TO MAJOR GENERAL RICHARD ANDERSON DURING THE EARLY MOMENTS OF THE BATTLE, "I CANNOT THINK WHAT HAS BECOME OF STUART; I OUGHT TO HAVE HEARD FROM HIM LONG BEFORE NOW. HE MAY HAVE MET WITH DISASTER, BUT I HOPE NOT. IN THE ABSENCE OF REPORTS FROM HIM, I AM IN IGNORANCE AS TO WHAT WE HAVE IN FRONT OF US HERE. IT MAY BE THE WHOLE FEDERAL ARMY, OR IT MAY BE ONLY A DETACHMENT." AS E. PORTER ALEXANDER LATER WROTE, "HOOKER'S CHANCELLORSVILLE CAMPAIGN HAD BEEN LOST BY THE ABSENCE OF HIS CAVALRY, AND LEE'S GETTYSBURG CAMPAIGN WAS SIMILARLY COMPROMISED." ALEXANDER WENT ON: "HAD HE WASTED NO TIME PAROLLING PRISONERS AND SAVING WAGONS, HIS RAID MIGHT HAVE BEEN SUCCESSFUL, AS RAIDS GO, FOR HIS WHOLE CASUALTIES WERE BUT 89 KILLED, WOUNDED, AND MISSING. BUT THE VENTURE WAS A STRATEGIC MISTAKE, FOR IT RESULTED IN THE BATTLE BEING ONE OF CHANCE COLLISION, WITH THE CONFEDERATES TAKING THE OFFENSIVE, WHEREAS THE PLAN OF THE CAMPAIGN HAD BEEN TO FIGHT A DEFENSIVE BATTLE."

Q 143 Quakers enlisted as Union soldiers. True or false?

A True, but the majority of their brethren and all pacifists served in hospitals, cared for sick soldiers in their homes, or worked among the Contrabands.

Q Who were Freedmen?

A Slaves who became free men after Congress passed the Confiscation Act of 1862. Under this act, Confederates who did not surrender within 60 days of the act's passage were to be punished by having their slaves freed. It also dealt with a problem that had plagued field commanders occupying Southern territory. As troops advanced, slaves sought refuge in Union camps, and Federal commanders were confused over their obligations to the refugees. Some freed the slaves, other sent them back to their master for lack of means to care for them. The Confiscation Act declared all slaves taking refuge behind Union lines captives of war who were to be set free.

DID YOU KNOW

As well as being war leader, President Lincoln also had responsibilities as the leader of his political party. The Republican Party was barely five years old when he took office. It was composed of former Whigs and Democrats, and its members had a wide range of opinions on key issues such as slavery. Lincoln worked hard to keep the Republican coalition together throughout the war. He knew that he needed the support of Congress and the public to win the war and to be reelected for a second term in 1864. To achieve this broad support, he included former Whigs and former Democrats in his cabinet and appointed men of all political backgrounds to military commands.

WAR IS CRUELTY, AND YOU CANNOT
REFINE IT
WILLIAM TECUMSEH SHERMAN

Q **What were Dunkards, Amanists, and Schwenkfelders?**

A Pacifist religious groups.

Q **Which European country displayed support for the North in the Civil War?**

A Russia. In the autumn of 1863 two Russian fleets entered American waters, one in the Atlantic and one in the Pacific. They put into New York and San Francisco harbors and spent the winter there. Many Northerners believed that the Tsar was sending England and France a message: that if they made war in support of the South, he would help the North.

Q **What was the largest and almost only battle fought on Ohio soil?**

A The Battle of Buffington Island/St. Georges Creek, July 19, 1863. A force of 2,460 cavalry under Confederate Brigadier General John H. Morgan had been raiding Ohio, pursued by an increasing number of Union troops and Ohio militia. Morgan attempted to recross the Ohio River into West Virginia, but was blocked and badly defeated by a combined force of 3,000 Union troops and gunboats. Morgan's men suffered 820 casualties, including 700 prisoners. Union losses were 25.

Q What was the Order of the Heroes of America?

A A Southern peace society active in North Carolina, southwestern Virginia, and eastern Tennessee. The group protected deserters, aided spies, and escaped prisoners, and supplied Federal authorities with information about Confederate troop movements and strengths to bring about a Confederate defeat.

Q Name two of its most famous members.

A General Ulysses S. Grant and President Abraham Lincoln.

> ## THE ENEMY IS ADVANCING IN STRONG FORCE; I WILL FIGHT HIM INCH BY INCH
> UNION GENERAL JOHN REYNOLDS,
> GETTYSBURG, JULY 1863

Q On a Southern plantation, what was the "big house"?

A The main mansion that housed the planter family, usually a two-or three-storey mansion. It was a visible symbol of the planter's wealth. Common features included a wide entrance hall leading into a dining room, a parlor, a library, and one or more sitting rooms. In these rooms a planter could display his wealth with European furnishings and imported artwork. On the upper floors, the bedrooms for family members and guests had luxurious decor. Nurseries for children were located on the top floors and could be reached by the servants' stairs at the back of the house.

DID YOU KNOW

WHEN THE CIVIL WAR BROKE OUT, BRAXTON BRAGG WAS MADE A BRIGADIER GENERAL IN THE CONFEDERATE ARMY. AT THE BATTLE OF SHILOH ON APRIL 6–7, 1862, HE SERVED AS A CORPS COMMANDER IN THE ARMY OF TENNESSEE (THEN CALLED THE ARMY OF THE MISSISSIPPI). TWO MONTHS LATER PRESIDENT DAVIS APPOINTED HIM THE ARMY OF TENNESSEE'S TOP COMMANDER IN PLACE OF PIERRE G.T. BEAUREGARD. BRAGG HELD THE POST UNTIL DECEMBER 1863. AT FIRST BRAGG DID WELL. HE RESTORED DISCIPLINE, THEN ORGANIZED A REMARKABLE CAMPAIGN THAT CARRIED THE ARMY FROM NORTHERN MISSISSIPPI INTO KENTUCKY. IT BRIEFLY APPEARED AS IF BRAGG MIGHT REACH THE OHIO RIVER, BUT AN INCONCLUSIVE BATTLE AT PERRYVILLE ON OCTOBER 8, 1862, CAUSED HIM TO WITHDRAW INTO CENTRAL TENNESSEE. THE RETREAT GAVE HIM THE REPUTATION OF BEING A GENERAL WHO COULD SNATCH DEFEAT FROM THE JAWS OF VICTORY.

Q What was the fate of the defeated Confederates after the Battle of Buffington Island/St. Georges Creek, Ohio, on July 19, 1863?

A After the battle, Confederate Brigadier General John H. Morgan and his men fled as far north as West Point, near Steubenville, Ohio, where they were captured. In retaliation for the poor treatment of Union prisoners of war in the South, he and his officers were put in the Ohio Penitentiary as common criminals.

Q What did the slogan that appeared in the Confederate press— "Plant Corn and Be Free, or Plant Cotton and Be Whipped"— mean?

A It was an appeal to plantation owners. The government wanted planters to switch voluntarily from the cash crop system, such as cotton, to a more diversified subsistence strategy that would include the planting of crops, such as corn, that could feed both the army and the civilian population.

Q Which battle failed to stop Lee's retreating Army of Northern Virginia in July 1863?

A The Battle of Manassas Gap/Wapping Heights, Virginia, a Union attack through the Manassas Gap in the Shenandoah Valley.

Q Which Indian tribe was defeated at the Battle of Big Mound, North Dakota, in July 1863?

A Union Brigadier General Henry Hastings Sibley defeated a large Sioux Indian force at Big Mound during operations against the Indians in North and South Dakota.

Q What was the Lawrence Massacre in August 1863?

A Guerrillas under William Quantrill attacked Lawrence, Kansas, well known as a hotbed of antislavery sentiment. On Quantrill's orders they burnt the town and murdered every adult male they encountered, as well as a small garrison of Union soldiers. In all, more than 150 people were killed and 200 dwellings destroyed.

DID YOU KNOW

THE UNION SENT 20,000 TROOPS TO QUELL THE ANTIDRAFT RIOTS IN NEW YORK. MORE VIOLENCE FOLLOWED AS SOLDIERS KILLED AT LEAST 82 RIOTERS. TWO POLICEMEN AND EIGHT SOLDIERS WERE ALSO KILLED. ORDER WAS RESTORED BY JULY 16, AND CONSCRIPTION IN THE CITY RESUMED ON AUGUST 19; BUT BITTERNESS BETWEEN THE COMMUNITIES IN NEW YORK CITY REMAINED.

"

WE RAN LIKE A HERD OF
WILD CATTLE
CONFEDERATE COLONEL WILLIAM C. OATES,
LITTLE ROUND TOP, GETTYSBURG, JULY 2, 1863

"

Q Name at least two men who fought with William Quantrill in the Civil War.

A His outfit included Frank and Jesse James and "Bloody Bill" Anderson.

Q What was General Order No. 11, issued by Union Brigadier General Thomas Ewing on August 25, 1863?

A Ewing was commander of the District of the Border. Order No. 11 required all the inhabitants of the Western Missouri counties of Jackson, Cass, and Bates not living within one mile of specified military posts to vacate their homes by September 9. Those who by that date established their loyalty to the Federal government with the commanding officer of the military station nearest their place of residence would be permitted to remove to any military station in the District of the Border or to any part of Kansas, except the counties on the eastern border of that state. Persons failing to establish their loyalty were to move out of the district completely or be subjected to military punishment.

Q Why did Ewing issue Order No. 11?

A In retaliation for the destruction of Lawrence, Kansas, and the massacre of its male citizens by William Quantrill's guerrillas.

Q Who were the Davis Guards?

A A Texan Confederate unit named for Jefferson Davis.

Q What were the Davis Guards also called?

A The Fighting Irishmen, because they were all Irish.

Q What was this unit's most famous action?

A The Battle of Sabine Pass/Fort Griffin, Texas, September 8, 1863. A Union flotilla of four gunboats and 18 troop transports, carrying 6,000 troops, steamed into Sabine Pass and up the Sabine River with the intention of reducing Fort Griffin and landing troops to begin occupying Texas. However, the Davis Guards (49 men and six cannon in Fort Griffin) sunk two of the gunboats, killed or wounded more than 100 Union troops, and took 300 prisoners, successfully turning back the invasion. The Confederates suffered no losses.

> ## WHY DO MEN FIGHT WHO WERE
> # BORN TO BE BROTHERS?
> ### CONFEDERATE GENERAL JAMES LONGSTREET

Q Where was the Battle of Devil's Backbone/Backbone Mountain in September 1863?

A Arkansas. Confederate forces temporarily checked a Union pursuit of Rebels from Fort Smith, but were eventually forced to retreat in disorder to Waldron.

Q Name the two commanders at the Battle of Chickamauga in September 1863.

A General William Rosecrans, commander of the Union Army of the Cumberland, and Confederate General Braxton Bragg, commander of the Army of Tennessee.

DID YOU KNOW

The Battle of Gettysburg was been fought on July 1–3, 1863. Although the battle turned back a Confederate invasion of the North, the Union victory came at a heavy cost. After the battle the Pennsylvania governor appointed a local businessman, David Wills, to purchase the land and arrange for the burial of the bodies. Wills formed a commission to collect funds from all the Union states to pay the expenses. He planned to have the cemetery officially dedicated in late October. Funeral oration was a highly developed type of public speech, and David Wills believed that the Gettysburg dedication deserved the country's greatest orator. Accordingly, he invited Edward Everett of Massachusetts to present the keynote address. Everett was a noted scholar and former secretary of state, and widely believed to be the nation's finest orator. Everett accepted the invitation, and the date of the ceremony was set for November 19.

Q **What was the decisive moment at the Battle of Chickamauga?**

A At 11:00 hours on September 20, the Union commander, Rosecrans, pulled Thomas Wood's division out of the right of his line to plug what he thought was a gap farther north. Fortunately for the Confederates, three of their divisions under Longstreet launched an attack into the gap left by Wood at precisely the same time. The Union's defensive position was shattered. As Longstreet's men came close to cutting his line of communication with Chattanooga, Rosecrans ordered a retreat.

Q **Who was the "Rock of Chickamauga"?**

A George H. Thomas, who made a stand on Snodgrass Hill, a wooded ridge on the northern end of the Union line. Thomas and his men held Bragg at bay as Rosecrans and most of the Union army withdrew into Chattanooga. For his efforts, Thomas won the Medal of Honor.

Q **Why was the Battle of Chickamauga a hollow victory for the Confederates?**

A Bragg was unable to follow it up with the final defeat of the Army of the Cumberland. At a cost of over 18,000 casualties, he could only push Rosecrans back to Chattanooga, and was unable to destroy him or force the surrender of his army by a siege.

Q **What was Robert E. Lee's plan at the Battle of Bristoe Station, Virginia, in October 1863?**

A To turn Meade's right flank and put himself between the Union army and its supply base at Centreville. He therefore led his army across the Rapidan River and moved toward Culpeper. Meade, however, discerned his opponent's strategy and ordered a retreat.

> " MY GOD! MY GOD! WHAT
> # WILL THE COUNTRY SAY?
> ABRAHAM LINCOLN, ON HEARING OF THE
> UNION DEFEAT AT CHANCELLORSVILLE, MAY 1863 "

Q **What happened at the Battle of Baxter Springs, Kansas, on October 6, 1863?**

A William Quantrill's guerrillas massacred 103 Union troops around the Union post of Baxter Springs.

Q **What were the "Buckland Races"?**

A The Battle of Buckland Mills/Buckland Races/Chestnut Hill on October 19, 1863. Confederate troops ambushed Union cavalry that were pursuing Lee's retreating army, following its defeat at Bristoe Station and an aborted advance on Centreville. The Union forces were chased for 5 miles (8 km), hence the name "Buckland Races."

DID YOU KNOW

THE PHOTOGRAPHER MATHEW BRADY'S CIVIL WAR ACTIVITIES RUINED HIM FINANCIALLY. AFTER THE WAR THERE SEEMED NOTHING PEOPLE WANTED LESS THAN REMINDERS OF THOSE DREADFUL DAYS. BRADY HAD SUNK INTO THE PROJECT HIS ENTIRE FORTUNE OF $100,000, A HUGE SUM AT THE TIME. WHEN A MARKET FOR HIS WORK FAILED TO MATERIALIZE, HE WAS FORCED INTO BANKRUPTCY. FINALLY, IN 1875 CONGRESS BOUGHT THE ENTIRE ARCHIVE FOR $25,000, BUT THAT SUM WAS QUICKLY EATEN UP BY BRADY'S CREDITORS. BRADY DIED NEARLY BLIND AND PENNILESS IN 1896, BUT HIS WORK, NOW A NATIONAL TREASURE, REMAINS THE GREATEST RECORD OF THE WAR.

Q Who was was in charge of all aspects of Union military railroads?

A Brigadier General Herman Haupt. Haupt accepted no payment for his services to the Union, and resigned his post in the autumn of 1863 to pursue his other railroad projects and concerns.

183

Q Who organized the Union's first sanitary fair?

A Mary Livermore and Jane Hoge of the U.S. Sanitary Commission. They encouraged people to donate items of interest that they could sell to raise funds.

Q Where was the fair held?

A Chicago in October 1863 (many Northern cities held sanitary fairs to raise funds to buy medical supplies for wounded soldiers and other types of relief). The Chicago fair ran for two weeks and drew 5,000 visitors. The entrance price was 75 cents, and the items on sale included artwork, musical instruments, toys, and clothes. President Lincoln donated the original draft of the Emancipation Proclamation, which sold at auction for $3,000. The Chicago fair raised a total of $100,000.

" WE'LL FIGHT THEM, SIR, 'TIL HELL FREEZES OVER, AND THEN, SIR, WE WILL FIGHT THEM ON THE ICE

CONFEDERATE SOLDIER
AT GETTYSBURG, JULY 1863 "

Q When did President Lincoln deliver his "Gettysburg Address"?

A November 19, 1863, which was a crisp, clear, autumn day, ideal conditions for the outdoor event. The ceremonies began at around noon. After the opening musical pieces and the prayers, Edward Everett, the nation's finest orator, stood and spoke from memory for two hours. Following Everett's well-received speech, a hymn was sung, and the president rose to make his remarks.

Q How long did it take Lincoln to deliver his speech?

A Unfolding a paper from his coat pocket, Lincoln delivered the 272-word address in his high, clear Kentucky-accented voice. Speaking slowly and loudly enough to be heard by the crowd of more than 10,000, he took about three minutes to make the speech.

Q What was the fate of the Confederate blockade runner *Terista*?

A Carrying 298 bales of cotton, she was captured by the USS *Granite* near the mouth of the Rio Grande, Texas, on November 14, 1863.

Q Who said of Ulysses S. Grant: "I can't spare this man—he fights"?

A President Lincoln.

Q Before his "Gettysburg Address" President Lincoln jotted his comments hurriedly on the back of an envelope shortly before the dedication. True or false?

A False. Lincoln prepared his remarks in advance, in Washington, and the speech went through several revisions. The president was a dedicated wordsmith who wrote carefully, weighing each word, and devoting much thought to his speeches.

Q Why was Chattanooga in southeastern Tennessee strategically important?

A It was located at the rail junction linking Virginia with Tennessee, Georgia, and pointed west. Without this vital rail terminus Confederate troops moving between different theaters of war would have to use a roundabout series of railroads in the Deep South. For the Union, Chattanooga was an objective because it could serve as a base for an attempt to capture Atlanta.

185

DID YOU KNOW

LINCOLN BEGAN HIS GETTYSBURG ADDRESS WITH A REFERENCE TO THE BIRTH OF THE UNITED STATES. THE DECLARATION OF INDEPENDENCE, HE EXPLAINED, HAD "DEDICATED" THE NATION "TO THE PROPOSITION THAT ALL MEN ARE CREATED EQUAL." HE THEN TURNED TO THE CURRENT WAR, WHICH HE SAID WAS PUTTING THAT PROPOSITION TO ITS GREATEST TEST. AFTER PRAISING THE "BRAVE MEN, LIVING AND DEAD," WHO HAD FOUGHT AT GETTYSBURG, LINCOLN CALLED ATTENTION TO THE FACT THAT THE LIVING MUST "BE DEDICATED HERE TO THE UNFINISHED WORK" THAT THE SOLDIERS HAD BEGUN. HE CLOSED BY CALLING ON AMERICANS TO "HIGHLY RESOLVE THAT THESE DEAD SHALL NOT HAVE DIED IN VAIN—THAT THIS NATION, UNDER GOD, SHALL HAVE A NEW BIRTH OF FREEDOM AND THAT GOVERNMENT OF THE PEOPLE, BY THE PEOPLE, FOR THE PEOPLE, SHALL NOT PERISH FROM THE EARTH."

Q What was the Battle above the Clouds?

A In October 1863 Ulysses S. Grant arrived to reinforce the Union army at Chattanooga. Elements of Grant's army scaled Lookout Mountain, and on November 24 Grant's army fought what became known as the Battle above the Clouds, which forced the Confederates out of a key position above Chattanooga. Following defeat at Lookout Mountain, the Confederates entrenched on Missionary Ridge, a strong position stretching south from the Tennessee River.

> " YES, WE'LL RALLY ROUND THE FLAG,
> WE'LL RALLY ONCE AGAIN,
> ## SHOUTING THE BATTLE-CRY
> ## OF FREEDOM
> GEORGE FREDERICK ROOT,
> *BATTLE-CRY OF FREEDOM* "

Q What happened at Chattanooga on November 25, 1863?

A In one of the war's most stunning victories, Union troops under George H. Thomas stormed Missionary Ridge and defeated the Confederates, who retreated south along the rail line to Atlanta in order to protect that key supply artery.

Q Why did the fall of Chattanooga change the course of the war?

A Union forces now had the supply base and jumping-off point they need to initiate a campaign against Atlanta. For the Confederacy the loss of Chattanooga completed the South's loss of the rail networks, food supplies, and manpower of central Tennessee.

1864

The South lost a number of strategic places in 1864, including Atlanta and Savannah, and on the battlefield her armies were ground down in a war of attrition. Sherman's March to the Sea devastated Georgia, and lowered Southern morale, and at Petersburg Grant pinned Lee's Army of Northern Virginia.

Q Why was the best enforcer of the naval blockade of the South the Confederacy itself?

A Until 1863 it was government policy not to sell cotton abroad but rather to observe an embargo intended to starve European textile mills of their vital raw material. Confederates hoped that the embargo would compel support for the Confederacy from key European powers, especially Britain. The embargo failed, and the Confederacy had missed the chance to export cotton at a time when most of its ports were open and the Union blockade was weakest.

> " I HAVE NOT SEEN IN THIS WAR A
> CAVALRY COMMAND OF 1,000 THAT
> ## WAS NOT AFRAID OF THE
> ## SIGHT OF A DOZEN
> ## INFANTRY BAYONETS
> WILLIAM SHERMAN, JANUARY 1864 "

Q To Jefferson Davis he was the "Stonewall of the West," to Robert E. Lee he was "a meteor shining from a clouded sky," and to Braxton Bragg he was an officer "ever alive to a success." Which Confederate general were they speaking of?

A Patrick R. Cleburne (1828–1864), who served with the Army of Tennessee and who was killed leading his men at the Battle of Franklin in November 1864.

Q How did Union Major General John Sedgwick meet his end?

A He was killed at Spotsylvania on May 9, 1864, by a Confederate sharpshooter.

DID YOU KNOW

FROM 1864 THE SINGLE-SHOT RIFLE MUSKET WAS BEING STEADILY REPLACED.
THE UNION ARMY BEGAN TO BE ISSUED WITH NEW RIFLES SUCH AS THE
SPENCER, WHICH WAS A BREECHLOADER THAT COULD FIRE SIX TO EIGHT
ROUNDS BEFORE IT NEEDED TO BE RELOADED. THE SPENCER CARTRIDGE WAS
MADE UP OF A COPPER CASE CONTAINING A LEAD BULLET AND POWDER CHARGE
WITH ITS OWN PRIMER. THIS MADE IT MORE RELIABLE THAN OTHER IGNITION
SYSTEMS, SUCH AS THOSE REQUIRING PRIMER CAPS OR TAPES. THE
CONFEDERATES COULD NOT MATCH THIS KIND OF FIREPOWER. EVEN IF THEY
MANAGED TO SALVAGE ABANDONED BREECHLOADING RIFLES FROM THE BATTLE-
FIELD, THEY DID NOT HAVE THE INDUSTRIAL RESOURCES IN THE SOUTH TO
MANUFACTURE THE NEW KIND OF METAL CARTRIDGES THEY FIRED. AS ONE
UNION SOLDIER WROTE OF HIS NEW REPEATING RIFLE: "I THINK THE JOHNNY
[REBS] ARE GETTING RATTLED. ... THEY SAY WE ARE NOT FAIR, THAT WE HAVE
GUNS THAT WE LOAD UP ON SUNDAY AND SHOOT ALL THE REST OF THE WEEK."

Q **Which flag became known as the representative Confederate battleflag?**

A The Fourth Bunting issue battleflag was introduced into the Army of Northern Virginia in the spring of 1864 and was in widespread use until the end of the war. It was similar in size to the Third issue, and featured the distinctive white border but differed in having larger stars. This flag became known as the representative Confederate battleflag due to its role in the surrenders of 1865 and the fact that it was adopted as the symbol of the United Confederate Veterans in 1906.

Q **What was Grant's overall strategy in 1864?**

A His main objective was to target the two biggest Confederate armies in the field: Lee's in northern Virginia and Joseph E. Johnston's at Atlanta, Georgia, while putting pressure on the Shenandoah Valley and Mobile. As he wrote to Sherman on April 4: "It is my design ... to work all parts of the army together, and somewhat toward a common center."

Q Which was the first Union regiment to be composed entirely of fugitive slaves?

A The 1st South Carolina Volunteers. Despite being lauded in the Northern press, its first recruits were acquired by sending white troops on raiding parties into the refugee camps and hauling back any able-bodied black men they could find.

Q What was the uniform of this regiment?

A A bright blue jacket, brighter red pantaloons, and a red fez (making them ideal targets for sharpshooters).

" IF SLAVERY IS NOT WRONG, NOTHING
IS WRONG
ABRAHAM LINCOLN, APRIL 1864 "

Q What were "trains" and "the cares"?

A "Trains" were horsedrawn wagon trains, whereas "the cares" generally meant railroads.

Q At which battle was the brother of Nathan Bedford Forrest killed?

A Jeffrey Forrest was killed at the Battle of Okolona, Mississippi, on February 22, 1864. A Union force moving toward Memphis after the Meridian campaign came under attack around Okolona and was harassed all the way to the state line.

DID YOU KNOW

ALTHOUGH THE ADMINISTRATIONS OF NORTH AND SOUTH PAID LITTLE ATTENTION TO PROPAGANDA WITHIN THEIR OWN BORDERS, THE IMPORTANCE OF THE BATTLE FOR OPINION IN EUROPE (ESPECIALLY BRITAIN AND FRANCE) WAS CLEAR TO ALL. FROM THE BEGINNING OF THE CONFLICT EUROPEAN INTERVENTION WAS SEEN AS A KEY FACTOR THAT COULD WIN OR LOSE THE WAR. BOTH THE CONFEDERACY AND THE UNION ACCOMPANIED THEIR DIPLOMATIC OVERTURES TO EUROPE WITH PROPAGANDA. THE LINCOLN ADMINISTRATION DISPATCHED A STEADY STREAM OF VISITORS TO EUROPE DURING THE COURSE OF THE WAR, MANY ESPECIALLY SELECTED TO APPEAL TO EUROPEAN PRESSURE GROUPS OR INTERESTS. UNION REPRESENTATIVES INCLUDED JOHN HUGHES, THE CATHOLIC ARCHBISHOP OF NEW YORK, WHOSE MISSION WAS TO GAIN THE SUPPORT OF THE PAPACY AND THE CATHOLIC RULERS OF EUROPE; BISHOP MCILVAINE OF THE PROTESTANT EPISCOPAL CHURCH, WHO WAS TO LOBBY THE ENGLISH CLERGY; AND THE NEW YORK POLITICAL OPERATOR THURLOW WEED, WHO WAS TO TRY TO PROMOTE THE UNION CAUSE AMONG EUROPEAN JOURNALISTS. DESPITE LINCOLN'S DOMESTIC RELUCTANCE TO MAKE THE WAR AN ANTISLAVERY CRUSADE, THE ISSUE WAS A TRUMP CARD IN EUROPEAN COUNTRIES, WHICH HAD ABOLISHED SLAVERY WITHIN THEIR OWN COLONIES DECADES PREVIOUSLY. UNION REPRESENTATIVES HELPED ORGANIZE PUBLIC MEETINGS IN BRITAIN, WHICH PASSED RESOLUTIONS ENDORSING EMANCIPATION.

Q What did "laudable pus" signal to Civil War military surgeons?

A This was believed to be the lining of a wound, being expelled so that clean tissue could replace it and the wound could heal.

Q Which city was called the "Gateway to the South"?

A Chattanooga.

Q Which state produced the most iron used by the Confederacy?

A Alabama, with an average annual output of 40,000 tons (40,640 tonnes) during four years of war.

Q What was the Black Horse Troop?

A A cavalry unit that served in the Army of Northern Virginia. It was actually organized in 1859, two years before the war broke out.

Q Who was Turner Ashby?

A A Confederate partisan leader.

DID YOU KNOW

THE GREATEST THREAT TO A SOLDIER'S LIFE WAS DISEASE. HISTORIANS ESTIMATE THAT DISEASES KILLED AT LEAST TWICE AS MANY CIVIL WAR SOLDIERS AS COMBAT WOUNDS. THAT WOULD MEAN THAT OF THE 620,000 SOLDIERS WHO DIED IN THE CIVIL WAR, AROUND 207,000 DIED FROM WOUNDS AND 413,000 FROM DISEASE. DISEASE DID MORE THAN JUST REDUCE THE NUMBER OF MEN AVAILABLE TO FIGHT; IT HAD A DIRECT EFFECT ON MANY MILITARY CAMPAIGNS. THE UNION'S FIRST ATTEMPT TO TAKE THE CITY OF VICKSBURG IN MISSISSIPPI IN 1862 FAILED LARGELY BECAUSE MORE THAN HALF THE TROOPS WERE SICK. DISEASE ALSO FIGURED IN LINCOLN'S DECISION TO ABANDON THE PENINSULAR CAMPAIGN IN VIRGINIA THAT SAME YEAR.

I PROPOSE TO FIGHT IT OUT ON
THIS LINE IF IT TAKES
ALL SUMMER
ULYSSES S. GRANT, MAY 1864

Q Which town was the "back door to the Confederacy"?

A Brownsville, Texas, from where goods were traded across the border with Mexico.

Q Where was the Battle of Middle Boggy Depot fought?

A Oklahoma, on February 13, 1864.

Q Which battle defeated a Union attempt to burn Richmond and kill President Davis?

A The Battle of Walkerton/Mantapike Hill, Virginia, on March 2, 1864. This abortive Union raid against Richmond's defenses ended in the destruction or capture of many of the attackers. Captured papers referred to the burning of Richmond and killing of President Davis as primary objectives.

Q What position did Lieutenant General Ulysses S. Grant assume on March 2, 1864?

A Commander of all the armies of the United States.

Q Which Union armies did William Sherman command at the beginning of 1864?

A The armies of the Tennessee, the Cumberland, and the Ohio.

Q What was Nathaniel Banks instructed to carry out by Grant at the beginning of April 1864?

A To take his Union forces and move from New Orleans, Louisiana, against the port of Mobile in Alabama.

Q Banks had his own ideas about what strategy he should follow. What were they?

A He decided to embark on a campaign northwest up the Red River. He envisioned a combined army and navy force, with troops and gunboats under David D. Porter, moving up the Red River to cooperate with another Union force under General Frederick Steele in capturing Shreveport, Louisiana, a major supply depot and gateway to Texas. Banks hoped to capture large supplies of cotton as well.

> " I WORKED NIGHT AND DAY FOR 12 YEARS
> ## TO PREVENT THE WAR,
> ## BUT I COULD NOT
> JEFFERSON DAVIS, JULY 1864 "

Q Why was Richmond, Virginia, so important to the Confederacy?

A As well as being the political center of the Confederacy, the city was a medical and manufacturing center, and the main supply depot for troops operating on the South's northeastern frontier. It was thus a primary target for the Union army.

Q Which Confederate guerrilla was declared an outlaw by the Union but held a captaincy in the Confederacy?

A William Quantrill.

DID YOU KNOW

FROM 1863 TO 1865 JOHN SINGLETON MOSBY IS ESTIMATED TO HAVE CAPTURED MORE THAN 1,000 UNION PRISONERS, MORE THAN 1,000 HORSES, LARGE AMOUNTS OF WEAPONS AND AMMUNITION, AND HUNDREDS OF THOUSANDS OF DOLLARS IN U.S. CURRENCY. MOSBY CAUSED LITTLE OR NO DIVERSION OF TROOPS FROM THE FIGHTING FRONTS. ALTHOUGH THE "GRAY GHOST" CONTROLLED THE ROADS AND FIELDS OF "MOSBY'S CONFEDERACY," HIS ACTIONS DID NOT HAVE ANY EFFECT ON THE EVENTUAL OUTCOME OF THE WAR. UNWILLING TO SURRENDER WITH ROBERT E. LEE, MOSBY DISBANDED HIS PARTISAN RANGERS ON APRIL 21, 1865, 11 DAYS AFTER LEE'S SURRENDER AT APPOMATTOX.

Q How was the Union naval flotilla under David D. Porter saved during the Red River Campaign in April 1864?

A Porter's naval flotilla was stranded by falling river levels at Alexandria and was almost lost to Confederates firing on the fleet from the banks of the river. Only the heroic construction of river dams near Alexandria by 3,000 soldiers, sailors, and marines rescued the marooned boats and allowed them to escape.

Q Who attacked the Union garrison at Fort Pillow, on the Mississippi River, in April 1864?

A Major General Nathan Bedford Forrest.

Q Why was the outcome of the battle at Fort Pillow so controversial?

A Forrest demanded unconditional surrender. The garrison refused and the Confederates overran the fort and drove the Federals down the river's bluff. Only 60 out of 262 of the Union black troops survived the fight. The Confederates were accused of massacring the black troops.

Q What was the most widely read daily newspaper in New York?

A The *New York Herald*, which spent freely on coverage of the conflict, and sent 63 reporters to the various battlefields.

Q Union Major General Fred Steele suffered two major defeats in Arkansas in April 1864. What were they?

A The Battle of Poison Spring (April 18), when a Union raid out of Camden to acquire corn was crushed by the Confederates on its return journey at Lee's Plantation, the Union force losing 198 supply wagons. The second was the Battle of Marks' Mills (April 25), when a Union supply train of 240 wagons was captured by Confederate forces. This defeat forced Steele to look to save his army rather than unite with the forces of Nathaniel Banks on the Red River.

" THEY COULDN'T HIT AN ELEPHANT
AT THIS DISTANCE
UNION GENERAL JOHN SEDGWICK,
MOMENTS BEFORE BEING SHOT DEAD
BY A CONFEDERATE SNIPER AT SPOTSYLVANIA "

Q Which group of soldiers used the rallying cry "Remember Fort Pillow"?

A Black Union troops, in response to the slaughter of black troops at Fort Pillow. It was a rallying cry among black troops in the last year of the war.

Q Where was Camp William Penn?

A Pennsylvania. Many of the Union's main military camps and supply depots were located in the state. Camp William Penn was in operation between July 4, 1863, and August 3, 1865.

DID YOU KNOW

At the Battle of Antietam in September 1862, the Confederate John B. Gordon suffered four wounds, the last a head wound that almost killed him. Shortly after Antietam he was promoted to brigadier general. Gordon served as a brigade commander at the Battle of Gettysburg in July 1863. He planned and carried out a brilliant attack at the Battle of the Wilderness in May 1864 and was promoted to major general on May 14. Gordon's abilities, combined with losses among Lee's officers, led to his promotion to division, and later army corps, command. At all levels he performed brilliantly. By April 1865 Gordon was in command of more than half of Lee's remaining troops. He surrendered along with Lee at Appomattox in April 1865.

Q What prevented the garrison of Fort Pillow from using its artillery during the battle.

A The Confederates seized the older outworks, with high knolls commanding the Union position, and Rebel sharpshooters on the knolls fired into the fort. The garrison could not depress its artillery enough to cover the approaches to the fort.

Q Why did General Robert E. Lee decide to fight in the Wilderness in May 1864?

A When Lee learnt of the Union presence (120,000 men of the Army of the Potomac), he decided to attack, knowing that fighting in the thick undergrowth of the Wilderness would neutralize General Grant's superior numbers.

Q Why was the Wilderness area of Virginia, near Chancellorsville, so called?

A It was a marshy area of dense woodland and scrub.

Q At which battle did General Ulysses S. Grant say, "I am heartily tired of hearing about what Lee is going to do. Some of you always seem to think he is suddenly going to … land in our rear and on both of our flanks at the same time. Go back to your command, and try to think what we are going to do ourselves, instead of what Lee is going to do."?

A The Battle of the Wilderness in May 1864, when a flustered officer approached him and said: "General, this is a crisis … I know Lee's methods well by past experience; he will throw his whole army between us and the Rapidan [River], and cut us off completely from our communications."

Q Name the protagonists at the Battle of Albemarle Sound, North Carolina, in May 1864.

A The ironclad CSS *Albemarle* attacked Union blockade ships on the Roanoke River. The action was inconclusive, with damage to both sides. The steam gunboat USS *Sassacus* rammed the *Albemarle*, which managed to disengage and fire two shells at close range, hitting the *Sassacus*' boiler, which exploded, seriously scalding several crew members.

DID YOU KNOW

In the Civil War the treatments for disease were often as bad as the diseases themselves. The most common treatment for many diseases was calomel, a medicine whose main ingredient was mercury. Calomel depleted the body's vital fluids—already a major problem in diarrhea—and in large doses it could cause mercury poisoning. Some doctors still believed in the ancient practice of bleeding sick patients, which served only to weaken them further. Not surprisingly, many soldiers tried to avoid seeing a doctor unless they were on the verge of death. One of the few effective drugs available in the war was quinine, which could prevent and treat malaria.

> # THE DEAD COVERED MORE THAN
> ## FIVE ACRES OF GROUND
> # ABOUT AS THICKLY AS
> # THEY COULD BE LAID
> #### CONFEDERATE SURVIVOR DESCRIBING UNION DEAD
> #### AT THE BATTLE OF COLD HARBOR

Q At the Battle of the Wilderness how was the Confederate General Longstreet wounded?

A On May 6 Longstreet's corps became muddled with Hill's, and Longstreet himself was shot and seriously wounded in the shoulder by one of his own side. He was out of action for several months.

Q What interrupted the fighting during the Battle of the Wilderness in May 1864?

A During the battle brush fires became such a problem that the fighting stopped at several points by mutual consent while soldiers of both sides cooperated in trying to save the wounded.

Q What were the tactical and strategic results of the Battle of the Wilderness in May 1864?

A The inconclusive battle cost Lee 8,700 casualties. Grant suffered 17,000 dead and wounded, but the heavy losses did not shake his resolve. For the first time, instead of ordering the Army of the Potomac to retreat, the usual move after initial Union defeats in Virginia, Grant ordered his troops to continue the advance south toward Spotsylvania. Lee would not shake off Grant until his surrender at Appomattox.

Q Which action commenced Union General Sherman's Atlanta Campaign?

A On May 4 Union General George Thomas began to move slowly east along the Western and Atlantic Railroad from Ringgold, Georgia.

Q Who was the "boy general"?

A George Armstrong Custer. On June 29, 1863, Custer received a general's star and command of the Union Michigan Brigade of cavalry. At 23, he was the youngest general in the Union Army. A private in the brigade declared that Custer had put "the very devil" into the regiments. The men had called him at first "the boy General of the Golden Lock."

Q What was the Burnside carbine?

A A cavalry .54-caliber carbine was designed and patented by Ambrose E. Burnside. It was manufactured in Rhode Island by the Bristol Firearms Company and, later, by its successor, the Burnside Rifle Company, from about 1857 to 1865.

> **IT'S ALL A DAMNED MESS! AND OUR**
> # TWO ARMIES AIN'T NOTHING BUT HOWLING MOBS!
> CONFEDERATE PRIVATE
> ON THE BATTLE OF THE WILDERNESS

Q Why was General Benjamin Butler nicknamed "Spoons"?

A In 1862 Butler had taken command in New Orleans following its surrender to Union forces. He and his men were deeply unpopular. Within a few months, charges of rampant corruption by Union officials under Butler's watch (including his brother) reached intolerable levels. No proof of wrongdoing touched the general personally, but rumors of his wrongdoings earned him the nickname "Spoons" (for allegedly stealing silverware from the mansions of the wealthy). President Lincoln eventually recalled Butler as commander of New Orleans and replaced him with General Nathaniel Banks.

DID YOU KNOW

In the Civil War the Western theater encompassed Kentucky and Tennessee, most of Mississippi and Alabama, and part of Louisiana —everything, essentially, between the Mississippi River and the Appalachian Mountains. The Confederate defensive line at the beginning of the war stretched from the Mississippi River to the Cumberland Gap in the Appalachian foothills. The strategic importance of the rivers and railroads in the West meant that many major battles were fought in the Western theater, and by 1864 it extended all the way to the Pacific Ocean.

Q At which battle was the Confederate Brigadier General Albert Jenkins killed?

A The Battle of Cloyd's Mountain, Virginia, on May 9, 1864. Three brigades of Union raiders in southwestern Virginia fought violent hand-to-hand actions on Cloyd's Mountain, resulting in a narrow Union victory and the death of Jenkins.

Q Who was Winslow Homer?

A A Civil War artist. Born in 1836, by 1857 he was a freelance illustrator for such magazines as *Ballou's Pictorial* and *Harper's Weekly*. The latter publication sent Homer to the front during the Civil War, where he did sketches of battle scenes and mundane camp life. Although these did not gain him much note at the time, they were to influence much of his later work. Back at his studio after the war, Homer set to work on several war-related paintings, among them "Sharpshooter on Picket Duty" and "Prisoners from the Front." After 1884 he lived the life of a recluse and died in 1910.

Q Which Union commander took charge of IX Corps of the Army of the Potomac in April 1864?

A Ambrose Burnside. Sent west to command the Department of the Ohio in March 1863, by August Burnside was in charge of Army of the Ohio. In April 1864 Burnside was transferred back to the Army of the Potomac, where he again took charge of IX Corps.

Q At which battle was "Jeb" Stuart killed?

A The Battle of Yellow Tavern, Virginia, on May 11, 1864. A Union cavalry raid against Richmond resulted in the defeat of Confederate cavalry at Yellow Tavern. During the battle "Jeb" Stuart was mortally wounded.

> " I AM SHORT A CHEEK-BONE AND AN EAR,
> ## BUT AM ABLE TO WHIP
> ## ALL HELL YET
> UNION GENERAL JOHN M. CORSE
> AT THE BATTLE OF ALLATOONA "

Q What was the CSS *Hunley*?

A A Confederate submarine. Comprising a cylindrical iron steam boiler as the main center section, she had tapered ends and was built for hand-power. She was designed for a crew of nine persons, eight to turn the hand-cranked propeller and one to steer and direct the boat. She had ballast tanks at each tapered end which could be flooded by valves or pumped dry by hand pumps. In addition, iron weights were bolted as extra ballast to the underside of her hull, which could be dropped off by unscrewing the heads of the bolts from inside the submarine if she needed additional buoyancy to rise in an emergency.

Q What was the subject of a petition signed by Patrick Cleburne and 12 other senior officers and presented to Jefferson Davis in January 1864?

A That slaves in the South should be offered military service in exchange for their freedom. Cleburne believed that by doing so the South would win foreign support and its manpower issues would be resolved, as well as the slavery dilemma. His superiors did not see his vision, and his idea was suppressed. Cleburne died while leading a charge on the Union breastworks on November 29, 1864, in Franklin, Tennessee.

Q What was the "Yankee cheesebox on a raft"?

A A nickname used by Confederate troops for the Federal ironclad USS *Monitor*. The innovative design of a low-profile hull and single turret reminded one southern wag of a "cheesebox on a raft." The name stuck, and was used by troops on both sides to refer to the vessel.

203

DID YOU KNOW

FOLLOWING THE BATTLE OF ANTIETAM ON SEPTEMBER 17, 1862, JAMES LONGSTREET WAS PROMOTED TO LIEUTENANT GENERAL AND GIVEN COMMAND OF I CORPS IN GENERAL ROBERT E. LEE'S ARMY OF NORTHERN VIRGINIA. IN THAT CAPACITY HE TOOK PART IN THE CONFEDERATE VICTORY AT FREDERICKSBURG ON DECEMBER 13, 1862, AND THE DECISIVE CONFEDERATE DEFEAT AT GETTYSBURG IN JULY 1863. LONGSTREET WENT ON TO RECEIVE A SEVERE SHOULDER WOUND IN THE WILDERNESS CAMPAIGN IN MAY 1864, BUT RETURNED TO COMMAND WITH A PARALYZED ARM AND SURRENDERED WITH LEE AT APPOMATTOX IN APRIL 1865.

Q What was the mascot of the Union 69th New York Regiment?

A An Irish Wolfhound.

Q What was a hospital flag?

A A yellow flag with the green "H" was adopted as a hospital flag by the U.S. Army under a General Order issued on January 4, 1864. Prior to that, the only flag used was a plain yellow flag. The Confederates used a plain yellow flag to fly over hospitals.

Q Were hospital flags also red?

A No. Red flags were flown at battlefield aid stations, which were actually located on the battlefield.

DID YOU KNOW

FOR THOSE HEALTHY ENOUGH TO GO INTO COMBAT, A WOUND OFTEN MEANT DEATH OR THE LOSS OF A LIMB. CIVIL WAR MUSKETS FIRED A VERY LARGE LEAD BULLET THAT TRAVELED AT A RELATIVELY SLOW SPEED, SO BULLETS CAUSED TERRIBLE WOUNDS. SOLDIERS WITH A HEAD OR GUT WOUND WERE OFTEN LEFT FOR DEAD. FOR ARM AND LEG WOUNDS AMPUTATION WAS THE USUAL TREATMENT TO PREVENT DEATH FROM GANGRENE INFECTION. SOME WOUNDED SOLDERS WERE LUCKY ENOUGH TO BE TREATED BY A SURGEON SUPPLIED WITH CHLOROFORM OR ETHER, ANESTHETICS THAT MADE OPERATIONS MORE BEARABLE. THOSE LESS LUCKY —ESPECIALLY IN THE POORLY SUPPLIED CONFEDERATE ARMIES—COULD EXPECT ONLY WHISKEY AND A BULLET TO BITE ON FOR THE PAIN. OPIUM WAS ALSO WIDELY USED AS A PAINKILLER.

> **IN MY OPINION I CAN HOLD THIS POST;**
> **IF YOU WANT IT COME**
> **AND TAKE IT**
>
> CLARK WEVER, OCTOBER 1864, RESPONDING
> TO A DEMAND FOR SURRENDER FROM
> CONFEDERATE GENERAL HOOD

Q Who was the first African-American to win the Medal of Honor?

A William H. Carney. A sergeant with Company C, 54th Massachusetts Colored Infantry, he won his medal at Fort Wagner, South Carolina, on July 18, 1863. However, the medal was not issued until May 23, 1900. The citation read: "When the color sergeant was shot down, this soldier grasped the flag, led the way to the parapet, and planted the colors thereon. When the troops fell back he brought off the flag, under a fierce fire in which he was twice severely wounded."

205

Q What was Grant's objective after the Battle of the Wilderness in May 1864?

A After the inconclusive Battle of the Wilderness, General Grant and the Union Army of the Potomac attempted to move south and east toward Richmond. Grant's objective was the road junction at Spotsylvania Court House, from where he could cut Lee's line of supplies and prevent his retreat to the Confederate capital.

Q Did Grant succeed in cutting Lee's supply line in May 1864?

A No. Both armies emerged from the tangled woodlands of the Wilderness on the night of May 7, but it was the Confederates who won the race to Spotsylvania. Lee established a strong, well-fortified defensive line north of the village, but his position had one weakness. A bulge, or salient, where his line followed a piece of high ground offered a tempting target for assault.

Q At which battle was the "Bloody Angle"?

A The Battle of Spotsylvania, Virginia, May 12, 1864. Grant attacked and achieved a breakthrough, capturing almost an entire division of Lee's army. The Confederates managed to plug the gap, and there followed 24 hours of hand-to-hand combat in drenching rain. This fight at the "Bloody Angle" was among the most desperate of the war. An oak tree with a 20 in (50 cm) diameter standing in the defensive lines was literally sawn down by bullets, and thousands of killed and wounded soldiers littered the earthworks. Bold Confederate counterattacks, at one point personally led by Lee, eventually restored the situation, but Lee was convinced of the need to withdraw to a stronger position. He did so beginning on May 14, and subsequent attacks by both armies on different parts of this new line were unsuccessful.

> **WAR, AT THE BEST, IS TERRIBLE, AND THIS WAR OF OURS ... IS ONE OF THE MOST TERRIBLE**
> ABRAHAM LINCOLN, JULY 1864

Q What was the Confederate "Roll of Honor"?

A Although the Confederate authorities wished to devise a medal for valor, similar to the Federal Medal of Honor, they were never able to issue a general medal for bravery and good conduct. In lieu of such an award, therefore, the Confederate Congress instituted a "Roll of Honor." This roll was to list the names of soldiers from each company who were singled out for valor or good conduct displayed during victorious battles. The names were to be selected by vote of the company members. A company could also decline to choose a name, and the honor could be awarded posthumously. The completed Roll was to be published and read in each regiment.

DID YOU KNOW

EVEN THE MOST DIEHARD FAN OF THE INDEPENDENT STATE HAD TO ADMIT THAT NO INDIVIDUAL SOUTHERN STATE COULD STAND AGAINST THE POWER OF THE UNITED STATES AND MAINTAIN ITS INDEPENDENCE. THEREFORE THE SECEDING STATES QUICKLY FORMED THEIR OWN UNION, FOR MUTUAL DEFENSE AS MUCH AS ANYTHING ELSE. THE NEW CONFEDERATE GOVERNMENT, LARGELY MADE UP OF INDIVIDUALS WHO SAW THEMSELVES AS FIGHTING A CONSERVATIVE WAR, IN DEFENSE OF PRINCIPLES DATING BACK TO THE ADOPTION OF THE U.S. CONSTITUTION, ESSENTIALLY ADOPTED THE U.S. CONSTITUTION FOR THEIR NEW NATION WITH ONLY MINOR CHANGES, SUCH AS THE LENGTH OF AND NUMBER OF TERMS OF THE PRESIDENT. A HANDFUL OF SOUTHERNERS FELT THAT THEY WERE UNITED AS A UNIQUE NATIONALITY, DIFFERENT FROM THOSE WHO LIVED IN THE NORTH, BUT SIMILAR TO THOSE THROUGHOUT THE SOUTH. "UNITY OF SENTIMENT, OF INSTITUTIONS, AND OF INTERESTS, ARE OUR CHIEF CHARACTERISTICS," EDITORIALIZED THE RICHMOND *DAILY DISPATCH* ON FEBRUARY 3, 1862. THEREFORE, THEY FELT A STRONG NATIONAL EFFORT WAS THE KEY TO GAINING INDEPENDENCE. THE RICHMOND *DAILY EXAMINER* EDITORIALIZED ON MAY 8, 1861, IN FAVOR OF NATIONAL CONSCRIPTION, ADDING, "WE NEED A DICTATOR." ALABAMA CONGRESSMAN J.L.M. CURRY CALLED FOR A BAN BY THE NATIONAL GOVERNMENT OF COTTON PLANTING, SO THAT FARMERS WOULD PLANT MORE NEEDED FOOD.

Q What was the "Stainless Banner"?

A The Confederate national flag, second pattern. This flag was authorized by the Confederate Congress in May 1863 and first saw official use in Richmond during the funeral of "Stonewall" Jackson. It continued to be flown throughout the Confederacy until March 1865.

DID YOU KNOW

Although religion was temporarily ignored at the war's beginning, as novel scenes and events took the men's attention, this changed as time went on. In order to keep on the right with God, waves of religious revivals, such as the tent meetings that were so familiar in rural Southern communities, swept the Army of Northern Virginia, beginning in the spring of 1863. But it wasn't enough. That July, Vicksburg fell and Lee was turned back at Gettysburg almost simultaneously. God was obviously displeased with His people. In consequence, revivals continued in the winter of 1863–64, as soldiers believed that their repentance would turn God from punishing a South that did not give enough thanks and praise to one that would reward their cause.

Q "Every man we hold, when released on parole or otherwise, becomes an active soldier against us at once either directly or indirectly. If we commence a system of exchange which liberates all prisoners taken, we will have to fight on until the whole South is exterminated." Which Union general said this in August 1864?

A Ulysses S. Grant.

Q What was the "Andersonville of the North"?

A This was a Union prison camp for Confederate soldiers at Fort Delaware, located on an island a few miles south of Wilmington, North Carolina. It was a damp and filthy place, and most of the 2,436 Confederate prisoners who died there during the war succumbed to scurvy and dysentery.

Q **What was the name of Robert E. Lee's horse?**

A Traveller, who was ridden by General Lee throughout most of the Civil War. The iron-gray horse was born in 1857 in Greenbrier County, West Virginia. He was first named Jeff Davis by Andrew Johnston, who bred him. He was renamed Greenbrier by the next owner, Captain Joseph M. Broun. Lee bought the gelding from Captain Broun for $200 in 1861 and renamed him Traveller.

Q **What was the life expectancy of horses in Civil War armies?**

" WHEREVER THE ENEMY GOES, LET OUR
TROOPS GO ALSO
ULYSSES S. GRANT, AUGUST 1864 "

A Six months.

Q **How did the Confederate spy Belle Boyd escape when the ship she was traveling on was captured by a Union vessel?**

A In 1862 Belle was arrested but released a month later as part of a prisoner exchange. In 1863 she was imprisoned once again and, this time, released suffering from typhoid. In 1864 she took refuge in England. When her ship was captured by a Union vessel, Belle charmed a Union naval officer, Sam Hardinge, into helping her. He was later court-martialled and discharged, and the two later married in England.

Q Why was the Confederate 43rd Regiment Mississippi Infantry nicknamed the "Camel Regiment"?

A The regimental mascot was a camel called Douglas. A Texan cavalryman recorded seeing it for the first time: "It was a new regiment, just out from home, and it seemed to us, from the amount of luggage they had, that they had brought about all their household goods along. This regiment is remembered for these distinct peculiarities. Aside from the weight and bulk of its baggage, they had the tallest man and the largest boy in the army, and the colonel used a camel to carry his private baggage."

Q What was so unusual about the USS *Onondaga*?

A It was the first double-turreted monitor in the Union navy. It saw service on the James River.

" CONQUER OR BE CONQUERED "
UNION ADMIRAL DAVID FARRAGUT

Q The Confederate government only awarded one medal for bravery. What was it?

A The Davis Guard Medal. The Confederate victory at Sabine Pass in Texas, and the part played in it by the Davis Guards, reached the Confederate Congress in Richmond, which quickly ordered that a special Davis Guard Medal be cast for each of the men who had taken part. The battle had saved upper Texas from Union occupation until the end of the war, and allowed east Texas to continue shipping cotton through the blockade and to act as the breadbasket for Confederate forces in Louisiana.

DID YOU KNOW

THROUGHOUT THE CIVIL WAR LEE'S LEADERSHIP STYLE WAS VERY AGGRES-
SIVE. WHY WAS THIS SO? PARTLY BECAUSE HE FLATLY HATED THE FORCES OF
THE UNION. HE CALLED FEDERALS "VANDALS" WHO CAUSED THE "RUIN &
PILLAGE" OF VIRGINIA WITH THEIR "PILLAGING", "BURNING", "ROBBING",
"MARAUDING," AND "ALARMING WOMEN & CHILDREN." "YOUR OLD HOME,
IF NOT DESTROYED BY OUR ENEMIES, HAS BEEN SO DESECRATED THAT I
CANNOT BEAR TO THINK OF IT," LEE WROTE TO A DAUGHTER ON
DECEMBER 25, 1861, ABOUT THEIR ARLINGTON ESTATE. "I SHOULD HAVE
PREFERRED IT TO HAVE BEEN WIPED FROM THE EARTH, ITS BEAUTIFUL HILL
SUNK, AND ITS SACRED TREES BURIED, RATHER THAN TO HAVE IT BEEN
DEGRADED BY THE PRESENCE OF THOSE WHO REVEL IN THE ILL THEY DO
FOR THEIR OWN SELFISH PURPOSES." PARTLY IT SEEMS TO HAVE SIMPLY BEEN
IN HIS CHARACTER TO ATTACK WHENEVER POSSIBLE. LONGSTREET WROTE
THAT AT GETTYSBURG, AFTER THE FIRST DAY'S SUCCESS: "HE SEEMED
UNDER SUBDUED EXCITEMENT, WHICH OCCASIONALLY TOOK POSSESSION OF
HIM WHEN 'THE HUNT WAS UP', AND THREATENED HIS SUPERB EQUIPOISE."

211

Q After the Battle of Spotsylvania in May 1864, why didn't Grant attack Lee's exhausted forces?

A Grant did not press his forces on for some eight days while he awaited the result of a landing of another Federal army on the Bermuda Hundred below Richmond. This attack, made by the newly created Army of the James under Major General Benjamin Butler, drew off five infantry brigades and a number of batteries from Lee's army, which could ill afford such losses on top of the ones taken in battle.

Q Where was the location of the horse hospital of the Army of Northern Virginia?

A Culpeper Court House, Virginia.

Q What was Grant's basic aim in the summer of 1864?

A Grant's strategy was to grind down the Confederate armies in a war of attrition and at the same time finish off the Southern economy by destroying its rich farm lands. In May 1864 he traveled with the Army of the Potomac, under George G. Meade, toward Robert E. Lee and Richmond.

Q Where was The South Carolina Military Academy?

A Charleston. Called The Citadel, it ceased operation as a college when Union troops entered Charleston and occupied the site.

> ❝ THE MEN CONTINUE THEIR DRUNKENNESS
> **& GAMBLING ALMOST**
> **WITHOUT REPROOF**
> UNION COLONEL CHARLES B. HAYDEN,
> 2D MICHIGAN VOLUNTEERS ❞

Q What was the pivotal moment at the Battle of New Market, Virginia, on May 15, 1864?

A As part of Grant's mission to destroy the railroad and canal complex at Lynchburg, Major General Franz Sigel advanced up the Shenandoah Valley along the Valley Pike with 10,000 men. At New Market he was attacked by a makeshift Confederate army of about 4,100 men commanded by Major General John C. Breckinridge. At one stage in the battle a Union battery withdrew from the line to replenish its ammunition, leaving a gap that Breckinridge exploited. He ordered his entire force forward, and the Union line collapsed. Threatened by Confederate cavalry on his left flank and rear, Sigel ordered a general withdrawal.

Q What was the first ship to be sunk by a submarine in the history of warfare?

A The USS *Housatonic*. In February 1864, the Confederate submarine *Hunley* detonated its torpedo under the USS *Housatonic*. The attack succeeded, and the *Housatonic* became the first ship to be sunk by a submarine. But the *Hunley* also went down with the *Housatonic*.

DID YOU KNOW

TORPEDOES WERE USED IN CONFEDERATE HARBOR DEFENSE. UNLIKE MODERN TORPEDOES, THEY DID NOT MOVE; AND, UNLIKE MODERN SEA MINES, THEY DID NOT USUALLY EXPLODE ON CONTACT WITH A SHIP. (RELIABLE CONTACT FUSES HAD NOT YET BEEN INVENTED.) INSTEAD, THEY WERE SIMPLY WATERTIGHT CYLINDERS PACKED WITH BLACK POWDER AND SUBMERGED. A CABLE OR OTHER DEVICE WAS USED TO KEEP THE TORPEDO IN PLACE. ANOTHER CABLE RAN TO AN OBSERVATION POST ON SHORE. WHEN AN ENEMY SHIP CAME CLOSE TO THE MINE, THE SHORE OBSERVERS WOULD DETONATE IT USING AN ELECTRIC CURRENT. ALTHOUGH INEFFICIENT BY LATER STANDARDS, THE TORPEDO WAS THE SINGLE MOST EFFECTIVE ELEMENT IN THE CONFEDERATE NAVAL ARSENAL. DURING THE WAR CONFEDERATE TORPEDOES CLAIMED 29 UNION WARSHIPS. THE SPAR TORPEDO WAS AN EXPLOSIVE PLACED AT THE END OF A SPAR AND ATTACHED TO THE BOW OF A SMALL BOAT. MANNED BY A CREW OF SAILORS, THE SPAR TORPEDO BOAT WOULD ROW UNDER COVER OF NIGHT UNTIL IT GOT THE TORPEDO NEXT TO THE HULL OF AN ENEMY VESSEL. THE TORPEDO WAS ATTACHED TO THE SPAR BY AN IRON SLIDE, WHICH COULD BE DETACHED FROM THE BOAT. THE TORPEDO WOULD THEN FLOAT UP AGAINST THE VESSEL'S HULL AND BE EXPLODED BY PULLING A SEPARATE LANYARD. WITH LUCK, THE TORPEDO-BOAT CREW WOULD ESCAPE TO SAFETY, WHILE THE ENEMY VESSEL WOULD BE DAMAGED OR SUNK.

Q What was the result of the Battle of Ware Bottom Church on May 20, 1864?

A Confederate forces made a major attack against the Bermuda Hundred Line near Ware Bottom Church, pushing back the Federal troops into their defenses and freeing up soldiers to provide reinforcements for General Lee at Cold Harbor.

DID YOU KNOW

SOUTHERN STATES NOT ONLY SENT MILITARY SUPPLIES AND CLOTHING TO LEE'S ARMY, THEY ALSO OFTEN STEPPED IN TO CARE FOR THEIR WOUNDED AND ILL SOLDIERS BY SETTING UP HOSPITALS OPEN ONLY TO SOLDIERS FROM THEIR PARTICULAR STATE, THUS COMPETING FOR RARE MEDICINES AND MEDICAL SUPPLIES WITH EACH OTHER AND LIMITING THE ARMY SURGEON GENERAL'S ABILITY TO RATIONALIZE RESOURCES SUCH AS BED SPACE MORE EFFICIENTLY. THE CONFEDERATE ARMY'S SURGEON GENERAL SAMUEL P. MOORE OBJECTED TO THESE. CHIMBORAZO HOSPITAL DIVISION MATRON PHEOBE YATES PEMBER WROTE: "HE WAS AVERSE TO ANY ARRANGEMENT OF THIS KIND, NOT FROM PREJUDICE, BUT A CONVICTION OF THE EXPENSE AND TROUBLE OF SMALL ESTABLISHMENTS OF THIS NATURE." STILL, HE WAS UNABLE TO PREVENT SUCH HOSPITALS FROM BEING SET UP. THE GEORGIA HOSPITAL AND RELIEF ASSOCIATION HAD ITS HEADQUARTERS IN RICHMOND ON MAIN STREET, BETWEEN 14TH AND 15TH STREETS, AND OVERSAW OPERATIONS AT FOUR HOSPITALS JUST FOR THAT STATE'S TROOPS. THE GEORGIA STATE LEGISLATURE GRANTED THE ORGANIZATION $200,000 IN 1861 AND ANOTHER $500,000 IN 1863 TO FURTHER ITS WORK. THE ALABAMA AID ASSOCIATION, PARTIALLY SUPPORTED BY A $1,000 GRANT BY THE STATE GOVERNMENT IN 1861, MAINTAINED THREE SEPARATE HOSPITALS FOR ITS SOLDIERS IN THE CITY, THE FIRST ONE OF WHICH WAS FULL BEFORE IT HAD ADMITTED 100 MEN. HOWEVER, THE STATE LEGISLATURE, WHICH HAD PREVIOUSLY FUNDED THIS OPERATION, REPEALED ALL LAWS FOR THE RELIEF OF ALABAMIANS IN VIRGINIA IN DECEMBER 1863. LOUISIANA AND SOUTH CAROLINA EACH HAD ONE HOSPITAL IN THE CITY.

Q At which battle was Confederate Major General Fitzhugh Lee beaten off by two African-American regiments?

A The Battle of Wilson's Wharf/Fort Pocahontas, Virginia, on May 24, 1864. Major General Fitzhugh Lee's cavalry attacked a Union supply depot at Wilson's Wharf but was beaten off.

> **IN DIXIE LAND WHERE I WAS BORN IN,**
> **EARLY ON A FROSTY MORNIN',**
> **LOOK AWAY, LOOK AWAY**
> "DIXIE", ANTHEM OF THE CONFEDERACY

Q Why was Cold Harbor crossroads, Virginia, so important in May 1864?

A At the end of May the Union Army of the Potomac was just 11 miles (18 km) northeast of Richmond. Lee had Grant's line of march south covered; but, to the east, on his far right flank, lay the Cold Harbor crossroads. Named after an old tavern, Cold Harbor was only a few miles north of the Chickahominy River, the last natural obstacle between the Union troops and Richmond. If Grant gained control of it, his route south was open once again. His far-left flank was at Bethesda Church, several miles north of Cold Harbor.

215

Q What was the last natural defense line before the city of Atlanta, Georgia?

A The Chattahoochie River.

Q Who assumed command of the Union Army of Tennessee in March 1864?

A James McPherson.

Q Why was the main Union attack at the Battle of Cold Harbor on June 3, 1864, a disaster?

A A 7-mile (11 km) front formed on the battlefield, extending from Bethesda Church to the Chickahominy River with Cold Harbor in the center. Lee's 58,000-strong army was in position first. The major Union attack began at 04:30 hours on June 3. It was a disaster from the start. Only three corps at the southern end of the Union line pressed forward. They were met by a devastating crossfire from entrenched Confederate infantry and artillery. One division alone lost more than 1000 men. A Union captain remembered "the dreadful storm of lead and iron seemed more like a volcanic blast than a battle." One Confederate general just called it murder. Within half an hour the assault stopped under the sheer weight of fire.

" BEFORE THIS WAR IS OVER, I INTEND
TO BE A MAJOR GENERAL
OR A CORPSE
CONFEDERATE GENERAL ISAAC TRIMBLE "

Q Did Grant call off the attack at Cold Harbor?

A Grant did not call off the attack until midday, ordering his men to dig in where they could. The two armies confronted each other along these battle lines until June 12. Grant later wrote that he regretted that the last attack at Cold Harbor was ever made.

Q What were the respective losses at Cold Harbor?

A Cold Harbor cost the Union army 7,000 casualties for no gain at all. The Confederates suffered only about 1,500 casualties.

DID YOU KNOW

IN EACH ARMY THE COMMISSARY OFFICER WAS TO PROVIDE FOOD, SOAP, CANDLES, AND, WHERE POSSIBLE, LUXURIES SUCH AS TOBACCO. HE HAD TO WORK WITH THE QUARTERMASTER TO GET TRANSPORTATION FOR THESE ITEMS. EACH COMMAND HAD A MEDICAL OFFICER, RANGING FROM THE ARMY'S MEDICAL DIRECTOR TO THE REGIMENTAL SURGEON. HE WAS IN CHARGE OF THE SOLDIERS' HEALTH, NOT ONLY TAKING CARE OF THE SICK AND WOUNDED BUT ALSO MAKING SUGGESTIONS TO THE COMMANDING GENERAL FOR IMPROVEMENTS IN LIVING CONDITIONS IN CAMP, DIET, AND THE LIKE, TO MAINTAIN THE HEALTH AND WELL-BEING OF THE SOLDIERS. THE ORDNANCE OFFICER WAS IN CHARGE OF MAKING SURE THE SOLDIERS WERE ARMED AND HAD SUFFICIENT SUPPLIES OF AMMUNITION FOR THEIR WEAPONS. THIS INVOLVED GETTING ENOUGH SUPPLIES FROM THE GOVERNMENT'S ORDNANCE DEPARTMENT OR FROM THE VARIOUS ARMORIES AND ARSENALS IN THE REAR BY TURNING IN THE CORRECT REQUISITIONS, KEEPING THE ITEMS WITH THE UNITS ON THEIR OWN WAGONS, ISSUING THEM AS NEEDED, AND BEING SURE THEY WERE MAINTAINED AND REPAIRED AS NECESSARY.

Q Who was Secretary of the Confederate navy?

A Stephen Mallory, who was a firm advocate of ironclad ships for the navy. However, his efforts to purchase ironclads from Britain and France came to nought. After the war Mallory was for a time imprisoned, before resuming his law practice in 1866.

Q Which brown and white bull terrier was captured twice by the Confederates?

A Jack, the mascot of the 102d Pennsylvania Volunteer Regiment. He conducted himself with such valor during the Civil War that the men of the 102d Pennsylvania exchanged a Confederate prisoner for him when he was captured and commissioned a portrait of him at the war's end.

Q What battle in June 1864 was a disaster for the Confederates in the Shenandoah Valley?

A The Battle of Piedmont, Virginia, on June 5. Around 8,000 Union troops under General David Hunter defeated 5,500 Confederates under General "Grumble" Jones at Piedmont. Jones was killed and the Federals took nearly 1,000 prisoners. Hunter advanced unimpeded to Staunton, where he was reinforced by Brigadier General George Crook's Army of West Virginia marching from the west. The combined Union force then advanced on Lynchburg.

Q List the consequences of the battle for the Confederates.

> **THERE CAN BE NO NEUTRALS IN THIS WAR, ONLY PATRIOTS, OR TRAITORS**
> Union Senator Stephen Douglas

A First, in response to Piedmont, Robert E. Lee rushed J. C. Breckinridge's division back to Rockfish Gap on June 7. Second, he was then forced to detach II Corps of the Army of Northern Virginia under General Jubal Early to confront Hunter at Lynchburg. Third, these moves limited Lee's ability to undertake operations around both Richmond and Petersburg.

Q Who was Frank of the Confederate 2d Kentucky Infantry?

A A dog and mascot of the regiment. He had his own haversack around his neck that carried his rations.

Q What wound did the Confederate General Longstreet suffer at the Battle of the Wilderness?

A He was shot through the throat.

DID YOU KNOW

ROBERT E. LEE TRIED TO BECOME A FRONTLINE COMMANDER SEVERAL TIMES DURING THE CLOSE FIGHTING IN THE 1864 CAMPAIGN. THE FIRST TIME WAS IN THE WILDERNESS WHEN LONGSTREET'S MEN ARRIVED JUST AS HILL'S CORPS BROKE UNDER A TREMENDOUS FEDERAL ATTACK. ONE OF LONGSTREET'S FIRST REGIMENTS WAS THE 4TH TEXAS, AND A MEMBER OF THIS REGIMENT LATER RECALLED, "AT THIS JUNCTURE, GENERAL LEE RODE UP NEAR OUR LINE. MOUNTED ON THE HANDSOME DAPPLE GRAY HORSE HE BESTRODE AT FREDERICKSBURG IN 1862, AND WHICH HE ALWAYS RODE ON THE BATTLEFIELD, HE WAS A PICTURE OF NOBLE GRACE THAT I CAN NEVER HOPE TO SEE AGAIN. HAVING GIVEN GENERAL GREGG AN ORDER TO ADVANCE AT ONCE AND CHECK THE ON-COMING ENEMY, HE ADDED: 'THE TEXAS BRIGADE ALWAYS HAS DRIVEN THE ENEMY, AND I WANT THEM TO DO IT NOW. AND TELL THEM, GENERAL, THAT THEY WILL FIGHT TODAY UNDER MY EYE—I WILL WATCH THEIR CONDUCT!' GREGG RODE OUT IN FRONT OF US, AND TOLD US WHAT GENERAL LEE HAD SAID, AND THEN GAVE THE COMMAND, 'FORWARD!' THE WORD HAD BARELY PASSED HIS LIPS WHEN GENERAL LEE HIMSELF CAME IN FRONT OF US, AS IF INTENDING TO LEAD US. THE MEN SHOUTED TO HIM TO COME BACK, THAT THEY WOULD NOT BUDGE AN INCH UNLESS HE DID SO, AND TO EMPHASIZE THE DEMAND, TWENTY OR MORE OF THEM SPRANG FORWARD AND MADE AN EFFORT TO LEAD OR PUSH HIS HORSE TO THE REAR. I WAS TOO FAR FROM HIM TO JOIN IN THIS ATTEMPT, OR, LIKE ANY OTHER MAN IN THE BRIGADE, I WOULD HAVE DONE SO. EXACTLY WHAT OCCURRED, NOT EVEN THOSE NEAREST LEE CAN TELL, BUT JUST AS THEY GOT 'TRAVELER' HEADED TO THE REAR, GENERAL LONGSTREET RODE UP AND SAID SOMETHING, WHEREUPON GENERAL LEE RODE SILENTLY BACK THROUGH OUR RANKS."

Q What was a Havelock?

A A white kepi cover with a long tail draping over the wearer's neck and shoulders. Named for Sir Henry Havelock, a British commander in India in the 1850s, it was worn early in the Civil War by Northerners and Southerners to ward off sunstroke. However, its use was discontinued when it was discovered that it cut off air circulation around the head and face.

Q How many stands of colors did a Union infantry regiment have?

A A stand of colors was a single color or flag. A Union infantry regiment carried two silk flags, or two stands of colors. The first was the national banner, with the regiment's number or name embroidered in silver thread on the center stripe. The second, or regimental, color had a blue field with the arms of the U.S. embroidered in silk on the center.

DID YOU KNOW

ROBERT E. LEE RARELY GAVE DIRECT ORDERS, MAKING SUGGESTIONS INSTEAD, AS WHEN HE SUGGESTED TO EWELL TO TAKE CEMETERY RIDGE THE FIRST EVENING OF GETTYSBURG. INDEED, HE RARELY DIRECTED HIS UNITS ON THE BATTLEFIELD ITSELF. AS ARTHUR FREMANTLE, A PROFESSIONAL BRITISH SOLDIER, WROTE AT GETTYSBURG: "AS SOON AS THE FIRING BEGAN, GENERAL LEE JOINED HILL JUST BELOW OUR TREE, AND HE REMAINED THERE NEARLY ALL THE TIME, LOOKING THROUGH HIS FIELD GLASS—SOMETIMES TALKING TO HILL AND SOMETIMES TO COLONEL LONG OF HIS STAFF. BUT GENERALLY HE SAT QUITE ALONE THE WHOLE TIME THE FIRING CONTINUED; HE ONLY SENT ONE MESSAGE, AND ONLY RECEIVED ONE REPORT. IT IS EVIDENTLY HIS SYSTEM TO ARRANGE THE PLAN THOROUGHLY WITH THE THREE CORPS COMMANDERS, AND THEN LEAVE TO THEM THE DUTY OF MODIFYING AND CARRYING IT OUT TO THE BEST OF THEIR ABILITIES."

Q How many stands of colors did a Confederate infantry regiment have?

A One—a battle flag.

Q Who was Loreta Jancta Velazquez?

A A Cuban-born widow of a Confederate soldier who died of an accidental gunshot injury early in the war. She left her New Orleans home, raised the Arkansas Grays, an infantry unit, at her own expense, dressed as a man, and fought with her unit.

" BRAVE MEN DIE IN BATTLE
UNION GENERAL WILLIAM ROSECRANS "

221

Q Which Union commander was defeated at the Battle of Brices Cross Roads/ Tishomingo Creek, Mississippi, on June 11, 1864?

A Brigadier General Samuel Sturgis. A Confederate cavalry corps under Nathan Bedford Forrest defeated a much larger Union force under Sturgis.

Q Which artist painted the picture entitled "Drum and Bugle Corps"?

A Winslow Homer.

Q Why was George Custer's intervention at the Battle of Trevilian Station in June 1864 so decisive?

A A Federal force under Major General David Hunter occupied Staunton, western terminus of the Virginia Central Railroad. General Grant sent his cavalry commander, Major General Philip Sheridan, with two divisions to join him. To meet this threat, Lee sent two brigades west under Breckinridge, as well as most of his cavalry under Wade Hampton. Hampton's cavalry headed off on a route parallel to Sheridan's, sending a part of his force on to Trevilian Station, 28 miles (45 km) west of Charlottesville, where he planned to meet Sheridan's troops. Hampton's plan was to have Fitzhugh Lee attack Sheridan's men from the east. As Lee was on the move, however, he was hit by a Union cavalry division, led by a brigade commanded by a young brigadier general, George A. Custer, that drove his brigades back, and captured a number of wagons.

❝ A GRAND AND AWFUL SPECTACLE IS PRESENTED TO THE BEHOLDER IN THIS BEAUTIFUL CITY
AN AIDE TO WILLIAM T. SHERMAN
ON THE BURNING OF ATLANTA **❞**

Q Why was the field artillery piece the "Parrot Gun" so called?

A In the late 1840s an exotic bird craze swept the United States. Parrots and parakeets were imported by the thousands. The birds became a major problem in cities. In response the authorities ordered the development of artillery pieces to solve the problem. Two models were speedily developed: a 10-pound parrot gun for medium and small birds, and a 20-pounder for the larger parrots. The guns proved a failure and were put into storage, only to be brought out again for use in the Civil War.

DID YOU KNOW

AFTER BRANDY STATION THE FEDERAL CAVALRY'S STAR SEEMED TO BE ON THE RISE, AS THE CONFEDERATE CAVALRY STAR SUNK. THE CONFEDERATE SYSTEM CALLED FOR EACH CAVALRYMAN TO PROVIDE HIS OWN HORSE, FOR WHICH HE WAS RECOMPENSED. IF THE HORSE WAS KILLED OR DIED IN SERVICE, HE WAS GIVEN TIME TO RETURN HOME AND OBTAIN A NEW ONE; THIS BECAME INCREASINGLY DIFFICULT AS HORSES DWINDLED IN NUMBER IN THE SOUTH AND THEIR COST BECAME PROHIBITIVE. THIS SYSTEM ALSO MEANT THAT A HIGH PROPORTION OF CONFEDERATE CAVALRYMEN WERE AWAY FROM THEIR UNIT AT ANY GIVEN TIME FINDING NEW HORSES, ITEMS THAT THE UNION ARMY SUPPLIED TO ALL ITS CAVALRYMEN AT THE FRONT. MOREOVER, THE CONFEDERATE COMMISSARY HAD PROBLEMS IN SUPPLYING ENOUGH FORAGE, ESPECIALLY IN THE WINTER, TO KEEP CAVALRY HORSES HEALTHY. THEN THERE WERE WEAPON PROBLEMS. UNION CAVALRYMEN WERE INCREASINGLY ARMED WITH BREECH-LOADING, MAGAZINE-FED CARBINES SUCH AS THE SPENCER WHICH HELD SEVEN SHOTS THAT COULD BE FIRED BEFORE BEING RELOADED. THEY RECEIVED WELL-MADE REVOLVERS AND SABERS. THE CONFEDERATE GOVERNMENT ACQUIRED A FACTORY IN RICHMOND THAT MADE COPIES OF THE BREECH-LOADING SHARPS CARBINE, BUT NEVER MADE THESE IN ENOUGH NUMBERS OR WITH HIGH ENOUGH QUALITY COMFORTABLY TO SUPPLY LEE'S HORSEMEN. FINALLY, THE CONFEDERATE ARMY PICKED AS ITS STANDARD CARBINE A COPY OF AN ALREADY OBSOLETE BRITISH ARMY MUZZLE-LOADING, SINGLE-SHOT CARBINE, BUT EVEN THESE WERE NEVER PRODUCED IN SUFFICIENT NUMBERS. NEITHER COULD THE SOUTH PRODUCE OR BUY ENOUGH REVOLVERS, AND MANY SOLDIERS WENT WITHOUT.

Q Who commanded the Confederate States Marine Corps?

A Commandant Colonel Lloyd J. Beall, a former army paymaster with no marine experience.

Q **What was Union General William Sherman's mission in the 1864 campaign?**

A Grant's plan for the 1864 campaign called for a concerted offensive by all Union armies at one time. Sherman controlled three of them, the armies of the Tennessee, the Cumberland, and the Ohio, and Grant instructed him to use this massive force to "break up" the Confederate Army of Tennessee. Grant also ordered Sherman to inflict as much damage as possible on Confederate supplies and war resources.

Q **Who was nicknamed "Old Jubilee"?**

A The Confederate commander Jubal Early.

WE WERE BLOCKADED ON EVERY SIDE, COULD GET NOTHING FROM WITHOUT

VICTORIA V. CLAYTON, WIFE OF
CONFEDERATE GENERAL HENRY D. CLAYTON

Q **Who commanded the Southern commerce raider CSS *Alabama*?**

A Captain Raphael Semmes.

Q **Did the *Alabama* kill enemy crews?**

A No. The sailors boarded the enemy merchantmen and took their seamen prisoner before destroying the vessels. When the *Alabama* grew too crowded, Semmes would designate the next captured merchantman a "cartel ship," place the prisoners on board, and let them sail to the nearest port.

DID YOU KNOW

WHEN GENERAL ULYSSES S. GRANT CAME EAST IN 1864 TO TAKE COMMAND OF ALL UNION ARMIES, HE MADE HIS HEADQUARTERS WITH THE UNION ARMY OF THE POTOMAC, A TACIT RECOGNITION THAT HE REGARD-ED THE ARMY OF NORTHERN VIRGINIA AS HIS MOST DANGEROUS OPPONENT. THE RESULTING OVERLAND CAMPAIGN, FROM MAY INTO JULY 1864, WAS A TITANIC STRUGGLE. THE BATTLES OF THE WILDERNESS, SPOTSYLVANIA, NORTH ANNA, AND COLD HARBOR LEFT THE EXHAUSTED ARMIES WITHIN SIGHT OF RICHMOND—LEE'S LEGIONS SHATTERED BY MORE THAN 30,000 ADDITIONAL CASUALTIES, INCLUDING 37 GENERAL OFFICERS. THE ARMIES SHIFTED INTO SIEGE WARFARE AT PETERSBURG FOR THE NEXT 10 MONTHS, BUT THE END WAS NEAR. LEE'S FORCES HELD OUT IN PETERSBURG UNTIL EARLY APRIL 1865, WHEN SUCCESSIVE OFFENSIVES BY GRANT'S ARMY FORCED LEE TO EVACUATE THE CITY.

Q What was the fate of the CSS *Alabama*?

A She was sunk outside Cherbourg, France, on June 19, 1864. Built in England, the *Alabama* mounted eight guns and could reach a speed of more than 13 knots under steam.

Q What was her record?

A Starting in August 1862, the *Alabama* destroyed 68 Union vessels in 22 months—without injuring the crews.

Q What happened to Semmes after the war?

A He was tried for cruelty to prisoners, though Semmes was cleared when Union captain after captain testified he had been "complete in his regard for the rights and privileges" of his prisoners.

Q What was a mortar?

A The mortar was a type of artillery used during the war. Mortars had a short, stubby barrel that could throw shells in a high arc at short range into fortifications. This made them ideal for sieges, and they were used in large numbers by the Union army. The largest mortars had a caliber of 13 in (33 cm) and were sometimes mounted on railroad flatcars.

Q Who was the governor of Georgia in the Civil War?

A Joseph Emerson Brown, governor of Georgia from 1857 to 1864 and staunch advocate of states' rights. Brown was extremely critical of attempts by the government in Richmond to centralize control of the Southern war effort.

> " TIME SETS ALL THINGS RIGHT.
> ERROR LIVES BUT A DAY.
> TRUTH IS ETERNAL
> GENERAL JAMES LONGSTREET "

Q What were contrabands?

A Freed Southern slaves.

Q What tasks did they perform?

A Many contrabands contributed to the Union war effort by working as laborers in the army.

DID YOU KNOW

THE QUESTION OF SEA-COAST DEFENSE WAS A MAJOR ONE FOR MOST OF THE SOUTHERN STATES, AND THE CONFEDERATE GOVERNMENT WAS CLEARLY NOT ABLE TO DEFEND EVERY INCH OF COASTLINE. TRADITIONALLY, HOWEVER, AMERICANS HAD ALWAYS HAD SEVERAL LEVELS OF MILITARY FORCES. THERE WOULD BE A NATIONAL ARMY THAT HANDLED OVERALL DEFENSE. AT THE SAME TIME, EACH STATE, IN THE NORTH AS WELL AS IN THE SOUTH, HAD ITS OWN MILITIA OR VOLUNTEERS WHO WERE NOT IN NATIONALIZED SERVICE, BUT SERVED UNDER COMMAND OF THE STATE GOVERNOR AS COMMANDER-IN-CHIEF. GOVERNOR BROWN CREATED HIS 1ST DIVISION, GEORGIA VOLUNTEERS, IN SEPTEMBER 1861 AFTER AN INSPECTION TOUR OF THE COAST CONVINCED HIM THAT THE STATE WAS THREATENED BY SEABORNE INVASION. MOST OF THESE TROOPS, HOWEVER —WHICH NEVER SAW ACTION EVEN THOUGH FORT PULASKI OUTSIDE SAVANNAH FELL WHILE ITS UNIT WAS IN EXISTENCE—WERE EVENTUALLY CONSCRIPTED INTO CONFEDERATE SERVICE. WHEN UNION RAIDERS, HOWEVER, BURNED SEVERAL NORTHERN GEORGIA RAILROAD BRIDGES, BROWN ORGANIZED THE RAILROAD BRIDGE GUARD IN MAY 1862. THIS FORCE WAS EXPANDED IN THE WINTER OF 1862–63 TO A TWO-REGIMENT-STRONG GEORGIA STATE LINE. IT WAS AUTHORIZED, ACCORDING TO THE LEGISLATURE, "TO BE EMPLOYED IN THE MILITARY SERVICE OF THE STATE FOR THE PROTECTION OF HER PEOPLE AGAINST INVADING FORCES OF THE ENEMY, AND FOR INTERNAL POLICE DUTY." OFFICIALLY, THIS FORCE WAS STILL CONSIDERED STATE MILITIA. IN FACT, THE CREATION OF THIS FORCE DID NOT SERIOUSLY AFFECT THE NUMBER OF MEN GEORGIA SENT INTO THE CONFEDERATE MILITARY (SOME 120,000), SINCE ITS VOLUNTEERS SEEM TO HAVE BEEN DISCHARGED VETERANS AND INDIVIDUALS WHOSE OCCUPATIONS LEGALLY EXEMPTED THEM FROM CONFEDERATE DUTY BUT WHO STILL WANTED TO BE OF SOME SERVICE.

Q What was the USS *Kearsarge* famous for?

A For sinking the Confederate raider CSS *Alabama* in June 1864. The Union frigate USS *Kearsarge* cornered the raider in the port of Cherbourg, France. The *Kearsarge* waited outside the port. The *Alabama* sailed out to fight but was sunk in a one-hour battle.

Q Who commanded the *Kearsarge*?

A Captain John A. Winslow.

Q Was the commander of the *Alabama* captured by the USS *Kearsarge*?

A No. Captain Raphael Semmes went over the side but was picked up by the *Deerhound*, a yacht filled with sightseers. They took him to England to avoid capture.

228

> " NEVER STAND AND TAKE A CHARGE.
> ## CHARGE THEM TOO
> NATHAN BEDFORD FORREST "

Q Who commanded the Union Army of the James in mid-1864?

A Major General Benjamin F. Butler, who on June 15 with his army landed at Bermuda Hundred, a neck of land north of City Point at the confluence of the James and Appomattox rivers, only 15 miles (25 km) south of Richmond.

Q Which battle in June 1864 opened up the Shenandoah Valley for a Confederate offensive into Maryland?

A The Battle of Lynchburg, Virginia, on June 17–18. A Union attempt to take the Confederate rail and canal depots at Lynchburg failed due to lack of supplies. Union Major General David Hunter's line of retreat through West Virginia took his army out of the war for nearly a month and opened the Shenandoah Valley for a Confederate advance into Maryland.

Q How many times did Harpers Ferry, western Virginia, change hands during the Civil War?

A Eight times between 1861 and 1865.

DID YOU KNOW

BY 1864 SOLDIERS WERE CHANGING THE WAY THEY WERE FIGHTING AS A RESULT OF BITTER EXPERIENCE. INFANTRY ATTACKS WERE NOW MADE IN SHORT RUSHES, WITH SOLDIERS GIVING EACH OTHER COVERING FIRE AS THEY RAN FROM ONE PLACE OF SAFETY TO ANOTHER. IN DEFENSE, GETTING OUT OF THE WAY OF ENEMY FIRE BECAME THE FIRST PRIORITY, AND ENTRENCHMENTS WERE WIDELY DUG. UNION GENERAL WILLIAM T. SHERMAN WROTE OF HIS MEN IN THE LAST YEAR OF WAR: "TROOPS HALTING FOR THE NIGHT OR FOR BATTLE FACED THE ENEMY; MOVED FORWARD TO GROUND WITH A GOOD OUTLOOK TO THE FRONT; STACKED ARMS; GATHERED LOGS, FENCE-RAILS; ANYTHING THAT WOULD STOP A BULLET; PILED THESE IN FRONT, AND DIGGING A DITCH BEHIND THREW THE DIRT FORWARD, AND MADE A PARAPET WHICH COVERED THEIR PERSONS AS PERFECTLY AS A GRANITE WALL."

Q Which Union commander was promoted to brigadier general in the field in June 1864?

A Joshua Lawrence Chamberlain. During Union assaults on Petersburg in June 1864, Chamberlain so impressed Ulysses S. Grant with his bravery that Grant promoted him to brigadier general in the field. Although wounded during the battle, Chamberlain soon returned to the front.

Q Why was Petersburg, Virginia, so important to the Confederates in the summer of 1864?

A It was a vital rail center, which supplied the Army of Northern Virginia.

" DAMN THE TORPEDOES! FOUR BELLS, CAPTAIN DRAYTON, GO AHEAD! "

DAVID FARRAGUT
AT THE BATTLE OF MOBILE BAY, AUGUST 1864

Q What stopped Grant taking Petersburg in mid-June 1864?

A Union General Grant sent 100,000 men of the Army of the Potomac south from Cold Harbor across the James River to swing west through Petersburg and attack Lee from the rear. However, the Union forces were stopped at Petersburg by a Confederate force hastily organized by General P.G.T. Beauregard.

Q What was the first Civil War battle site to have a monument?

A Manassas, Virginia, in 1864.

DID YOU KNOW

NATHAN BEDFORD FORREST WAS GIVEN A CAVALRY DIVISION IN THE ARMY OF TENNESSEE IN THE SUMMER OF 1863 AND WAS PROMOTED WITHIN WEEKS TO THE COMMAND OF THE CAVALRY CORPS. HE DISTINGUISHED HIMSELF AT THE BATTLE OF CHICKAMAUGA, AND IN DECEMBER WAS PROMOTED TO THE RANK OF MAJOR GENERAL. ON APRIL 12, 1864, DURING FORREST'S CAPTURE OF FORT PILLOW, TENNESSEE, HIS MEN KILLED BOTH WOUNDED BLACK TROOPS AS THEY LAY AND OTHERS THAT HAD SURRENDERED. BY JUNE FORREST WAS IN MISSISSIPPI. ON THE 10TH HE DESTROYED A UNION COLUMN OF 8,000 MEN UNDER SAMUEL D. STURGIS AT BRICE'S CROSSROADS. HE FOLLOWED THIS VICTORY WITH A BRIEF OCCUPATION OF MEMPHIS IN AUGUST. BY THE END OF 1864 FORREST AND HIS CAVALRY WERE RAIDING UNION SUPPLY DEPOTS AND SUPPLY LINES ACROSS TENNESSEE.

Q What were the color of the facings on the uniforms of Confederate officers for the artillery, infantry, medical, and cavalry?

A Officers indicated their affiliation with colored facing on their coats or jackets: red for artillery, yellow for cavalry, light blue for infantry, and black for medical.

Q In the Confederate army, what rank did three gold stars on the collar indicate?

A Colonel. Lieutenant colonels wore two stars on their collars.

Q What was distinctive about the uniform of the Union Garibaldi Guard of New York City?

A Its members wore an Italian-style uniform featuring a broad flat hat adorned with chicken feathers.

Q List the shoulder board insignia worn by officer ranks in the Union army.

A On their shoulder boards major generals commanding armies wore three stars, the center star being larger than the others. Major generals wore two stars; brigadier generals, one star; colonels sported an eagle; lieutenant colonels, two silver embroidered leaves; majors, two gold embroidered leaves; captains, two groups of two gold bars; a 1st lieutenant, a gold bar; and 2nd lieutenants wore boards with no insignia.

Q What was distinctive about Union Marine Corps uniforms?

A U.S. Marine uniforms were mostly the same as army uniforms, except that bandsmen wore brilliant red coats. The shako (discontinued in army, artillery, and cavalry units), regulation Marine headgear in the early war years, was replaced by the kepi. Marines were distinguished by their cap insignia: a bugle with an M in the center.

> ## DUTY IS THE SUBLIMEST WORD IN
> # OUR LANGUAGE
> ### ROBERT E. LEE

Q What was a Hardee hat?

A In 1855, Secretary of War Jefferson Davis was instrumental in the creation of two regiments of cavalry. A board of officers, appointed to consider their equipment, recommended a distinctive hat for the cavalry. Because this happened during Davis' tenure the hat is some-times called the Jeff Davis hat. It also was referred to as the Hardee hat, after William Joseph Hardee, an officer of the 2nd Cavalry. The hat was made of black felt and had various insignia.

Q How many Native Americans fought for the Union cause in the Civil War?

A An estimated 3,600.

Q Which Confederate units defeated an attempt to take Petersburg on June 9, 1864?

A Home Guard forces under General P.G.T. Beauregard.

DID YOU KNOW

MANY SOLDIERS IN THE ARMY OF NORTHERN VIRGINIA CAME FROM STATES THAT WERE UNABLE TO SUPPLY THEIR SOLDIERS' NEEDS, LARGELY BECAUSE THEY WERE CUT OFF FROM THEM BY UNION FORCES. MATRON PEMBER WROTE TO A FRIEND IN GEORGIA IN FEBRUARY 1864, "WE ARE NOW A MARYLAND HOSPITAL AT MY PARTICULAR REQUEST. THE VIRGINIANS ARE NOT SO KIND IN FEELING AND ACT TO THEIR SISTER STATE (LIKE THE GEORGIANS TO SO. CA.) AND SO MY LOVE OF EQUITY AND JUSTICE WAS AROUSED AND I HAVE TAKEN THEM ALL (I SUPPOSE I MUST NOT SAY TO MY BOSOM) UNDER MY PROTECTIVE WING." INDEED, EVEN THE CONFEDERATE ARMY SENT ITS SOLDIERS TO HOSPITALS ACCORDING TO STATES, WITH CHIMBORAZO, THE LARGEST HOSPITAL CENTER IN ITS SYSTEM, RECEIVING SICK AND WOUNDED FROM STATES LARGELY BEHIND ENEMY LINES, KENTUCKY, MARYLAND, MISSOURI, AND TENNESSEE, AS WELL AS VIRGINIA ITSELF. THOSE NEEDING HOSPITALIZATION FROM OTHER STATES WERE SENT ELSEWHERE. THE PROBLEM WITH THE POLICY OF HAVING HOSPITALS AND MEDICAL AID SOCIETIES FOR UNIQUE STATES WAS THAT NOT ACTING THROUGH THE CENTRAL GOVERNMENT'S ARMY MEDICAL DEPARTMENT CERTAINLY FORCED UP PRICES AND MADE SOME MEDICINES SCARCE IN SOME STATE HOSPITALS WHILE THEY WERE PLENTIFUL IN OTHERS.

Q What was Union General Sherman's strategy against Johnston in Georgia in May and June 1864?

A On May 5, General Sherman and his three Union armies, totaling nearly 100,000 men, began moving south out of Tennessee toward Atlanta, Georgia. Johnston's 60,000 Confederate troops tried to block the Union advance by entrenching across its path and inviting an assault against their prepared defences. The campaign became one of maneuver as Sherman moved to get behind Johnston, and the latter shifted to block him. For a month the two forces moved deeper into Georgia as they battled each other, yet Sherman avoided committing his troops to a full attack. Instead, he used his superior numbers to turn Johnston out of his defenses.

Q Why had Sherman abandoned trying to protect his supply lines while he rested at Atlanta?

A His supply line, the railroad from Chattanooga, Tennessee, was under constant attack by the Confederate Army of Tennessee. After several weeks trying to protect the railroad, Sherman realized it was an impossible task.

> " I CAN MAKE MEN
> FOLLOW ME TO HELL
> UNION GENERAL PHILIP KEARNY "

Q What was his alternative plan?

A He decided instead to march to Savannah, a port on the Atlantic Coast 220 miles (352 km) away. On the march his men would live off the land. The capture of Savannah would enable Union ships to supply the army and give Sherman a secure base from which to operate.

DID YOU KNOW

IN 1853 THE BRITISH ARMY ADOPTED A 0.577-CALIBER RIFLED MUSKET THAT FIRED A LEAD CONICAL BALL WITH A BOXWOOD OR CLAY PLUG IN ITS REAR THAT WOULD BE SHOVED FORWARD BY EXPANDING GASES ON FIRING TO ENGAGE THE BALL IN THE LANDS AND GROOVES. THE U.S. ARMY FOUND THIS PLUG UNNECESSARY WHEN IT ADOPTED ITS OWN RIFLED MUSKET, A 0.58-CALIBER MODEL, IN 1855. WHILE THIS WAS THE STANDARD ARMY INFANTRY WEAPON AT THE BEGINNING OF THE CIVIL WAR, THERE WERE RELATIVELY FEW OF THEM AVAILABLE, BOTH NORTH AND SOUTH. THE STANDARD WEAPON ACTUALLY ON HAND FOR MOST VOLUNTEER UNITS WAS THE TRIED-AND-TRUE M1842 PERCUSSION CAP, 0.69-CALIBER SMOOTHBORE MUSKET. HOWEVER, BOTH SIDES KNEW THAT THE RANGE OFFERED BY THE MINIÉ RIFLE MUSKET MADE IT THE MOST DESIRABLE WEAPON AVAILABLE, AND SOUGHT TO ARM THEIR TROOPS WITH IT.

Q Why did General Sherman attack the Confederates on Kennesaw Mountain on June 27, 1864?

A By mid-June Johnston's Confederate troops had fallen back to a ridgeline anchored by Kennesaw Mountain, west of Marietta, Georgia. Believing that Johnston's line was stretched too thin, Sherman decided to attack.

Q What happened when Sherman attacked at Kennesaw Mountain?

A Union formations advanced toward the well-entrenched Confederates. Diversionary attacks against the Confederate flanks had little effect. An assault against Pigeon Hill, south of Kennesaw Mountain, was met by deadly fire, forcing the attackers to withdraw. The main assault occurred just south of Pigeon Hill, where 8,000 Union troops were ordered to advance at a run using only fixed bayonets. The advance soon degenerated into confusion as men were halted by concentrated fire from the earthworks to their front. By noon Sherman's men could take no more. The battle had proved to be a disaster.

Q What strategy did Sherman adopt after the Battle of Kennesaw Mountain?

A After the battle Sherman decided to return to his strategy of maneuver, flanking Johnston to the west and racing for the Chattahoochie River and Atlanta. Johnston had no choice but to move south, hoping once again to entice Sherman into battle on ground favorable to defence.

Q Which city did the Weldon Railroad supply?

236

A Petersburg. In June 1864, during the Battle of Jerusalem Plank Road/First Battle of Weldon, the Union's II and IV Corps moved to cut the railroad. They did not reach the railroad, but increased the extent of their siege lines.

Q Which railroad ran along Kennesaw Mountain?

A The Western & Atlantic Railroad. On June 22, 1864, at the Battle of Kolb's Farm, Sherman sought to envelop Confederate defensive lines protecting the Western & Atlantic Railroad along Kennesaw Mountain. The attack failed, but cost the Confederacy over 1,000 men.

Q Who commanded the Army of Northern Virginia's II Corps in 1864?

A Jubal Anderson Early.

Q What happened to this commander at the Battle of Second Manassas?

A He was badly wounded and lost a leg.

DID YOU KNOW

ALTHOUGH ROBERT E. LEE WAS UNFAILINGLY GRACIOUS TO VISITORS AND THOSE WHO SAW HIM ONLY OCCASIONALLY, HE DID HAVE A TEMPER AND WAS NOT ALWAYS EASY TO WORK WITH. WALTER H. TAYLOR WROTE HOME ON AUGUST 15, 1864, "THE GENERAL AND I LOST TEMPER WITH EACH OTHER YESTERDAY, AND OF COURSE I WAS AFTERWARDS DISGUSTED AT MY ALLOWING MYSELF TO BE PLACED IN A POSITION WHERE I APPEAR TO SUCH DISADVANTAGE. I COULDN'T HELP IT, HOWEVER; HE IS SO UNREASONABLE AND PROVOKING AT TIMES. I MIGHT SERVE UNDER HIM FOR TEN YEARS TO COME AND COULDN'T LOVE HIM AT THE END OF THAT PERIOD." AFTER THE WAR, TAYLOR BECAME ONE OF LEE'S BIGGEST SUPPORTERS AND LATER WROTE THAT: "HE WAS NOT ONE OF THOSE INVARIABLY AMIABLE MEN WHOSE TEMPER IS NEVER RUFFLED; BUT WHEN WE CONSIDER THE IMMENSE BURDEN WHICH RESTED UPON HIM, AND THE NUMBERLESS CAUSES FOR ANNOYANCE WITH WHICH HE HAD TO CONTEND, THE OCCASIONAL CROPPING-OUT OF TEMPER WHICH WE, WHO WERE CONSTANTLY NEAR HIM, WITNESSED, ONLY SHOWED HOW GREAT WAS HIS HABITUAL SELF-COMMAND."

Q What was unusual about the staff of the Confederate cavalry commander "Jeb" Stuart?

A It included one person who was only on the staff because of his excellence in playing the banjo.

DID YOU KNOW

ONCE IN THE LINES AROUND PETERSBURG, THE WAR OF MANEUVER THAT MARKED PREVIOUS CIVIL WAR ACTIONS ENDED, AND THE FIGHTING BEGAN TO RESEMBLE THAT OF EUROPE IN 1914–18. J.B. POLLEY, OF THE 4TH TEXAS, DESCRIBED HOW MISERABLE LIFE IN THESE TRENCHES WAS IN THE SUMMER OF 1864, "UNDER A HOT, ALMOST BLISTERING SUN, AND WITH ONLY THE SHADE MADE BY BLANKETS AND TENT-CLOTHS, STRETCHED ACROSS SUCH RAILS AND PLANKS AS COULD BE BROUGHT LONG DISTANCES ON THE SHOULDERS OF ITS MEN THROUGH AN INCESSANT STORM OF BULLETS, TO PROTECT THEM FROM ITS HEAT AND GLARE. THERE WAS LITTLE BREEZE, SCANT RAIN, AND MUCH DUST. THE OPPOSING LINES TOO CLOSE TOGETHER TO PERMIT EITHER SIDE TO SEND PICKETS TO THE FRONT, THE WATCHING OF EACH OTHER AND THE GUARDING AGAINST SURPRISE WAS DONE IN AND FROM THE MAIN LINES, AND LEST THE VIGILANCE EXERCISED THERE PROVE INSUFFICIENT, EACH SIDE MAINTAINED A RIFLE FIRE, WHICH, ALTHOUGH IN THE DAYTIME SOMEWHAT SCATTERING AND PERFUNCTORY, WAS AT NIGHT AN UNCEASING VOLLEY. THROUGH THIS STORM OF BULLETS HAD TO COME ON THE SHOULDERS OF COMMISSARY SERGEANTS AND SUCH MEN AS WERE DETAILED TO ASSIST THEM, THE RATIONS ON WHICH SOUL AND BODY WERE BARELY KEPT TOGETHER. THE CORN-BREAD, A POUND A DAY TO THE MAN, WAS COOKED BY DETAILS FAR IN THE REAR; THE BACON, A SCANT FOURTH OF A POUND PER DIEM TO THE MAN, OR THE SAME QUANTITY OF TOUGH, LEAN BEEF, WAS BROUGHT, UNCOOKED, ON THE SAME SHOULDERS, AS WERE ALSO, BUT ONLY AT LONG INTERVALS, THE SMALL SUPPLIES OF BEANS, PEAS, RICE, AND SUGAR THEN PROCURABLE. COFFEE—NOT MORE THAN THIRTY BEANS TO THE MAN— WAS A RARITY."

IN THE NAME OF GOD AND HUMANITY
I PROTEST!
GENERAL JOHN BELL HOOD'S
COMPLAINT AGAINST GENERAL WILLIAM T. SHERMAN'S
ORDER TO EVACUATE ATLANTA

Q Why did Lee's tactics after the Battle of Cold Harbor ultimately work against him?

A The reasons for Lee's success also became the reasons for his later failure. Lee had succeeded by deploying in front of his enemy and then digging in where the advanced defensive weapons of the day— the rifled musket and cannon—could break up any offensive that could be launched against him. But in so doing he had also moved into positions where he could not maneuver either, and most major Confederate successes, such as Chancellorsville, had come about because of superior maneuverability. Once the Army of Northern Virginia lost this and became immobilized, numbers became the all-important factor, and the numbers game was one that the Confederates could never win.

Q The Weldon Railroad was torn up at which battle in June 1864?

A The Battle of Ream's Station, Virginia, on June 29. A Union raid destroyed 60 miles (96 km) of track of the Weldon Railroad, but lost large numbers of men (around 600) in a major engagement at Ream's Station. Despite this and other local successes, it was clear that Lee's army was now pinned down around Richmond, and was growing steadily weaker.

Q In the Confederate army, what was the Veteran Reserve Corps?

A Units of men physically unable to survive campaign life but still able to do duty.

Q Which Union commander was nicknamed "goggle-eyed snapping turtle"?

A Major General George Meade, commander of the Army of the Potomac.

Q What prompted Lee to launch an assault up the Shenandoah Valley in June 1864?

A Robert E. Lee was desirous of another Jacksonian assault up the Shenandoah Valley, into Maryland if possible, to force the authorities in Washington to weaken Grant's army significantly to shore up the city's defenses.

> **" HOLD ON WITH A BULL-DOG WHIP AND CHEW AND CHOKE AS MUCH AS POSSIBLE"**
> LINCOLN'S ADVICE TO GRANT BEFORE PETERSBURG

Q Lee committed a quarter of the Army of Northern Virginia to the Shenandoah Valley expedition in June 1864. True or false?

A True. Lee ordered Early to drive toward Washington. Early's II Corps, amounting to a quarter of the entire Army of Northern Virginia, moved into the Valley on June 23. He turned north, and quickly reoccupied Winchester on July 2. Early then sent part of his army to Harpers Ferry, while the rest headed toward Martinsburg, West Virginia. Then, he united his command in Maryland, just across the Potomac River.

DID YOU KNOW

OF VIRGINIA'S TOTAL POPULATION IN 1860, ONLY 528,897 WERE WHITE MALES. THERE WERE ANOTHER 249,483 MALE SLAVES WHO COULD BE USED TO PRODUCE FOOD ON THE FARMS, WORK THE FACTORIES TO PRODUCE WAR GOODS, AND ASSIST IN BUILDING FORTIFICATIONS AND THE LIKE, BUT THEY NEEDED CAREFUL WATCHING, WHICH WOULD CREATE A MANPOWER DRAIN ON THE NUMBER OF WHITE MALES AVAILABLE TO BE SENT AWAY TO FIGHT. SOME 518,514 VIRGINIANS WERE FEMALE. TRADITIONALLY, ESPECIALLY IN THE SOUTH, THESE WOMEN WOULD NOT HAVE WORKED OUTSIDE THE HOME. HOWEVER, THEY COULD BE USED BOTH ON FARMS AND PLANTATIONS TO OVERSEE FOODSTUFF PRODUCTION, AND IN THE CITIES IN MANUFACTURING FACILITIES. MANY OF THEM, TO SUPPLEMENT THEIR MEAGER INCOMES, WOULD EVENTUALLY WORK AS SEAMSTRESSES PRODUCING UNIFORMS FOR THE RICHMOND CLOTHING MANUFACTORY, WRAPPERS OF PAPER CARTRIDGES IN THE RICHMOND ARMORY, AND EVEN SIGNERS OF CONFEDERATE CURRENCY. IN SUCH A WAY, THEY, TOO, BECAME AN ECONOMIC ASSET.

Q Name at least two of Ulysses S. Grant's favorite horses.

A His favourite horse was Cincinnati, but he also rode Methuselah, Randy, Fox, Jeff Davis and Kangaroo.

Q Who was the dog called Stonewall?

A Soldiers of the Confederate Richmond Howitzers kept a dog called Stonewall. Stonewall was given rides in the safety of a limber chest during battle. He was taught to attend roll call, sitting on his haunches in line.

Q Who was Dennis Hart Mahan?

A The most important military theorist in the United States between 1830 and 1860. A graduate of West Point, his works included *Complete Treatise on Field Fortifications* (1836), *Summary on the Cause of Permanent Fortifications and of the Attack and Defense of Permanent Works* (1850), and *An Elementary Course of Military Engineering* (two volumes, 1866–67).

DID YOU KNOW

MOST MAJOR MANUFACTURING FACILITIES IN THE SOUTH WERE EITHER IN VIRGINIA OR LOUISIANA, WHICH WAS TOO FAR AWAY TO BE A MAJOR CONTRIBUTOR TO THE EASTERN WAR EFFORT. VIRGINIA'S IRON-FOUNDING VOLUME HAD GROWN FROM A VALUE OF $409,836 IN 1850 TO $809,955 IN 1860, WHICH WAS THE BEST IN THE SOUTH, ALTHOUGH FAR FROM THE $5,912,698 WORTH OF VALUE IN NEW YORK, OR $3,092,347 IN PENNSYLVANIA. VIRGINIA PRODUCED 9,542,627 BUSHELS OF COAL, MOSTLY IN WESTERN VIRGINIA IN 1860, CONSIDERABLY BELOW THE 66,994,295 PRODUCED IN PENNSYLVANIA. THE STATE PRODUCED 1,500 TONS (1,524 TONNES) OF COPPER, VITALLY IMPORTANT IN ARMS MANUFACTURE. TRANSPORTATION WOULD BE A MAJOR PROBLEM, BOTH IN GETTING TROOPS WHERE THEY WERE NEEDED AND IN MOVING SUPPLIES TO TROOPS IN THE FIELD. VIRGINIA STARTED THE WAR WITH 1,771.16 MILES (2,833.8 KM) OF RAILROAD TRACK; COMPARE THIS WITH THE 2,542.49 MILES (4,067.9 KM) IN MORE INDUSTRIALIZED PENNSYLVANIA AT THE SAME TIME. THERE WERE 20 DIFFERENT RAILROAD COMPANIES IN THE STATE, MANY WITH TRACK GAUGES THAT DIFFERED FROM CONNECTING LINES. SOME, SUCH AS THE ALEXANDRIA AND WASHINGTON WITH ITS 6.12 MILES (9.79 KM) OF TRACK, WERE TINY. THE MAJOR LINES THE ARMY WOULD DEPEND ON WOULD BE THE RICHMOND AND DANVILLE, WITH 143 MILES (228 KM) OF TRACK, THE ORANGE AND ALEXANDRIA WITH 156.7 MILES (250.72 KM), THE VIRGINIA CENTRAL WITH 189.19 MILES (302.7 KM), AND THE RICHMOND, FREDERICKSBURG AND POTOMAC WITH 78.5 MILES (125.6 KM).

Q Where was the North's tobacco-producing center?

A Under the pressure of war, tobacco manufacturing shifted quickly from the South to the North. New York City became the North's tobacco-manufacturing center, servicing the area once dominated by Virginia tobacco planters.

> THE WHOLE ARMY IS BURNING WITH AN
> INSATIABLE DESIRE TO
> ## WREAK VIOLENCE UPON
> ## SOUTH CAROLINA
> UNION GENERAL WILLIAM T. SHERMAN

Q Was tobacco part of army rations?

A Yes. For years the U.S. Navy had supplied its sailors with tobacco rations. In February 1864, the Confederate government followed suit and included tobacco as part of the army's rations. When not fighting each other, Confederate and Union soldiers would often exchange goods. The traditional swap was Northern coffee for Southern tobacco. Confederate officers did not receive the tobacco rations granted to soldiers. Nevertheless, Confederate officers favored the more fashionable smoking of cigars.

Q Who ran the Confederate spy service?

A Colonel William Norris. His command extended to patrols watching for enemy movements along the Potomac River and to agents operating in Northern cities, such as Washington, D.C., New York, and Baltimore.

Q In the Union Army of the Potomac, what was unusual about Ferrero's Division of IX Corps, and Hinks' Division of XVIII Corps?

A They were composed entirely of black regiments. In the first attack on Petersburg, June 15, 1864, Hinks' Division achieved a brilliant success, capturing the line of works in its front, and seven pieces of artillery.

Q Which Union regiment had a lodge of masons?

A The 10th New York (National Zouaves), raised in New York City. The regiment had a working lodge of Master Masons in the regiment, the National Zouave Lodge, which founded a lodge room in a casemate at Fort Monroe. It had 34 members.

> " LIVELY SKIRMISHING TODAY, CAUGHT
> # AND KILLED 17 OR 20 LICE,
> ## ALL FAT
> EUGENE FORBES, UNION PRISONER IN ANDERSONVILLE "

Q In the Union army, what was notable about the First Michigan Engineers?

A It was a regiment composed almost entirely of mechanics and engineers. Like the other engineer commands, it was a large regiment—1,800 strong—containing 12 companies of 150 men each.

Q Why did Jubal Early send a cavalry brigade to Baltimore in July 1864?

A Early sent one cavalry brigade to Baltimore to try to free some 18,000 Confederates held prisoner at Point Lookout, while the rest of his forces marched on Washington.

DID YOU KNOW

ON JUNE 15, 1864, GRANT SENT 100,000 MEN OF THE ARMY OF THE POTOMAC SOUTH FROM COLD HARBOR ACROSS THE JAMES RIVER TO SWING WEST THROUGH PETERSBURG AND ATTACK LEE FROM THE REAR. HOWEVER, THE UNION FORCES WERE STOPPED AT PETERSBURG BY GENERAL P.G.T. BEAUREGARD. TWO DAYS LATER LEE ORDERED MOST OF HIS ARMY SOUTH TO REINFORCE PETERSBURG, WHICH WAS A VITAL RAIL CENTER. CONFEDERATE FORCES SET UP LINES OF FORTIFICATIONS SOUTH-EAST OF THE CITY THAT COULD NOT BE BREACHED BY FRONTAL ASSAULT. INSTEAD, GRANT KEPT HIS ARMY ATTACKING TO THE WEST AND SOUTH. HIS OBJECTIVES WERE THE TWO RAILROADS THAT WERE SUPPLYING LEE'S ARMY AND THE APPOMATTOX RIVER, WHICH MARKED LEE'S LINE OF RETREAT TO THE WEST. IN LATE AUGUST UNION FORCES CUT THE RAILROAD RUNNING SOUTH. GRANT ATTACKED AGAIN IN LATE SEPTEMBER AND LATE OCTOBER, EXTENDING THE SIEGE LINES TO 35 MILES (56 KM) AND THREATENING THE LAST RAIL LINE OPEN TO LEE. LEE'S POSITION WAS NOW DESPERATE. THIS STALEMATE CONTINUED UNTIL FEBRUARY 1865, WHEN GRANT RENEWED HIS ATTACKS. ON MARCH 29 GRANT BEGAN HIS FINAL PUSH, SENDING 125,000 MEN TO FLANK LEE'S TRENCH LINE. AT THE BATTLE OF FIVE FORKS ON APRIL 1 THEY OVERWHELMED A CONFEDERATE FORCE OF 10,000 AND THREATENED TO CUT OFF LEE'S LINE OF RETREAT. LEE PULLED OUT OF PETERSBURG ON APRIL 2, RETREATING WESTWARD. IT WAS THE BEGINNING OF THE END FOR HIS ARMY.

245

Q The Union Wisconsin 8th Infantry was also known as the "Eagle Regiment." Why?

A Because of the live American eagle it carried through the war, perched conspicuously on a staff beside the colors.

Q What ransoms did Early extract from Hagerstown and Frederick in July 1864?

A $20,000 from Hagerstown and $200,000 from Frederick.

Q Give the names of the three divisional commanders in the Army of the Potomac's Cavalry Corps in April 1864?

A Upon the reorganization of the Army of the Potomac in April 1864, Major General Philip Sheridan was placed in command of the Cavalry Corps. The three divisions were commanded by Generals Torbert, Gregg (D.M.), and Wilson, and contained 32 regiments of cavalry, numbering 12,424 men.

Q Which Union division in the Army of the Potomac became so reduced in numbers that it was withdrawn from the field in 1864?

A Sykes's Division of Regulars. Commanded by Major General George Sykes, the division included the Second, Third, Fourth, Sixth, Tenth, Eleventh, Twelfth, Fourteenth, and Seventeenth United States Infantry. The regiments were small, seldom having more than eight companies to a regiment. At Gaines' Mill and at Gettysburg, they sustained a terrible percentage of loss.

" IF WE WHIP THE YANKEES
GOOD AGAIN,
THEY WILL QUIT
IN DISGUST
ROBERT E. LEE, SPRING 1864 "

Q Where was the largest military prison in the North?

A The largest military prison in the North was located at Elmira, N.Y. It consisted of an open stockade or prison pen. In it were held 11,916 prisoners, of whom 5,994 died, or 50 percent.

DID YOU KNOW

CAVALRY FOUND ITS GREATEST POTENTIAL IN THE RAID. BOTH SIDES RAIDED INTO ENEMY TERRITORY, BUT J.E.B. STUART'S ARMY OF NORTHERN VIRGINIA CAVALRY, STARTING WITH ITS RIDE CLEARLY AROUND THE ARMY OF THE POTOMAC DURING THE PENINSULAR CAMPAIGN OF 1862, LED ITS COMMANDER TO CONCENTRATE ON RAIDS ABOVE ALMOST EVERYTHING ELSE. IT CAN BE ARGUED, HOWEVER, THAT HIS LOVE OF A RAID, BRINGING BACK BOOTY TO THE MAIN ARMY, HELPED COST THE CONFEDERACY THE BATTLE OF GETTYSBURG, SINCE LEE'S MAIN FORCE HAD FEW CAVALRYMAN WITH WHOM TO RECONNOITRE UNION POSITIONS, AND INSTEAD ALLOWED THE ARMY OF NORTHERN VIRGINIA TO LURCH INTO AN UNWANTED BATTLE ON GROUND NOT OF ITS CHOOSING. RAIDS WERE USED TO GATHER INTELLIGENCE ABOUT AN ENEMY FORCE, SUCH AS THE PENINSULAR CAMPAIGN RAID, OR DESTROY ENEMY EQUIPMENT AND MORALE, SUCH AS RAIDS INTO PENNSYLVANIA LATER IN THE WAR. OBJECTIVES WERE OFTEN RAILROADS, TELEGRAPH LINES (STUART'S CAVALRYMEN INCLUDED TRAINED TELEGRAPH OPERATORS WHO COULD TAP INTO UNION TELEGRAPH LINES BOTH TO GAIN INTELLIGENCE AND TO SEND MISLEADING MESSAGES), SUPPLY BASES, WAGON TRAINS (WHICH SLOWED STUART'S RAID DURING THE GETTYSBURG CAMPAIGN), GARRISONS, AND TOWNS AND CITIES. THEY COULD EITHER SERVE AS AN END IN THEMSELVES OR AS A DIVERSION THAT DISTRACTED THE ENEMY, WHILE THE MAIN ARMY WAS SOMEWHERE ELSE. IN EITHER CASE, THE AIM OF THE RAID'S COMMANDER WAS TO AVOID PITCHED BATTLE AND COME HOME WITH AS FEW CASUALTIES AS POSSIBLE, WHILE STILL SECURING THE RAID'S OBJECTIVE. MOREOVER, TO BE A SUCCESS, THE RESULTS OF THE RAID HAD TO BE SOMETHING BEYOND SIMPLE LOOT OR DESTRUCTION OF PROPERTY; IT HAD TO CONTRIBUTE TO THE OVERALL PLAN OF THE ARMY.

Q What was the "Battle that Saved Washington"?

A The Battle of Monocacy, July 9, 1864. As Early pushed up the Shenandoah Valley, Federals largely drawn from the Baltimore garrison under regional commander Major General Lew Wallace rushed to get between Early and Washington. At the Monocacy River southeast of Frederick, Wallace drew up his battle lines and clashed with Early's men. Wallace's makeshift force, which included some nine-months regiments from Ohio, fought surprisingly well. They fell back across the river after some hard fighting, and the Confederates managed to cross the river after them. Finally, Gordon's men swept the Union troops aside and took the field. However, it was too late to continue forward; Wallace had bought a full day for Washington to prepare its defences. Monocacy was thus the "Battle that Saved Washington."

> **IT WAS A BLIND AND BLOODY HUNT TO**
> # THE DEATH
> UNION SOLDIER, MAY 1864

Q Was Early's move against Washington a success?

A Within the city there was serious concern at the approach of Early's corps, but not the same level of panic as there had been in 1862 and 1863. Veteran Reserve Corps units made up of men physically unable to survive campaign life but still able to do duty manned the forts as Grant detached his VI Corps and sent it north. On July 11 Early's men reached the city limits and scouted Federal positions. They could tell they were too strong to take. Early withdrew slowly back into the Valley. The move on Washington was, however, a success. Grant's forces had been reduced in number and, with attention drawn back north, had been stalemated. The Valley was in Confederate hands once again.

DID YOU KNOW

WHILE INFANTRY COULD START FIRING WITH EFFECT AS FAR AWAY AS 500 YARDS (457 M) FROM AN ATTACKING ENEMY, SUCH AN EVENT RARELY HAPPENED. FIRING AT THIS DISTANCE WAS LARGELY WASTED, WITH THE FIRE TENDING TO BE VERY WILD, OFTEN HIGH, TEARING UP TREES' LIMBS RATHER THAN ENEMY SOLDIERS. SOUTH CAROLINA INFANTRYMAN BARRY BENSON NOTED THAT IN A WOODED AREA NEAR WHERE THE BATTLE OF FREDERICKSBURG WAS FOUGHT, THE TREES WERE "SPOTTED AND SCARRED WITH THE MARKS OF BULLETS, MOST OF THEM JUST OVERHEAD, WHICH SHOWS THAT THE AVERAGE AIM IS TOO HIGH. IN ONE TREE WE FOUND A RAMROD WHICH HAD BEEN SHOT INTO IT AND WONDERFULLY BENT AND TWISTED IT WAS." NOT ALL THIS FAULTY AIMING WAS DUE TO A LACK OF TRAINING; BLACK POWDER WHEN FIRED MAKES CLOUDS OF DENSE WHITE SMOKE THAT, ESPECIALLY WHEN IT IS QUITE HUMID, HANGS LOW IN THE AIR AND MAKES EVERYTHING ANY DISTANCE AWAY INVISIBLE.

249

Q Estimate the maximum range of the M1855 rifled musket.

A 900 yards (822 m).

Q In the artillery, how did gunners actually aim their field pieces?

A There were no long-range or indirect fire-control methods at this time, so all firing had to be done with the gunner actually sighting down the tube as if he were firing a big rifle. This limited the use of longer-range cannon.

Q What were the fighting ranges of Civil War artillery?

A On average, 2000 yards (1828 m) against enemy batteries and 500 yards (457 m) against infantry.

Q Which weapon types made up a Civil War field artillery battery?

A In theory a battery would consist of both guns and howitzers. However, in the Southern armies the types of artillery pieces varied so widely that a battery usually consisted of whatever guns were available, the number of horses alive to pull them, and the amount of ordnance on hand to fire.

Q What was the Army of Northern Virginia's main supplier of weapons?

A The U.S. Army Ordnance Department, i.e. captured from the enemy.

DID YOU KNOW

ON THE BATTLEFIELD INFANTRY ATTACKS WERE GENERALLY TO BE MADE BY WAVES OF INFANTRY, EACH WAVE SOME 250–300 YARDS (228–274 M) BEHIND THE ONE AHEAD OF IT. THIS WAS TO ALLOW A SPACE FOR ENEMY ROUNDS TO FALL BETWEEN THE WAVES WITHOUT HURTING ANYONE. IN FACT, THE INFANTRY TENDED TO BUNCH UP IN THE ATTACK, EACH UNIT WANTING TO REACH ITS DESTINATION AS QUICKLY AS POSSIBLE. ATTACKS ALSO COULD BE MADE IN A COLUMN OF COMPANIES BY A REGIMENT OR A COLUMN OF REGIMENTS BY A BRIGADE. THIS HAD THE EFFECT OF PUTTING A LARGE NUMBER OF MEN IN A VERY SMALL AREA, A NUMBER CAPABLE OF BREAKING THROUGH VIRTUALLY ANY ENEMY LINE. HOWEVER, THIS ALSO SUBJECTED THE MEN AT THE HEAD OF THE COLUMN TO DESTRUCTIVE FIRE FROM FRONT AND THE FLANKS, WHILE ONLY ALLOWING RETURN FIRE FROM THE HEAD OF THE COLUMN AND SKIRMISHERS ALONG THE FLANKS. THEREFORE, SUCH AN ATTACK COULD ONLY BE MADE SUCCESSFULLY OVER RELATIVELY SHORT DISTANCES, WITH THE ATTACKING COLUMN PREFERABLY BEING HIDDEN BY WOODS OR TERRAIN UNTIL CLOSE TO ITS OBJECTIVES.

" I WILL CHARGE HELL FOR
THAT OLD MAN
CONFEDERATE SOLDIER
ABOUT ROBERT E. LEE

Q **Name a foreign source of weapons for the Confederate armies.**

A Southern buyers managed to obtain virtually the entire output of the London Armoury Company Ltd., which made fine versions of the 1853 Pattern British Army rifled musket, with interchangeable parts just like the Enfield-made versions. By February 1863 the company had shipped 70,980 of these weapons to the Confederacy, along with numbers of rifles and carbines. Given other sources, the Confederacy received 81,049 Enfield-type weapons by March 1863. The London Armoury also produced an excellent revolver, the 0.44-caliber, five-shot Kerr, of which the Confederates obtained about 9,000. On top of that, Confederate buyers also obtained some 100,000 0.54-caliber Austrian Lorenz rifled muskets, which were also a first-class battlefield weapon.

Q **What was an Arkansas toothpick?**

A A knife.

Q **What was "Bragg's Body Guard"?**

A Body lice.

Q **Aside from fighting, what other uses did a bayonet have?**

A A meat spit, candle holder, and entrenching tool.

Q Whose home was Arlington Mansion?

A Robert E. Lee. Lee was at Arlington on April 20, 1861 when he made his decision to resign his commission in the U.S. Army.

Q Why did escaped slaves make excellent Union spies?

A They were often able to get close to sources of information because as servants their presence was ignored by officials and officers discussing war matters. John Scobell was an effective black agent employed by Pinkerton in the Union secret service.

> " GENERAL SHERMAN WILL NEVER
> GO TO HELL, HE'LL FLANK THE DEVIL
> ## AND MAKE HEAVEN IN
> ## SPITE OF THE GUARDS
> CONFEDERATE SOLDIER, 1864 "

Q What new strategy did Grant adopt in July 1864?

A Having decided that he was unable to destroy Lee's army in the field north of Richmond, he determined to head south, link up with the Army of the James and capture Petersburg, south of Richmond, forcing Lee to fight there.

Q Who was Harriet Tubman?

A Harriet Tubman, better known for her prewar work as a conductor on the Underground Railroad helping runaway slaves to freedom, also spied for the Union during the war.

DID YOU KNOW

PUTTING TOGETHER A RAIDING PARTY REQUIRED SOME THOUGHT. THE PLANS HAD TO BE DETAILED, SPELLING OUT EXACTLY WHAT WAS TO BE ACCOMPLISHED, YET FLEXIBLE ENOUGH TO ALLOW FOR CHANGING DEVELOPMENTS AND TARGETS OF OPPORTUNITY. MAPS OF THE AREA TO BE RAIDED HAD TO BE ACCURATE, AND SCOUTS WHO ACTUALLY KNEW THE GROUND HAD TO ACCOMPANY THE RAIDING PARTY. THE PARTY ITSELF HAD TO BE SMALL ENOUGH TO BE ABLE TO MOVE QUICKLY BUT LARGE ENOUGH TO ACCOMPLISH WHAT IT HAD TO DO AND BE PREPARED TO DEFEND ITSELF IF CORNERED. THE COMMANDER OF THE RAID HAD TO BE CLEVER, COOLHEADED, AND ABLE TO MEET SUDDEN CHANGES IN THE SITUATION WITH FLEXIBILITY. HE HAD TO BE ABLE TO EXERCISE STRICT AUTHORITY OVER HIS COMMAND, YET AT THE SAME TIME BE WILLING TO ALLOW SUBORDINATES TO EXERCISE INDEPENDENT THOUGHT WHEN NECESSARY. INDEED, HE NEEDED SUBORDINATE OFFICERS WHO WERE CAPABLE OF INDEPENDENT THINKING, JUST AS HE NEEDED ENLISTED MEN WHO WERE ABLE TO SPEND LONG HOURS IN THE SADDLE, ROUGH IT IN ALL KINDS OF WEATHER, FIGHT WHEN CALLED ON, AND USE AN AXE ON TELEGRAPH POLES OR RAILROAD TIES. ALL OF THIS WOULD HAVE TO BE DONE WITH THE LEAST POSSIBLE EQUIPMENT CARRIED, SO AS NOT TO SLOW DOWN THE RAID. AND THE ENTIRE PROJECT WOULD HAVE TO BE PUT TOGETHER AND LAUNCHED WITH THE GREATEST SECRECY, SOMETHING NOT COMMON IN THE DAYS OF UNCENSORED NEWSPAPERS AND LITTLE CONCEPT OF OFFICIAL SECRETS.

253

Q In Union and Confederate armies, which officer took charge of prisoners.

A The provost marshal.

Q Which state was known as the "Old Dominion"?

A Virginia.

> **GENERAL GRANT WILL NOT RETREAT.**
> # HE WILL MOVE HIS ARMY
> # TO SPOTSYLVANIA
> ROBERT E. LEE, MAY 1864

Q What were the punishments for desertion?

A Dishonorable discharge, branding of the body ("C" for coward, "D" for deserter), imprisonment, hard labor, or the death sentence.

Q Why was Confederate General Joseph E. Johnston replaced as commander of Atlanta in July 1864?

A Confederate President Davis considered the defense of Atlanta by Johnston to be unacceptably passive.

Q Johnston's replacement would prove to be a disaster. Why?

A On July 17 he replaced Johnston with John Bell Hood, a commander known for his aggressiveness. Until Hood's appointment the campaign had been primarily one of maneuver; as soon as he took charge, it changed to one of headlong battle. Hood attacked part of William T. Sherman's force, George H. Thomas' Army of the Cumberland, at Peachtree Creek. The determined assault by the Confederate Army of Tennessee threatened to overrun the Union troops at various locations. However, the Union troops held, and the Confederates were forced to retire. Hood lost nearly 5,000 men compared with fewer than 2,000 Union casualties.

Q Why was Atlanta, Georgia, so important to the Confederacy?

A It was a vital transportation and logistics center, with several major railroads in the area, such as the Western & Atlantic Railroad, which connected the city with Chattanooga, Tennessee, to the north. In addition, a series of roads radiated out from the city in all directions, connecting Atlanta with neighboring towns and states. This transportation network meant Atlanta rapidly became a concentration point for the Confederate stores, and warehouses were soon filled with food, forage, supplies, ammunition, clothing, and other equipment critical to the Confederate armies operating in the west.

Q What did John Bell Hood do after his defeat at Peachtree Creek?

A He withdrew his main army from Atlanta's outer line to the inner line as a bait for Sherman to follow. He also sent William J. Hardee with his corps to attack the unprotected Union left and rear, east of the city.

255

DID YOU KNOW

In 1864 General Sherman advanced on the industrial and transportation center of Atlanta, Georgia, 100 miles (160 km) southeast of Chattanooga. It took from May to September 1864, but eventually Sherman fought his way into the city. Sherman decided to abandon the city and march to a new base at the port of Savannah, Georgia, on the Atlantic coast. The march would take several weeks, but Sherman reasoned his troops could live off the countryside through which they passed. Sherman left Atlanta with 60,000 men on November 15, 1864. On December 21 Sherman captured Savannah. After resupplying his army, Sherman began a march through the Carolinas on February 1. This second march was intended to link up with Grant's army. Before this happened, Lee surrendered on April 9, 1865.

Q What was the decisive moment in the Battle of Atlanta on July 22, 1864?

A Although Hood outmaneuvered Sherman, two of his divisions were repulsed by Major General James B. McPherson's reserves. The Confederate attack stalled on the Union rear but began to roll up the left flank (at this time a Confederate soldier killed McPherson when he rode out to observe the fighting). Determined attacks continued, but the Union forces held. The decisive moment came at 16:00 hours, when Confederate forces in the center were repulsed by 20 cannon on a knoll near Sherman's headquarters. Major General John A. Logan's XV Army Corps then counterattacked to restore the Union line.

> " I FEEL THAT I WOULD LIKE TO SHOOT A YANKEE, AND YET I KNOW THAT THIS **WOULD NOT BE IN HARMONY WITH THE SPIRIT OF CHRISTIANITY**
> WILLIAM NUGET OF MISSISSIPPI "

Q What was the result of the Battle of Atlanta?

A Hood lost 8,000 casualties; Union losses were 3,600. The defeat also meant he would have to abandon Atlanta.

Q Who were the opposing commanders at the Second Battle of Winchester, Virginia, on July 24, 1864?

A Confederate General Jubal Early and Union Brigadier General George Crook.

DID YOU KNOW

FOLLOWING HIS CAPTURE OF ATLANTA, UNION GENERAL WILLIAM T. SHERMAN RESTED HIS ARMY AND PLANNED HIS NEXT MOVE. HIS SUPPLY LINE, THE RAILROAD FROM CHATTANOOGA, TENNESSEE, WAS UNDER CONSTANT ATTACK BY THE CONFEDERATE ARMY OF TENNESSEE. AFTER SEVERAL WEEKS TRYING TO PROTECT THE RAILROAD, SHERMAN REALIZED IT WAS AN IMPOSSIBLE TASK. HE DECIDED INSTEAD TO MARCH TO SAVANNAH, A PORT ON THE ATLANTIC COAST 220 MILES (352 KM) AWAY. ON THE MARCH HIS MEN WOULD LIVE OFF THE LAND. THE CAPTURE OF SAVANNAH WOULD ENABLE UNION SHIPS TO SUPPLY THE ARMY AND GIVE SHERMAN A SECURE BASE FROM WHICH TO OPERATE. SHERMAN ALSO HOPED TO STRIKE A PSYCHOLOGICAL BLOW TO THE CONFEDERACY. ABANDONING THE SUPPLY LINE WAS RISKY, BUT SHERMAN WAS CONFIDENT THAT GEORGIA FARMS PRODUCED MORE THAN ENOUGH TO FEED HIS TROOPS. THERE WAS ALSO A SECOND RISK. SHERMAN INTENDED TO TURN AWAY FROM THE CONFEDERATE ARMY OF TENNESSEE, LEAVING IT FREE TO TRY AND INVADE UNION-OCCUPIED TENNESSEE. TO COUNTER THIS THREAT, SHERMAN SENT 35,000 TROOPS BACK TO DEFEND NASHVILLE. THEN HE BURNED EVERYTHING OF MILITARY VALUE IN ATLANTA, AND ON NOVEMBER 15 SET OUT WITH 60,000 MEN TO SAVANNAH.

257

Q What were Ulysses S. Grant's actions after the Second Battle of Winchester?

A As a result of this defeat and the burning of Chambersburg, Pennsylvania, on July 30, Grant returned VI and XIX Corps and appointed Sheridan as commander of Union forces in the Shenandoah Valley.

Q Which Pennsylvania town was set on fire on July 30, 1864?

A Chambersburg. Two cavalry brigades under Confederate General Jubal Early rode in and set fire to the town.

Q What was distinctive about Union troops of the 48th Pennsylvania Infantry?

A The regiment was made up of former coal miners.

Q What plan did they hatch while in the siege lines before Petersburg?

A They came up with the idea of digging a tunnel under the enemy lines, planting gunpowder at the end of it, and blowing up one of the enemy forts. Army engineers declared their plan impossible since they would have to dig a tunnel 500 ft (152 m) long, and no mine had ever been dug so far.

DID YOU KNOW

GRANT'S 1864 STRATEGY WAS TO GRIND DOWN THE CONFEDERATE ARMIES IN A WAR OF ATTRITION AND AT THE SAME TIME FINISH OFF THE SOUTHERN ECONOMY BY DESTROYING ITS RICH FARM LANDS. IN MAY 1864 HE TRAVELED WITH THE ARMY OF THE POTOMAC, UNDER GEORGE G. MEADE, TOWARD ROBERT E. LEE AND RICHMOND. THE SIX-WEEK OVERLAND CAMPAIGN WAS A BLOODY AFFAIR THAT RESULTED IN 60,000 CASUALTIES. DESPITE THE HIGH COST IN MEN AND REPEATED TACTICAL REVERSES, GRANT KEPT MOVING FORWARD RELENTLESSLY. THE ARMY OF THE POTOMAC FORCED LEE'S ARMY BACK TO PETERSBURG AND BESIEGED IT FOR 10 MONTHS. MEANWHILE, GRANT'S SUBORDINATE, SHERMAN, MARCHED THROUGH GEORGIA FROM ATLANTA TO THE SEA, DESTROYING ENEMY SUPPLY LINES AND CUTTING A SWATHE OF DESTRUCTION THROUGH THE STATE. BY THE TIME SHERMAN REACHED THE COAST, HIS TROOPS HAD CAUSED $100 MILLION IN DAMAGE. SHERMAN THEN TURNED NORTH AND DESOLATED THE CAROLINAS.

Q Was their plan put into action?

A Yes. The men's commanding officer, Colonel Henry Pleasants, a mining engineer before the war, believed in the idea. He persuaded his corps commander, Ambrose E. Burnside, of its worth and soon had the regiment at work on the project. The 48th Pennsylvania took a month to dig a tunnel 511 ft (156 m) long, into which was put 4 tons (3.6 tonnes) of powder.

" ONE MORE YEAR OF "STONEWALL" WOULD

HAVE SAVED US
Mary Chestnut, January 1864 **"**

Q Why did the Federals fail at the Battle of the Crater outside Petersburg on July 30, 1864?

A The Union mine was detonated, and the explosion blasted a crater in the Confederate lines beneath Pegram's Salient nearly 200 ft (61 m) long, 30 ft (9.1 m) deep, and 60 ft (18.2 m) wide. Then Union troops attacked. Unit after unit charged into and around the crater, where thousands of soldiers milled around in confusion. The Confederates quickly recovered and launched several counterattacks led by Major General William Mahone. The breach was sealed off, and the Federals lost 5,000 men for no result.

Q What action did Grant take against Burnside as a result of this defeat?

A Burnside was relieved of his command.

" JUNE 3, 1864, COLD HARBOR, VIRGINIA.
I WAS KILLED
LAST ENTRY IN THE DIARY OF A UNION SOLDIER **"**

Q Which two forts protected the entrance to Mobile Bay, Alabama?

A Fort Morgan with 40 guns and Fort Gaines with 16 guns.

Q Who led the Union naval assault on Mobile Bay in August 1864?

A David Farragut.

Q Which military facility was located at City Point, Virginia?

A A vast Union supply depot.

Q At the Battle of Mobile Bay what happened to the Confederate ironclad CSS *Tennessee*?

A For almost two hours the *Tennessee* continued the fight alone against the entire Union fleet. Its six-inch-thick iron armor was pounded with solid shot. At least three Union ships repeatedly rammed the *Tennessee* at full speed. Surrounded by enemy ships, the badly damaged *Tennessee* surrendered.

Q Who was the Confederate commander at the Battle of Mobile Bay?

A Franklin Buchanan, who had at his disposal the powerful ironclad CSS *Tennessee*, three wooden ships, 427 men, and 22 guns.

Q At the Battle of Mobile Bay, what action taken by David Farragut was decisive in winning the battle?

A The Union ironclad USS *Tecumseh* fired the first shot as the Union fleet entered the bay on August 5. Wooden ships were fastened together in pairs to face the heavy fire from Fort Morgan. The *Tecumseh* hit a mine and sank. At its sinking the captain of the leading ship, the USS *Brooklyn*, halted in confusion and signaled for advice from Farragut. From his flagship, the USS *Hartford*, Farragut issued his famous rallying order: "Damn the torpedoes! Go ahead!" The *Hartford* then led the rest of the Union fleet into the bay without losing another vessel. They soon overwhelmed the three wooden Confederate ships.

Q What was the result of the battle?

A The city of Mobile remained in Confederate hands for eight months, but the Union achieved its goal of closing the port.

261

DID YOU KNOW

AFTER THE CAPTURE OF NEW ORLEANS, MOBILE, ALABAMA, WAS THE ONLY SIGNIFICANT CONFEDERATE PORT LEFT ON THE GULF OF MEXICO. ON AUGUST 5, 1864, DAVID FARRAGUT LED AN ATTACK ON MOBILE BAY, WHICH WAS PROTECTED BY SEA MINES (THEN CALLED TORPEDOES) AS WELL AS BY FORT MORGAN AND A CONFEDERATE FLEET. BLINDED BY THE SMOKE OF BATTLE, FARRAGUT CLIMBED THE RIGGING OF HIS SHIP AND HAD HIMSELF LASHED TO THE MAST SO THAT HE COULD SEE TO DIRECT OPERATIONS. SHORTLY AFTERWARD ONE OF HIS SHIPS STRUCK A TORPEDO (NOW KNOWN AS A SEA MINE) AND SANK. THIS DISASTER BROUGHT THE FLEET TO A POTENTIALLY FATAL STANDSTILL BEFORE THE BIG GUNS OF FORT MORGAN. FARRAGUT'S CRY—"DAMN THE TORPEDOES! GO AHEAD!"—RALLIED THE UNION FLEET, WHICH WENT ON TO WIN THE BATTLE. THIS WAS FARRAGUT'S LAST BATTLE. AS A NATIONAL HERO HE WAS AWARDED THE RANK OF ADMIRAL IN 1866. HE DIED IN 1870.

Q What were gabions?

A Cylindrical wicker baskets several feet high, filled with dirt and stones, usually used to reinforce fieldworks.

Q Grant's objective in August 1864 to strike the Confederates so they would have to abandon their strong Petersburg defenses resulted in which battle?

A The Battle of Globe Tavern/Yellow Tavern/Blick's Station.

Q Did he succeed?

A No, although he did succeed in extending his siege lines west and cutting Petersburg's main rail connection with Wilmington, North Carolina. Thereafter Confederates had to unload rail cars at Stony Creek Station, prior to a 30-mile (48-km) wagon haul up Boydton Plank Road to reach Petersburg.

DID YOU KNOW

THE 1864 RED RIVER EXPEDITION, THE THIRD PHASE OF THE UNION RIVER WAR IN THE WEST, WAS THE LEAST SUCCESSFUL. PORTER AND GENERAL NATHANIEL P. BANKS DECIDED TO MOVE UP THE RED RIVER AND INTO TEXAS, OPENING A GATEWAY INTO THE CONFEDERACY'S TRANS-MISSISSIPPI REGION. PORTER'S GUNBOATS CAPTURED ALEXANDRIA, LOUISIANA, IN MID-MARCH, BUT BANKS AND HIS GROUND FORCES SUFFERED A DEFEAT AT MANSFIELD, LOUISIANA, AND RETREATED. FALLING WATER LEVELS IN THE RED RIVER ALMOST STRANDED PORTER'S FLEET AT ALEXANDRIA, BUT 3,000 UNION SOLDIERS HASTILY BUILT DAMS TO RETAIN THE WATER TO ALLOW THE BOATS TO ESCAPE.

Q What were "hot shots"?

A Solid iron shot heated in a furnace and fired at wooden vessels. Shot furnaces were found in seacoast fortifications as well as on board ships. Hot shots were less effective against ironclads.

Q Were female spies hanged if caught?

A Although the punishment for spying was execution, female spies were not hanged if caught. In practice, many other spies were also only imprisoned.

> **"**
>
> ## ATLANTA IS OURS,
> # AND FAIRLY WON
> SHERMAN TO LINCOLN, SEPTEMBER 1864
> **"**

Q Who were the opposing commanders at the Battle of Front Royal on August 16, 1864?

A Union Brigadier General Wesley Merritt and Confederate Lieutenant General Richard Anderson.

Q What were the objectives of Major General Nathan Bedford Forrest's raid on Union-held Memphis, Tennessee, in August 1864?

A To capture three Union generals located there, to release Southern prisoners from Irving Block Prison, and to cause the recall of Union forces from Northern Mississippi.

Q Was Nathan Bedford Forrest's raid against Memphis a success?

A One Union general was not at his quarters and another escaped to Fort Pickering dressed in his night shirt. The attack on Irving Block Prison also failed because Union troops held up the raiders. After two hours in Memphis, Forrest decided to withdraw, cutting telegraph wires, taking 500 prisoners and large quantities of supplies, including many horses. Forrest had failed in Memphis, but his raid forced Union forces to move from northern Mississippi to provide protection.

Q At which battle was Confederate cavalry routed in West Virginia in August 1864?

A The Battle of Moorefield on August 7.

" THE CONSEQUENCES OF THIS DAY'S
WORK WILL BE TO THE
LASTING ADVANTAGE ...
OF THE COUNTRY
LINCOLN ON HIS ELECTION SUCCESS,
NOVEMBER 1864 "

Q Why was Nashville so important to the Union?

A Nashville on the Cumberland River rivaled Washington, D.C., in importance. A 90-mile (144 km) military railroad, built and operated by Union troops, gave Nashville access to steamboats operating on the Tennessee River. Connected with Louisville by rail, Nashville became one vast storehouse for Union forces.

DID YOU KNOW

THE ARMY OF NORTHERN VIRGINIA'S ARTILLERY COMMANDER WAS WILLIAM NELSON PENDLETON, THE OLDEST OF LEE'S COMMANDERS AND ONE WHO WAS SOMETIMES MISTAKEN FOR LEE BY OUTSIDERS. HE HAD BEEN BORN IN RICHMOND IN 1809 AND ATTENDED A PRIVATE SCHOOL THERE. HE WAS APPOINTED TO WEST POINT AND GRADUATED FIFTH IN THE CLASS OF 1830. HOWEVER, HE SPENT LITTLE TIME IN THE ARMY, INSTEAD RESIGNING TO TEACH AND THEN ENTERING THE EPISCOPAL PRIESTHOOD. HE WAS ORDAINED IN 1838 AND BECAME A FULL-TIME PRIEST IN 1847. HE WAS APPOINTED RECTOR OF GRACE CHURCH, LEXINGTON, VIRGINIA, IN 1853 AND HELD THAT POST, WITH TIME OFF FOR WARTIME DUTY, UNTIL HIS DEATH IN 1883. PENDLETON HELPED ORGANIZE THE ROCKBRIDGE ARTILLERY IN 1860 AND BECAME ITS CAPTAIN; HE NAMED THE FOUR GUNS MATTHEW, MARK, LUKE, AND JOHN. JOSEPH E. JOHNSTON PLUCKED HIM FROM THE RANKS OF BATTERY COMMANDERS TO BECOME CHIEF OF ARTILLERY, APPOINTING HIM A BRIGADIER GENERAL ON MARCH 26, 1862. HE HELD THAT POST UNTIL THE SURRENDER IN 1865.

Q Who did Grant appoint to command Union forces in the Shenandoah Valley in July 1864?

A General Philip H. Sheridan.

Q Which Union corps were involved at the The Battle of Globe Tavern/Yellow Tavern/Blick's Station in August 1864?

A Units of the Union IX and II Corps, under Major General G.K. Warren.

Q At the end of August 1864 Sherman decided that the Confederate position at Atlanta was too strong. What tactics did he use to capture the city?

A At the end of July, John Bell Hood's Confederates had retreated into Atlanta and were being bombarded by Sherman's forces. Sherman realized that the city was too strongly defended to be taken by direct assault. On August 25, he withdrew most of his army, moving it to cut the railroads west and south of Atlanta. If he could cut the Confederates' supply line, he reasoned, they would be forced out of the city.

Q Why was the cotton press at Piedras Negras on the Mexico side of the Rio Grande built?

A To handle the huge quantities of Confederate cotton coming across the Rio Grande.

DID YOU KNOW

JOHN WILKES BOOTH (1838–1865) WAS BORN INTO A LEADING THEATRICAL FAMILY ON MAY 10, 1838, NEAR BEL AIR IN THE SLAVE STATE OF MARYLAND. THE BOOTH HOME WAS 25 MILES (40 KM) SOUTH OF THE BORDER WITH THE FREE NORTH. BOOTH WAS PRO-SLAVERY FROM AN EARLY AGE AND THUS BECAME FERVENTLY ANTI-LINCOLN. BOOTH WAS IN GREAT DEMAND AS AN ACTOR IN WASHINGTON, D.C., DURING THE WAR YEARS. ON NOVEMBER 9, 1863, PRESIDENT LINCOLN SAW BOOTH STAR IN *THE MARBLE HEART* BY CHARLES SELBY AT FORD'S THEATRE. AS THE WAR WENT ON, BOOTH BECAME INCREASINGLY UPSET BY CONFEDERATE DEFEATS AND BEGAN TO GAIN A REPUTATION FOR BOUTS OF WILD BEHAVIOR. IN MAY 1864 BOOTH GAVE UP ACTING. HE DABBLED IN THE OIL BUSINESS AND MAY HAVE BECOME A SOUTHERN SPY, SMUGGLING QUININE AND OTHER MEDICINES TO THE CONFEDERATE ARMY. IN NOVEMBER BOOTH MOVED TO WASHINGTON, WHERE HE AND OTHERS DEVISED VARIOUS PLOTS TO KIDNAP THE PRESIDENT. THEY INTENDED TO RANSOM LINCOLN FOR THE RETURN OF CONFEDERATE PRISONERS OF WAR. BUT THEIR ATTEMPTS ALL FAILED.

Q Did Sherman succeed in forcing the Confederates out of Atlanta in August 1864?

A Yes. Hood interpreted Sherman's movements as a retreat. When he received reports of Union troops near Jonesborough, just south of Atlanta on the Macon and Western Railroad, he figured them to be only a raiding party and sent troops under William J. Hardee to destroy them. Hood's miscalculation had dire consequences. Hardee was surprised to encounter virtually the entire Union force near Jonesborough. Six Union army corps had moved in an arc around the Atlanta defenses. Hardee made an ineffective attack, and the Confederates suffered high losses. This failure forced the other Confederate corps, under Stephen D. Lee, back to a defensive position along the Macon and Western Railroad.

Q What was the result of Sherman cutting the railroad line north of Jonesborough on September 1, 1864?

A Once the last supply line was cut, Hood's Confederates were forced to evacuate Atlanta.

" I CAN MAKE GEORGIA HOWL
GENERAL SHERMAN, NOVEMBER 1864 "

Q What was significant about the fall of Atlanta to the Union?

A The Battle of Jonesborough and the subsequent loss of Atlanta removed any doubt that the Confederacy would be defeated. Sherman's forces suffered 1,150 casualties at Jonesborough, and 35,000 for the entire Atlanta Campaign, but they had given Lincoln the victory that he badly needed. The mismanaged attacks at Jonesborough also showed the command failures that plagued the Confederate Army of Tennessee.

Q Which state supplied cattle to Virginia?

A Texas. Texas cattlemen supplied beef to Southerners east of the Mississippi River until the summer of 1862, when the Union navy took control of the river.

Q What was the "Great Beefsteak Raid"?

A By September 1864, short of cattle, the Confederates in Virginia had been reduced to cattle raids on Union troops. However, on September 16 General Wade Hampton and his cavalrymen appeared at Coggins Point in the rear of the Union army on the James River. They carried off the entire beef supply of 2,486 cattle. The "Great Beefsteak Raid," as it was called, brought joy and relief to the hungry Rebels.

Q What action did Sherman take following his capture of Atlanta in September 1864?

A After taking the city, he ordered all civilians to leave their homes, declaring Atlanta to be a military encampment.

Q Who was Lincoln's running mate in the 1864 election?

A War Democrat Andrew Johnson of Tennessee.

> " I CLAIM NOT TO HAVE
> CONTROLLED EVENTS, BUT CONFESS
> ## PLAINLY THAT EVENTS
> ## HAVE CONTROLLED ME "
> ABRAHAM LINCOLN, APRIL 1864

DID YOU KNOW

As Sherman's men headed southeast after taking Atlanta, the Confederates turned back to Tennessee as predicted to embark on an ill-fated invasion. This left no forces to oppose Sherman except Confederate cavalry and Georgia militia. As a result, Sherman was able to spread his army along a path 60 miles (96 km) wide. By moving in such a dispersed pattern, his army greatly eased the task of supplying itself from the countryside. Parties of foragers set forth each day to scour the land for pork, beef, corn, and other foods. As the troops advanced, they paused regularly to wreck railroads and burn factories, cotton gins, and anything else that might be valuable to the Confederate war effort. In many cases the authorized foraging was accompanied by theft and vandalism, officially deplored but unofficially tolerated. There were also thousands of lawless stragglers following the army, who were beyond military control.

Q Why was the Third Battle of Winchester, Virginia, on September 19, 1864, so important?

A It was a key engagement of Union General Philip H. Sheridan's Shenandoah Valley Campaign, in which his aim was to destroy the South's "breadbasket."

Q What was the result of the battle?

A The battle took place east of the town. Confederate General Jubal A. Early was outnumbered nearly three to one. Nevertheless, the Confederates fought stubbornly all day, but their lines eventually broke. After losing nearly a quarter of his men, Early retreated through the town.

Q **What did the Confederate cavalry do at the Battle of Fisher's Hill, Virginia, in September 1864?**

A Nothing. Jubal A. Early's 9,500 Confederates took up a strong defensive position at Fisher's Hill, south of Strasburg. General Philip Sheridan's Union army of 30,000 advanced and occupied important high ground. Union troops outflanked Early and attacked at 16:00 hours on September 22. The Confederate cavalry did nothing and the infantry was unable to withstand the assault. The Rebel defense collapsed as Sheridan's other troops joined in the assault.

Q **What was the result of the Battle of Fisher's Hill?**

A Early retreated to Rockfish Gap near Waynesboro, opening the Shenandoah Valley to a Union "scorched earth" invasion.

Q Which battle in Virginia, at the end of September 1864, forced Robert E. Lee to pull in troops from Petersburg to defend the city of Richmond?

A The Battle of Chaffin's Farm/New Market Heights. It was an assault by the Union's Army of the James against Richmond's defenses north of the James River.

Q Grant's attack at Peebles' Farm in September 1864 was designed to achieve what?

A To cut Confederate lines of communication southwest of Petersburg. He despatched forces to hit Lee's right, extending the lines west and driving toward the South Side Railroad and the Appomattox River.

Q Was the attack successful?

A Not entirely. The Union V Corps, followed by IX Corps, struck southwest of Petersburg at Peebles' Farm, toward Poplar Springs Church. The Federals were initially successful, but General A.P. Hill counterattacked and opened a gap between the two corps.

> " I BEG TO PRESENT YOU AS A CHRISTMAS
> # GIFT, THE CITY OF SAVANNAH
> SHERMAN TO LINCOLN, DECEMBER 22, 1864 "

Q What was the result of the battle?

A It extended the Union siege lines and again stretched the resources of the Confederate defenders.

Q Which battle in October 1864 signaled that the Union had taken control of the Shenandoah Valley?

A The Battle of Tom's Brook/Woodstock Races. The Union routed Confederate forces at Tom's Brook during intense raiding and scorched-earth missions.

Q At which battle did General Robert E. Lee launch a bloody and futile attack against the Union far-right flank around Richmond?

A The Battle of Darbytown/New Market Roads/Fourmile Creek, Virginia, on October 7, 1864.

" I THINK WE MAY

WHIP THE KEARSARGE
CAPTAIN RAPHAEL SEMMES
OF THE CONFEDERATE SHIP *ALABAMA*, JUNE 1864 "

Q Why was the Battle of Cedar Creek, Virginia, on October 19, 1864, a disaster for the Confederacy?

A The Confederate Army of the Valley under General Jubal A. Early (21,000 men) surprised the Federal army at Cedar Creek and routed VIII and XIX Army Corps. However, the Union commander, Major General Philip Sheridan, arrived from Winchester, rallied his troops, and launched a counterattack that defeated the Confederates. Confederate losses were 2,910; Union casualties were 5,665. This defeat was a disaster for the South because it broke the back of the Confederate army in the Shenandoah Valley.

DID YOU KNOW

ONCE UNDER WAY, A CIVIL WAR CAVALRY RAID WAS LED BY SCOUTS, FOLLOWED BY A SMALL GROUP MAKING UP AN ADVANCE GUARD, ABOUT HALF A MILE (800 M) AHEAD OF THE MAIN COLUMN. PATROLS WERE SENT ALONG THE FLANKS, ABOUT 1 MILE (1.6 KM) OR LESS FROM THE MAIN COLUMN. STUART'S CAVALRY INCLUDED HORSE ARTILLERY (ONE BATTERY ACCOMPANIED THE RIDE AROUND THE ARMY OF THE POTOMAC IN JUNE 1862) AND THIS, WITH ANY WAGONS, MOVED IN THE CENTER OF THE COLUMN. FINALLY A REARGUARD FOLLOWED, ROUNDING UP STRAGGLERS AND DOING SUCH THINGS AS BURNING BRIDGES BEHIND THEM AS NECESSARY. THE COLUMN MOVED AT VARYING RATES OF MARCH. MOSTLY THE UNITS MOVED OFF AT THE TROT, BUT FROM TIME TO TIME THEY WOULD SWITCH TO A CANTER OR EVEN A GALLOP FOR SHORT PERIODS TO VARY THE MARCH. THE RATE OF MARCH WOULD BE AT LEAST 3 MILES (5 KM) AN HOUR, WITH A 10-MINUTE BREAK EVERY HOUR OR SO, OR MORE IN BAD WEATHER. AT NOON, THE COLUMN WOULD HALT FOR DINNER, AND AGAIN FOR ANOTHER MEAL IN THE EVENING. THIS PRECEDED A TYPICAL HALT AND CAMP AT NIGHT, USUALLY AFTER ABOUT 20 HOURS IN THE SADDLE, WHEN IT BECAME HARD TO KEEP A COLUMN TOGETHER.

273

Q What was the St. Albans Raid in October 1864?

A A group of about 20 disguised Confederate cavalrymen, led by Southern agent George Sanders and Lieutenant Bennett Young, left Quebec, Canada, and rode into St. Albans, a town in Vermont 15 miles (22 km) across the border.

Q Why was it significant?

A It was the northernmost engagement of the Civil War.

Q What was Hood's objective when he led 30,000 Confederates of the Army of Tennessee north out of Alabama in late 1864?

A His objective was to recapture Tennessee and put pressure on General William T. Sherman to call a halt to his campaign through Georgia. By the end of the month Hood had advanced his army north through Pulaski and Columbia, and had turned back a Union force of 27,000 outside Franklin. This battle cost Hood's army more than 6,200 casualties, including six generals, but Hood did not stop. On December 2, the Confederates were south of Nashville facing the strong Union fortifications that ringed the city. With winter coming on, Hood ordered his men to dig in for a siege.

" THE SIDES AND BOTTOM OF THE CHASM WERE LITERALLY LINED WITH YANKEE DEAD
CONFEDERATE JOURNALIST AT THE CRATER, JULY 1864 "

Q Who was the Union commander defending Nashville in December 1864?

A George H. Thomas, the commander of the Union Army of the Cumberland.

Q The Battle of Nashville, Tennessee, in December 1864 resulted in the resignation of which general?

A The Confederate Army of Tennessee was routed. It numbered barely 17,000 men and had lost most of its equipment. Hood retreated to Tupelo, Mississippi, and in January resigned his command. In contrast, Thomas was promoted to major general.

Q How did the Confederates escape from Savannah, Georgia, while besieged by General Sherman in December 1863?

A They escaped across a hastily constructed pontoon bridge over the Savannah River during the night and disappeared into South Carolina.

1865

THE FINAL YEAR OF THE WAR SAW SHERMAN MARCH
THROUGH THE CAROLINAS AND GRANT BREAK THE
CONFEDERATE DEFENSE OF PETERSBURG. LEE WAS
CAUGHT AT APPOMATTOX, WHERE HE SURRENDERED
ON APRIL 9. A SUCCESSION OF CONFEDERATE
SURRENDERS FOLLOWED, BRINGING AN END TO A
WAR THAT HAD COST MORE THAN 600,000 LIVES.

Q Why was the city of Savannah strategically important?

A It was well defended, had strong fortifications on all sides, and the surrounding network of swamps and rivers formed a natural barrier to a hostile army. Its strategic importance was immense. Capturing Savannah gave General William T. Sherman a secure base deep inside Confederate territory and a port where supplies could be brought in for his army.

Q What was Sherman's March to the Sea?

A In mid-November 1864, leaving Atlanta in flames, two huge columns of Union troops headed toward Savannah, cutting a huge swathe of destruction as they marched through the fertile Georgia countryside. Sherman entered Savannah unopposed.

> WITH MALICE TOWARD NONE;
> WITH CHARITY FOR ALL;
> ## WITH FIRMNESS IN THE RIGHT
> ABRAHAM LINCOLN, MARCH 1865

Q What was significant about the fall of Fort Fisher, North Carolina, to the Union in January 1865?

A It meant that the Union could now attack Wilmington, the South's last open seaport on the Atlantic coast.

Q Why were Sherman and his troops eager to punish the state of South Carolina in early 1865?

A The state was considered to be the "cradle of secession," and many Union troops wanted to make it pay for being the cause of so much suffering.

DID YOU KNOW

DURING SHERMAN'S MARCH TO THE SEA SOME OF THE MOST BADLY TREATED WERE THE AFRICAN-AMERICAN SLAVES LIBERATED BY THE UNION ARMY. ON ONE OCCASION A UNION GENERAL BURNED A BRIDGE OVER A CREEK TO PREVENT ANY AFRICAN-AMERICANS FROM FOLLOWING. HUNDREDS OF SLAVES FOUND THEIR PATH TO FREEDOM BLOCKED, AND SOME DROWNED TRYING TO SWIM THE STREAM AND ESCAPE. SHERMAN CAPTURED SAVANNAH ON DECEMBER 21, 1864. HIS NEXT MOVE WAS TO JOIN FORCES WITH ULYSSES S. GRANT IN VIRGINIA AND DEFEAT ROBERT E. LEE'S ARMY. SHERMAN CONSIDERED MOVING HIS TROOPS BY SEA FROM SAVANNAH BUT THEN DETERMINED ON A SECOND MARCH THROUGH THE CAROLINAS. THE MARCH BEGAN ON FEBRUARY 1, 1865. THIS MARCH WAS MORE CHALLENGING THAN THE FIRST. THERE WERE MORE CONFEDERATE TROOPS OBSTRUCTING SHERMAN'S ADVANCE, AS WELL AS SEVERAL SWAMPY RIVERS. WINTER RAINS HAD TURNED THE ROADS TO MUD. NEVERTHELESS, THE UNION TROOPS SURPRISED THE CONFEDERATE COMMAND WITH THE SPEED OF THEIR ADVANCE.

Q **Which Confederate army defended South Carolina in 1865?**

A The Confederate Army of Tennessee, led by Joseph E. Johnston from February, and numbering fewer than 10,000 men. Sherman had 60,000 troops.

Q **What was Sherman's plan after capturing Savannah in December 1864?**

A Union General William T. Sherman, having completed his infamous March to the Sea, during which his army had stormed from Atlanta to Savannah in just five weeks, destroying everything in its path, vowed to push on through the Carolinas into Virginia.

Q What happened on board the *River Queen* in Hampton Roads, Virginia, in February 1865?

A A peace conference between North and South, with President Lincoln attending. It failed to reach a diplomatic ending to the war. Representing the Confederacy were Robert M.T. Hunter, John A. Campbell, and Vice President Stephens.

Q What was a Gatling Gun?

A A rapid-fire weapon that had six barrels mounted in a revolving frame.

Q What was the most glaring problem with the first Gatling Guns?

A The bores were tapered, and often the barrels and chambers did not exactly align. This affected accuracy and velocity.

DID YOU KNOW

THE GATLING WAS A SIX-BARRELED GUN THAT USED A ROTATING MECHANISM TO LOAD, FIRE, AND EJECT ITS AMMUNITION AT A (THEN) PHENOMENAL RATE OF 200 ROUNDS PER MINUTE. THE GUN HAD SEVERAL SERIOUS DRAWBACKS. IT WAS TOO BIG AND HEAVY TO BE MANEUVERABLE IN ROUGH COUNTRY; AND USED BLACK POWDER, WHICH PRODUCED DENSE CLOUDS OF SMOKE THAT OBSCURED THE TARGET. THESE PROBLEMS WERE EVENTUALLY SOLVED BY INVENTORS AROUND THE WORLD OVER THE NEXT 30 YEARS. DURING THE CIVIL WAR ONLY 12 GATLING GUNS WERE USED BY THE UNION ARMY. THEY WERE BOUGHT PRIVATELY BY GENERAL BENJAMIN BUTLER IN 1864. GATLING HIMSELF SINCERELY BELIEVED HIS INVENTION WOULD BRING AN END TO WAR BECAUSE THE CARNAGE HIS NEW WEAPON COULD INFLICT WOULD MAKE ANY FUTURE WAR UNTHINKABLE.

> " I HATE NEWSPAPERMEN.
> I REGARD THEM AS SPIES,
> ## WHICH, IN TRUTH,
> ## THEY ARE
> Union General William T. Sherman "

Q Name two carbines used by Union cavalry during the war.

A Sharps carbine and Spencer breechloading repeater, which could fire seven rounds before reloading. By 1865 the Union army had issued more than 80,000 Sharps and 90,000 Spencers to its cavalrymen. In contrast, the Confederates began the war with muzzleloaders and even shotguns. Most of the breechloaders they used later were captured from Union forces.

Q Did Union forces start the fire that destroyed large parts of Columbia, South Carolina, in February 1865?

A As Union troops entered Columbia, someone set fire to bales of cotton that had been piled in the streets. High winds helped to spread the blaze, and more than half the city was destroyed before the flames were brought under control. Whether the fire was started by retreating Confederates or by arriving Union troops has remained a matter of controversy.

Q Which Confederate spy published her memoirs in 1865?

A Belle Boyd. Her memoirs were titled *Belle Boyd in Camp and Prison*. In England she became an actress and then made her American stage debut in 1868. She continued her life on stage as a lecturer, entertaining audiences with her experiences.

Q Which battle defeated the last of Early's force in the Shenandoah Valley?

A The Battle of Waynesboro, Virginia, on March 2, 1865. More than 1,500 Confederates, the last of Early's force in the Shenandoah Valley, were captured by two Federal cavalry divisions at Waynesboro. Early escaped with 100 men.

Q What was the Freedmen's Bureau?

A This Union bureau was designed to protect the interests of former slaves. This included helping them to find new employment and to improve educational and health facilities.

Q Who did Lincoln defeat to be reelected as president?

A The Democrat and former army commander George McClellan, by nearly 500,000 votes.

> ❝ I DON'T CARE A DAMN FOR THEIR GUNS.
> ## WHAT I WANT IS THE SOUTHSIDE RAILROAD!
> GENERAL PHILIP H. SHERIDAN
> AT THE BATTLE OF FIVE FORKS ❞

Q What was a major factor in Lincoln's victory?

A Lincoln's success was due to Sherman's capture of Atlanta, a victory that lifted spirits throughout the North and revitalized the Lincoln campaign.

DID YOU KNOW

AS PRISONER NUMBERS ROSE, BOTH THE UNION AND CONFEDERACY HAD TO RESORT TO USING VAST OPEN-AIR ENCLOSURES TO HOLD THEM. THE UNION WAR DEPARTMENT OPENED THE NOTORIOUS ELMIRA PRISON IN NEW YORK STATE IN MAY 1864. BY AUGUST IT WAS FILLED WITH 10,000 CONFEDERATES, HALF OF THEM LIVING IN TENTS ON A BADLY DRAINED, POLLUTED SWAMP. BY NOVEMBER MORE THAN 700 MEN HAD DIED FROM TYPHOID, DYSENTERY, PNEUMONIA, OR SMALLPOX, AND 1,000 MEN A DAY WERE FALLING SICK. SOME DIED FROM SCURVY DUE TO A LACK OF FRESH VEGETABLES IN THEIR RATIONS. IN FEBRUARY 1864 THE CONFEDERATES OPENED CAMP SUMTER NEAR ANDERSONVILLE IN GEORGIA. THE CAMP WAS MEANT TO RELIEVE THE PRESSURE ON PRISONS AROUND RICHMOND, BUT MEN WERE SENT THERE WITHOUT ANY REGARD TO CONDITIONS INSIDE OR HOW THE AUTHORITIES MIGHT FEED THEM. BY JULY MORE THAN 32,000 MEN WERE CROWDED INTO THE CAMP WITHOUT ANY SHELTER FROM THE SUN AND ON STARVATION RATIONS. THE TERRIBLE CONDITIONS SUFFERED BY UNION PRISONERS AT ANDERSONVILLE WERE FIRST PUBLICIZED IN THE NORTH IN LATE 1864, WHEN A PAMPHLET PUBLISHED IN BOSTON RECORDED THE EXPERIENCES OF PRISONERS WHO HAD SURVIVED. MANY UNION SOLDIERS GAVE GRAPHIC DESCRIPTIONS OF LIFE IN THE CAMP.

281

Q With what words did President Lincoln end his Second Inaugural Address in March 1865?

A "With malice toward none."

Q What was significant about the Confederate victory at the Battle of Natural Bridge, Florida, in March 1865?

A It meant that Tallahassee, the state capital, remained out of Union hands for the remainder of the war, unlike any of the other Southern capitals east of the Mississippi River.

THE WAR IS OVER.
THE REBELS ARE OUR
COUNTRYMEN AGAIN

ULYSSES S. GRANT, APRIL 9, 1865

Q **What factors impeded the ability of the Army of Northern Virginia to make rapid marches in early 1865?**

A Lee's horses were too weak from a lack of forage to pull the army's guns and wagons as quickly as could those well-fed animals of the Army of the Potomac. Indeed, Lee's men were considerably worse off in terms of diet than their enemies, and feeding the Confederates on a march, considering the supply problems, would be problematic. New shoes, which wore out rapidly on forced marches, could not be supplied to Lee's army once it moved away from the depots of Richmond. Once separated from Richmond, ammunition resupply would also be extremely difficult. Finally, it was difficult enough to keep his troops doing their duty in the trenches: on the march where possibilities for desertion would be even greater, it would be almost impossible, and the desertion rate would be bound to jump tremendously.

Q **Estimate Confederate strength in the east and west in March 1865.**

A In the Carolinas the Confederates had some 13,500 men under Joseph E. Johnston to oppose 80,000 Union troops only 120 miles (192 km) south of the Petersburg siege. Lee had, as of March 1, 56,000 men against Grant's nearly 100,000.

Q When was the Confederate national flag, third pattern, introduced?

A This was the last flag officially adopted by the South and was issued in limited numbers on March 4, 1865, barely a month before the end of the war. It was a variation of the second pattern flag, and its distinctive red band was introduced to prevent the "Stainless Banner" from being mistaken for a white flag of surrender.

Q Which law was passed by the Confederate Congress on March 13, 1865, concerning black troops?

A In a radical departure from Southern ideology, the law authorized the use of black troops.

DID YOU KNOW

ON FEBRUARY 20, 1865, GENERAL LONGSTREET HAD AN INFORMAL MEETING WITH THE NEW COMMANDER OF THE FEDERALS' ARMY OF THE JAMES, MAJOR GENERAL EDWARD O. ORD, DURING WHICH ORD SUGGESTED THAT LEE AND GRANT SHOULD MEET AND DISCUSS HOW THE MILITARY COULD STOP THE WAR. LONGSTREET PASSED THIS INFORMATION ON TO LEE. LEE THEN WROTE TO GRANT ON MARCH 2, PROPOSING "TO MEET YOU AT SUCH CONVENIENT TIME AND PLACE AS YOU MAY DESIGNATE, WITH THE HOPE THAT UPON AN INTERCHANGE OF VIEWS IT MAY BE FOUND PRACTICABLE TO SUBMIT THE SUBJECTS OF CONTROVERSY BETWEEN THE BELLIGERENTS TO A CONVENTION." ON MARCH 3 LINCOLN ORDERED THAT GRANT COULD "HAVE NO CONFERENCE WITH GENERAL LEE UNLESS IT BE FOR THE CAPITULATION OF GENL. LEE'S ARMY." GRANT REPLIED TO LEE THE FOLLOWING DAY THAT HE HAD "NO AUTHORITY TO ACCEDE TO YOUR PROPOSITION FOR A CONVENTION ON THE SUBJECT PROPOSED."

DID YOU KNOW

Q The Confederate Lieutenant General William Hardee was also an author. What was the title of his famous work?

A The military manual *Rifle and Infantry Tactics*, first published in 1855.

Q At which battle did Hardee command Confederate forces in mid-March 1865?

A The Battle of Averasborough/Smiths Ferry/Black River, North Carolina, on March 16. Union cavalry fought a day-long engagement with Lieutenant General Hardee's Confederate corps, deployed across the Raleigh Road near Smithville. The Confederates eventually retreated after inflicting heavy casualties.

Q Was the Union blockade of the South a success?

A The effectiveness of the blockade remains a matter of dispute. Judged by the proportion of blockade-runners that got in and out of Confederate ports, it was never completely effective. In 1861, for example, vessels made the trip successfully nine times out of ten, though the ratio fell to five in ten in 1865. The blockade appears more effective when the volume of wartime shipping is compared with prewar levels. Viewed from this perspective, the blockade reduced Confederate seaborne supply by more than two-thirds.

Q What was the Lost Cause?

A The idea that the Confederates' cause had been noble but doomed.

Q Who was a leading advocate of the Lost Cause after the war?

A Jubal Early. After the war Early lived for a time in Mexico and then in Canada. He returned to Virginia to practise law and continued to fight the Civil War with pen and printing press. Early became a leading advocate of the Lost Cause.

> THERE IS NOTHING LEFT FOR ME TO DO
> BUT TO GO AND SEE GENERAL GRANT,
> ## AND I WOULD RATHER DIE
> ## A THOUSAND DEATHS
> ROBERT E. LEE
> TO HIS STAFF, APRIL 9, 1865

Q April 12, 1865, was a notable day for the Union commander Joshua Lawrence Chamberlain. Why?

A He was breveted major general and on the same day he had the honor of receiving the formal surrender of Robert E. Lee's men. As the Confederates handed over their arms, Chamberlain brought his own men to attention in salute.

Q What did Chamberlain do after the war?

A After the Civil War Chamberlain refused a commission in the regular army. Instead, he served as governor of Maine (1866–1870) and was then president of Bowdoin College from 1871 to 1883. He spent his later years as a businessman and was involved in the construction of a railroad in Florida.

" WE HAVE NOW ENTERED UPON
A NEW PHASE OF
THE STRUGGLE
JEFFERSON DAVIS, APRIL 1865 "

Q What were the titles of his works that recorded his wartime service?

A *The Passing of Armies: An Account Of The Final Campaign Of The Army Of The Potomac*, *"Bayonet! Forward": My Civil War Reminiscences*, and *Through Blood and Fire at Gettysburg*.

DID YOU KNOW

THE DESTRUCTION BY UNION TROOPS IN SOUTH CAROLINA WAS MUCH MORE WIDESPREAD THAN IN GEORGIA. THE WORST SINGLE EVENT WAS THE BURNING OF COLUMBIA, THE STATE CAPITAL, ON FEBRUARY 17–18, 1865. BY EARLY MARCH SHERMAN'S ARMY HAD CROSSED INTO NORTH CAROLINA. JOSEPH E. JOHNSTON'S CONFEDERATES TRIED TO STOP ITS PROGRESS AT BENTONVILLE ON MARCH 19–21, BUT FAILED. SHERMAN'S MARCHES THROUGH GEORGIA AND THE CAROLINAS HAD BEEN DECISIVE. THEY SHOWED HOW WEAK THE CONFEDERACY HAD BECOME, WHILE THEIR DESTRUCTIVENESS TOTALLY DEMORALIZED THE SOUTH'S POPULATION AND HASTENED ITS DEFEAT.

Q Which general was nicknamed "Stonewall Jackson of the West"?

A Major General Patrick R. Cleburne, killed at the Battle of Franklin in November 1864.

Q Where there any black officers in the Union army?

A No. Although black regiments were raised to fight for the Union, their officers were always white.

Q In early 1865, who was the Confederate commander in Georgia and the Carolinas?

A Pierre Gustave Toutant Beauregard. In February he ordered Charleston to be evacuated. In April, after the loss of Richmond and the Army of Northern Virginia, he was one of the senior figures who urged Davis to negotiate the surrender of the last Confederate forces to end the war.

Q What happened to Jefferson Davis after the war?

A After the war Davis was imprisoned by the Union. After his release Davis and his wife wrote long, self-vindicating memoirs. They did not do well at the time and shed little light behind the scenes. Davis died on December 6, 1889, in New Orleans.

Q Was Davis revered after his death?

A While Robert E. Lee became almost saint-like to the Southern people during the late nineteenth century, some blamed the president for the Confederacy's defeat. Many others, however, revered Davis' memory.

Q Was Davis a good war leader?

A Not really. In his military appointments Davis clung to his favorites far too long and could not work with people whom he disliked. For this reason Pierre G. T. Beauregard, a general who perhaps could have forged a victorious strategy for the Confederates, was relegated to a relatively minor role.

DID YOU KNOW

THE ARMY OF THE POTOMAC HAD THREE GREAT MOMENTS. THE FIRST OCCURRED ON JULY 1–3, 1863, WHEN IT DECISIVELY REBUFFED LEE'S INVASION OF PENNSYLVANIA AT GETTYSBURG. THE SECOND TOOK PLACE ON APRIL 1, 1865, WHEN IT CRACKED OPEN THE FLANK OF LEE'S ARMY DEFENDING THE PETERSBURG TRENCHES IN THE BATTLE OF FIVE FORKS. THE BATTLE SET THE STAGE FOR LEE'S RETREAT FROM RICHMOND AND PETERSBURG. THE ARMY OF THE POTOMAC PURSUED, AND EIGHT DAYS LATER IT ENJOYED A THIRD GREAT MOMENT BY FORCING THE SURRENDER OF LEE'S ARMY AT APPOMATTOX COURT HOUSE.

“ TROOPS GREATLY DEMORALIZED, BREAKING
INTO AND DESTROYING THE
PUBLIC STORES
CONFEDERATE CAPTAIN JOHN TAYLOR WOOD,
APRIL 1865 **”**

Q Who was elected president of Washington College in
Lexington, Virginia, in August 1865?

A Robert E. Lee.

Q Was Robert E. Lee an "unreconstructed Rebel" to the end?

A No. For the rest of his life Lee served as an example of reconcilia-
tion for all Americans, working to heal the wounds of civil war.

289

Q Was James Longstreet revered in the South after the war?

A No. After the war Longstreet was disliked in the South because he
joined the Republican Party and accepted a succession of appointments from president and former Union general Ulysses S. Grant. Many
Southerners also blamed Longstreet for the defeat at Gettysburg, in
particular for his delay in making an attack on July 2.

Q Which Confederate general was killed by a Union sniper at Petersburg, Virginia, in April 1865?

A Ambrose Powell Hill.

Q Which battle in March 1865 failed to halt the Union advance in North Carolina?

A The Battle of Bentonville/Bentonsville. By early March Sherman's army had crossed into North Carolina. Joseph E. Johnston tried to stop its progress at Bentonville. Johnston eventually retreated. Union forces pursued, driving back the Confederate rearguard. The Federal pursuit was eventually halted at Hannah's Creek after heavy fighting. This Union victory cost Johnston's army 3,092 casualties. Union losses were 1,646.

Q Where was the Spanish Fort?

A Alabama. A Confederate-held position on the shore of Mobile Bay, it was taken by Major General E.R.S. Canby's XIII and XVI Corps in April 1865 after a long siege.

Q How did river transportation aid the North cause?

A River transportation was invaluable for moving large numbers of Union troops and their supplies long distances to war theaters in the South.

> " I HAD REASON TO BELIEVE THAT
> THE SPIRIT OF THE ARMY IN
> ## NORTH CAROLINA WAS UNBROKEN
> JEFFERSON DAVIS, APRIL 1865 "

DID YOU KNOW

By early 1865 the situation in the South was deteriorating rapidly. Fort Fisher, defending Wilmington, North Carolina, the last port open to blockade runners, fell to Federal assault on January 15, 1865. This meant that no longer would imported food, munitions, and clothing be available to Lee's men. In the west, a huge Federal Army—General Sherman's Army of the Tennessee—marched through Georgia virtually unopposed from Atlanta to Savannah, then in January turned and headed north toward Richmond through the Carolinas. The main Confederate Army to oppose Sherman had been destroyed by Union Major General George Thomas at Nashville during the battle of December 16–17, with a great deal of help from the poor strategy and tactics practised by its commander, General John Bell Hood. All of this further affected morale in the trenches of Petersburg, as more and more men became convinced that their cause was already lost.

Q Why did Lee attack Fort Stedman outside Petersburg in March 1865?

A Lee had instructed Major General John B. Gordon to study the Federal lines and come up with a plan to save the army. Gordon found a spot, called Fort Stedman, which was relatively close to the Confederate trenches, that he thought could be overwhelmed in a night attack, after which his troops could then spread out to take the flanking works.

Q Was the attack successful?

A No. Stedman was taken, but a full Union division moved forward and formed a crescent around the Confederates now trapped in Fort Stedman. The area between the lines was covered with Union fire, so escape was difficult at best. No Confederate reinforcements were available, due in part to train breakdowns.

Q What was the result of the attack on Fort Stedman?

A Some 10 percent of Lee's entire army, around 4,000 men, was trapped in the fort and forced to surrender. Moreover, Union troops had counterattacked, capturing a long section of the Confederate picket posts, putting Lee's lines in even greater danger. Union casualties were fewer than 1,500 officers and men. The Fort Stedman assault would be the last attack of the Army of Northern Virginia. The next day Sheridan's troops, fresh from clearing the Valley of the remnants of Early's forces, crossed the James and headed toward the Army of the Potomac. These additional numbers would make a successful Confederate defense even less likely. Lee began to prepare to abandon Petersburg and, with it, Richmond itself.

> **GRANT STOOD BY ME WHEN I WAS CRAZY, AND I STOOD BY HIM WHEN HE WAS DRUNK**
> SHERMAN, ABOUT GRANT

Q What happened to John Bell Gordon after the war?

A After the war Gordon returned to Georgia, where he was elected U.S. senator three times and governor of Georgia once. He was a driving force behind the Confederate veterans' movement and wrote an influential memoir of his wartime service.

DID YOU KNOW

PHILIP SHERIDAN'S ACTIONS IN EARLY 1865, CULMINATING IN HIS CAPTURE OF 6,000 MEN AND SIX GENERALS AT SAYLER'S CREEK ON APRIL 6, 1865, HELPED BRING THE CIVIL WAR TO AN END. AFTER THE WAR HE WAS SENT TO TEXAS WITH 50,000 SOLDIERS TO THREATEN THE FRENCH REGIME IN MEXICO. AFTER A YEAR'S NEGOTIATIONS THE FRENCH WITHDREW IN 1867. SHERIDAN DIED ON AUGUST 5, 1888, DAYS AFTER FINISHING HIS MEMOIRS.

Q Contraband camps were usually terrible places. Why?

A The former slaves were often neglected and abused by their Union protectors. Northern soldiers almost resented being assigned to duty guarding and policing contraband camps. They insisted they had enlisted to save the Union, not to "nursemaid" black refugees, and they vented their frustration on their hapless charges. In addition, the soldiers often assigned the refugees onerous jobs that the soldiers hated to perform themselves.

293

Q At the end of March 1865, why was Lee's position at Petersburg precarious?

A The Federals were skirmishing at Lewis's Farm near Gravelly Run, at the junction of the Quaker and Boydton Roads (the scene of the sharpest fighting) and on the Vaughan Road near Hatcher's Run. Further west, Sheridan's cavalry headed toward Dinwiddie Court House south of Five Forks, to be joined by two full Union corps. Rain, more than Confederate defenders, slowed the Union advance. On March 30 the Union II Corps pressed closer to the Confederate line at Hatcher's Run, while V Corps took a line toward Gravelly Run. Cavalry struck Fitzhugh Lee's troops at Five Forks, but the Confederate defenders held their line. Elsewhere, Union reconnaissance suggested to Grant that Lee had so weakened his position to save his right that a general advance on the Confederate line was now possible. In fact, Lee had only 1,000 men per 1 mile (1.6 km) to defend 11 miles (17 km) of trenches.

Q The Battle of Dinwiddie Court House in March 1865 forced the Confederates to retire to where?

A A flanking march by the Union II and V Corps against the Petersburg defenses was temporarily stopped by the Confederates north and northwest of Dinwiddie Court House. However, the Rebels eventually had to retreat to Five Forks.

Q At the Battle of Five Forks on April 1, 1865, where was the Confederate commander?

A As the Confederates waited for a Federal advance in the late morning of April 1, George Pickett, the Rebel commander, and Fitzhugh Lee joined Major General Thomas Rosser for a lunch of fresh shad which the cavalry general had just brought back from the Nottoway River.

> " MY LIFE HAS BEEN A BATTLE
> ## FROM THE START
> NATHAN BEDFORD FORREST "

Q What was Grant afraid of as he besieged Petersburg?

A He feared that his adversary, General Robert E. Lee, would attempt to evacuate the city's defenses and escape westward to join a Confederate army in North Carolina.

Q What did he therefore do?

A To prevent Lee's escape, Grant planned an offensive to cut off his remaining escape routes to the west. On March 31, elements of the Union Army of the Potomac under Philip H. Sheridan fought a sharp engagement with George Pickett's Confederates at Dinwiddie, west of Petersburg.

Q Was it deliberate policy to mistreat prisoners during the Civil War?

A Today, it is commonly held that both sides were guilty of mistreating prisoners during the war. In most cases the sufferings of the prisoners had more to do with official incompetence and a lack of food and resources than with a deliberate policy of letting enemy prisoners die.

Q Why was Five Forks, Virginia, so called?

A From the hamlet known as Five Forks five different roads radiated like spokes on a wheel.

Q Why was it so critical to the Confederates in 1865?

A One road led directly north to Lee's last remaining supply line, the Southside Railroad.

DID YOU KNOW

DAILY RATIONS AT ANDERSONVILLE WERE TWO OUNCES OF PORK, USUALLY HALF ROTTING, PLUS A LITTLE RICE AND CORN BREAD. PRISONERS LACKED WOOD FOR A COOKING FIRE OR A PAN TO COOK IN. STARVATION, SICKNESS, AND DEPRESSION WERE RIFE, AND MANY PRISONERS EITHER LAY MOTIONLESS OR STALKED VACANTLY UP AND DOWN. BY AUGUST 1864 THERE WERE 35,000 MEN IN ANDERSONVILLE, AND THE DEATH TOLL FROM STARVATION AND DISEASE HAD CLIMBED TO 100 A DAY. BY APRIL 1865 THE TOTAL NUMBER OF DEATHS IN THE CAMP HAD REACHED 13,000, ALTHOUGH THIS MAY BE AN UNDERESTIMATE. THERE WERE CALLS IN THE NORTH FOR RETRIBUTION AGAINST THE OFFICERS RESPONSIBLE. IMMEDIATELY AFTER THE WAR ENDED, THE CAMP COMMANDANT, HENRY WIRZ, WAS TRIED BY A U.S. MILITARY TRIBUNAL, CHARGED WITH CRUELTY AND CONSPIRACY TO KILL UNION PRISONERS OF WAR. HE WAS FOUND GUILTY AND HANGED IN 1865.

Q The Confederate defeat at Five Forks on April 1, 1865, had dire consequences for the South. What were they?

A On receiving word of the defeat at Five Forks, Lee was forced to make preparations to evacuate Petersburg, and Grant planned a climactic assault. While the Battle of Five Forks alone did not end the Petersburg campaign, the disastrous defeat helped to seal the fate of Lee's Army of Northern Virginia.

Q What action did Grant take the day after the Battle of Five Forks?

A He attacked the Petersburg defenses. The Confederates began to retreat from Petersburg and their capital of Richmond. The Confederate situation was now desperate.

Q When Lee's army marched west in April 1865, why did it halt at Amelia Court House?

A Lee lost a day waiting for supplies for his hungry and tired men at Amelia Court House on the Richmond and Danville Railroad. The desperately needed supplies never arrived, and the hungry soldiers searched in vain for food in the ravaged countryside nearby.

" I WAS TOO WEAK TO DEFEND,
SO I ATTACKED
ROBERT E. LEE, APRIL 1865

DID YOU KNOW

ON THE NIGHT OF GOOD FRIDAY (APRIL 14) 1865 LINCOLN ATTENDED A PERFORMANCE OF *OUR AMERICAN COUSIN* AT FORD'S THEATRE. DURING THE THIRD ACT OF TOM TAYLOR'S PLAY, JOHN WILKES BOOTH ENTERED THE UNGUARDED PRESIDENTIAL BOX AND SHOT LINCOLN THROUGH THE BACK OF THE HEAD WITH A PISTOL. DESPITE HAVING BROKEN HIS LEFT LEG AS HE LANDED ON THE STAGE, BOOTH ESCAPED ON HORSEBACK. TWELVE DAYS LATER UNION TROOPS CAUGHT UP WITH HIM ON THE FARM OF RICHARD GARRETT NEAR BOWLING GREEN, VIRGINIA. THE SOLDIERS SET FIRE TO THE TOBACCO BARN IN WHICH THE ASSASSIN WAS HIDING. BOOTH DIED IN THE ENSUING BATTLE, EITHER SHOT THROUGH THE NECK BY SERGEANT BOSTON CORBETT OR BY HIS OWN HAND.

Q **Did President Lincoln visit Richmond in 1865?**

A Yes. By the end of April 2 the Confederate capital had been abandoned by its army and government and left as an open city for the looters and fire razers. The first Federal units arrived on the morning of Monday, April 3, and the United States flag was raised over the former capitol building. The city surrendered, order was restored, and on April 4 Abraham Lincoln made an official visit.

Q **Which Confederate hero was defeated at Selma on April 2, 1865?**

A Nathan Bedford Forrest. Three divisions of Union cavalry commanded by Major General James H. Wilson defeated Nathan B. Forrest's defense of the town of Selma. The defeat of Forrest was a major blow to Southern morale.

THE FIRST OF THE
UNLIMITED INDUSTRIAL WARS
WAS THE CIVIL WAR
IN AMERICA
J.F.C. FULLER

Q Did the Army of Northern Virginia make a night march in April 1865?

A Yes. In early April Union cavalry under Sheridan had outpaced Lee and blocked his route south at Jetersville on the Richmond and Danville Railroad. Lee was forced to set out west for Farmville, ordering supplies to be sent from Lynchburg. Union forces caught up with the army's rear. Lee led his men on a rapid night march west to Rice's Station on the Southside Railroad. Many sick and starving soldiers dropped out through sheer exhaustion.

Q What happened to Jefferson Davis when the Confederates abandoned Richmond?

A President Davis and his cabinet fled Richmond. They attempted to run a government until May 2.

Q Why was the Battle of Sayler's Creek/Hillsman Farm, Virginia, on April 6, 1865, a calamity for the Army of Northern Virginia?

A The straggling rear of the Confederate army was battered by a sustained assault from Union troops near Sayler's Creek. The fighting had a devastating effect. Between 7,000 and 8,000 of Lee's army—about one-third of those who had marched from Amelia Court House—were killed, wounded, or captured.

Q What was Lee's reply when General Grant asked for his surrender on April 7, 1865?

A Lee replied that he did not think the cause was yet hopeless, but asked for terms.

Q Which Confederate general told Lee that his men had been fought "to a frazzle" in April 1865?

A John Bell Gordon. On April 9, Gordon's Confederate infantry and Fitzhugh Lee's cavalry attacked, with Longstreet following in support. Gordon's men hit the breastworks the Federals had hurriedly prepared and overran them. Gordon then fought hard to hold Federal infantry and cavalry, but sent word back to Lee that he had been fought "to a frazzle" and needed support immediately.

DID YOU KNOW

A NUMBER OF LEE'S SENIOR OFFICERS SUGGESTED NOT SURRENDERING THE ARMY, BUT ORDERING IT DISPERSED, WITH THE MEN MAKING THEIR WAY INDIVIDUALLY EITHER TO JOHNSTON'S ARMY IN NORTH CAROLINA, BACK TO THEIR HOME STATES TO CONTINUE FIGHTING THERE, OR HEADING INTO THE HILLS TO FIGHT A PROLONGED GUERRILLA WAR. LEE REJECTED ALL THESE SUGGESTIONS. SHORTLY BEFORE THE SURRENDER, LEE HELD A COUNCIL OF WAR WITH SENIOR OFFICERS AND THREE POSSIBILITIES WERE DISCUSSED. ONE WAS TO SURRENDER IMMEDIATELY; THE SECOND WAS TO ABANDON ALL BAGGAGE AND CUT THROUGH GRANT'S LINES QUICKLY AND MAKE A WAY TO JOHNSTON'S ARMY. THE SECOND IDEA WAS DISCARDED BECAUSE THE ARMY COULD NOT FIGHT LONG WITHOUT THE AMMUNITION IN ITS WAGONS. THE THIRD, GORDON LATER WROTE, WAS "TO DISBAND AND ALLOW THE TROOPS TO GET AWAY AS BEST THEY COULD, AND REFORM AT SOME DESIGNATED POINT." THIS WAS REJECTED "BECAUSE A DISPERSION OVER THE COUNTRY WOULD BE A DREADFUL INFLICTION UPON OUR IMPOVERISHED PEOPLE, AND BECAUSE IT WAS MOST IMPROBABLE THAT ALL THE MEN WOULD REACH THE RALLYING-POINT."

Q When Lee decided to see Grant to discuss surrender terms, what were his words?

A "There is nothing left for me to do but to go and see General Grant, and I would rather die a thousand deaths."

Q On what date did Lee surrender the Army of Northern Virginia?

A April 9, 1865—Palm Sunday.

Q Where was the surrender document signed?

A In the parlor of Wilbur McLean's house at Appomattox Court House.

Q Name at least two Confederate generals captured at the Battle of Sayler's Creek?

A Six generals were captured: Richard S. Ewell, George W.C. Lee, Joseph B. Kershaw, Montgomery Corse, Dudley M. DuBose, and Eppa Hunton.

❝ I MET YOU ONCE BEFORE, GENERAL LEE, WHILE WE WERE SERVING IN MEXICO
GRANT TO LEE AT APPOMATTOX,
APRIL 9, 1865 **❞**

INDEX

303

304